Undermining American Hegemony

Advancing a new approach to the study of international order, this book highlights the stakes disguised by traditional theoretical languages of power transitions and hegemonic wars. Rather than direct challenges to US military power, the most consequential undermining of hegemony is routine, bottom-up processes of *international goods substitution*: a slow hollowing out of the existing order through competition to seek or offer alternative sources for economic, military, or social goods. Studying how actors gain access to alternative suppliers of these public goods, this volume shows how states consequently move away from the liberal international order. Examining unfamiliar – but crucial – cases, it takes the reader on a journey from local Faroese politics, to Russian election observers in Central Asia, to South American drug lords. Broadening the debate about the role of public goods in international politics, this book offers a new perspective of one of the key issues of our time.

Morten Skumsrud Andersen is a Senior Research Fellow at the Norwegian Institute of International Affairs (NUPI), in the Research group on Global order and Diplomacy. Andersen has published on theoretical and empirical topics of International Relations, including the history of empires and hierarchy in international politics, conceptual history, NGOs, and practice theory.

Alexander Cooley is the Claire Tow Professor of Political Science at Barnard College and Director of Columbia University's Harriman Institute (2016–present). Cooley is the author and/or editor of seven academic books, serves on several international advisory boards, and has testified for the United States Congress and Helsinki Commission.

Daniel H. Nexon is Professor of Government and Foreign Service at Georgetown University. He is the author or editor of three other books and the former lead editor of *International Studies Quarterly*. During 2009–2010 he worked in the Office of the Secretary of Defense (Policy) in the Russia, Ukraine, and Eurasia office. In 2016 he was one of two coordinators for a group of volunteers that worked on foreign policy issues for the Bernie Sanders campaign, and he remains active in debates about progressive foreign policy.

Undermining American Hegemony

Goods Substitution in World Politics

Edited by

MORTEN SKUMSRUD ANDERSEN
Norwegian Institute of International Affairs
ALEXANDER COOLEY
Barnard College, Columbia University
DANIEL H. NEXON
Georgetown University, Washington, DC

Shaftesbury Road, Cambridge CB2 8EA, United Kingdom

One Liberty Plaza, 20th Floor, New York, NY 10006, USA

477 Williamstown Road, Port Melbourne, VIC 3207, Australia

314–321, 3rd Floor, Plot 3, Splendor Forum, Jasola District Centre, New Delhi – 110025, India

103 Penang Road, #05–06/07, Visioncrest Commercial, Singapore 238467

Cambridge University Press is part of Cambridge University Press & Assessment, a department of the University of Cambridge.

We share the University's mission to contribute to society through the pursuit of education, learning and research at the highest international levels of excellence.

www.cambridge.org
Information on this title: www.cambridge.org/9781108949323

DOI: 10.1017/9781108954129

© Cambridge University Press & Assessment 2021

This publication is in copyright. Subject to statutory exception and to the provisions of relevant collective licensing agreements, no reproduction of any part may take place without the written permission of Cambridge University Press & Assessment.

First published 2021
First paperback edition 2024

A catalogue record for this publication is available from the British Library

ISBN   978-1-108-84497-0   Hardback
ISBN   978-1-108-94932-3   Paperback

Cambridge University Press & Assessment has no responsibility for the persistence or accuracy of URLs for external or third-party internet websites referred to in this publication and does not guarantee that any content on such websites is, or will remain, accurate or appropriate.

Contents

List of Figures	*page* vii	
List of Contributors	viii	
Preface	ix	
List of Abbreviations	xii	

1 Goods Substitution and the Logics of International Order Transformation 1
DANIEL H. NEXON, ALEXANDER COOLEY, AND MORTEN SKUMSRUD ANDERSEN

2 Goods Substitution and Counter-Hegemonic Strategies 29
ALEXANDER COOLEY AND DANIEL H. NEXON

3 International Rankings As Normative Goods: Hegemony and the Quest for Social Status 62
BAHAR RUMELILI AND ANN TOWNS

4 China and the Asian Infrastructure Investment Bank: Undermining Hegemony through Goods Substitution? 88
JULIA BADER

5 The Silk Road to Goods Substitution: Central Asia and the Rise of New Post-Western International Orders 104
ALEXANDER COOLEY

6 Goods Substitution in the USA's Back Yard: Colombia's Diversification Strategies under Conditions of Hierarchy 125
MORTEN SKUMSRUD ANDERSEN

7 Goods Substitution at High Latitude: Undermining Hegemony from below in the North Atlantic 151
REBECCA ADLER-NISSEN, BENJAMIN DE CARVALHO AND HALVARD LEIRA

8 Reflections on the Volume   177
   OLE JACOB SENDING AND IVER B. NEUMANN

Bibliography   189
Index   218

Figures

1.1	Dimensions of international order	*page* 11
2.1	Revisionism, an alternative typology	37
2.2	Implications for power -political maneuvers on US-led order: The example of the BRICS	44
5.1	Central Asian trade with Russia and China, annual, 2001–15	114
5.2	Post–Soviet era debt to multilateral organizations as a share of overall external debt, Kyrgyzstan and Tajikistan	117

Contributors

Rebecca Adler-Nissen, Professor at the Department of Political Science at the University of Copenhagen.
Morten Skumsrud Andersen, Senior Research Fellow in the Research Group on Global Order and Diplomacy at the Norwegian Institute of International Affairs.
Julia Bader, Professor at the University of Amsterdam.
Alexander Cooley, Claire Tow Professor of Political Science at Barnard College and Director of Columbia University's Harriman Institute.
Benjamin de Carvalho, Senior Research Fellow at the Norwegian Institute of International Affairs.
Halvard Leira, Research Professor at the Norwegian Institute of International Affairs.
Iver B. Neumann, Director of the Fridtjof Nansen Institute, Norway.
Daniel H. Nexon, Associate Professor in the School of Foreign Service and the Department of Government at Georgetown University.
Bahar Rumelili, Professor and Jean Monnet Chair at the Department of International Relations at Koç University, Istanbul.
Ole Jacob Sending, Research Director at the Norwegian Institute of International Affairs.
Ann Towns, Professor of Political Science at the University of Gothenburg.

Preface

We finalized this volume during the 2020 COVID-19 pandemic, not long after the United States and China engaged in a particularly fierce round of blaming one another for the initial spread of the virus. Many countries – in Asia, Europe, the Middle East, and elsewhere – closed borders as they struggled to cope with both the economic and the public health effects of the crisis. Political analysts and pundits are currently talking about 'deglobalization' – reducing economic interdependence and enhancing economic self-sufficiency. American President Donald Trump announced he was suspending support for the World Health Organization (WHO), and then that he would withdraw the United States entirely from WHO.

While it currently remains unclear if Trump will actually follow through on this threat, numerous commentators note that the United States has conspicuously avoided playing the kind of global leadership role that it assumed during previous pandemics. Meanwhile, China and Russia have publicly offered emergency medical supplies and advisors, especially to hard-hit European countries like Italy, Spain, and Serbia – where friendly politicians, at least initially, positively contrasted these efforts with those of the European Union (EU).

This political posturing is only the latest in a growing trend of *goods substitution* in international relations. For over a decade, new patrons – usually emerging powers including China, Russia, and Gulf States – have been providing a range of international goods once primarily supplied by the United States, its Western allies, and Western-dominated institutions of global governance.

This volume is a companion to Alexander Cooley and Daniel Nexon's monograph, *Exit from Hegemony: The Unraveling of American Global Order*, which looks at a number of different factors driving the erosion of US leadership. While that book numbers goods substitution among those factors, this volume provides a more sustained – and much more theoretically developed – examination of its dynamics.

As the distinguished contributors in this volume show, the process of international goods substitution has been quietly undermining the American 'patronage monopoly' (really more of a cartel, and never truly complete) in the economic, security, and even normative domains. This monopoly served as the foundation of the American-led liberal international order. Its erosion therefore matters a great deal for the texture of world politics.

Some symptoms of rising goods substitution have been highly visible – including the establishment of new development institutions such as the Asian Infrastructure Investment Bank (AIIB). Others, such as the rise of 'bad faith' international election observers, have operated in more obscure areas of global governance. The net effect of the rising salience of the politics of international goods substitution has been to hollow out aspects of American leadership, both in regions where Washington has traditionally dominated – such as Latin America and the North Atlantic – as well as in those already more susceptible to, say, Russian and Chinese influence, including Central Asia.

The current salience of goods substitution, we contend, stems from how power transitions affect more general dynamics associated with contestation over international order. But the analytical importance of international goods substitution extends beyond power transitions in general, and the current power transition in particular. We offer the concept as an integrative, synthetic approach that includes many traditional concerns in the study of power politics, including balancing and divide-and-rule strategies.

The funding for this project was provided by the Research Council of Norway under the project 'Undermining Hegemony' (project no. 240647). Beginning with a pilot in 2015, the full project, spearheaded by the Norwegian Institute of International Affairs (NUPI), ran from 2016 to 2018 and featured intensive workshops and meetings in Italy, Spain, and Norway, as well as within sessions of the International Studies Association. We are extremely grateful to our NUPI colleagues Iver B. Neumann, Benjamin de Carvalho, and Halvard Leira for their leadership and flexibility with regard to the evolution of the project, as well as other NUPI researchers for their feedback and support.

Because this project lasted for many years and received invaluable input from so many different friends and colleagues, we cannot possibly acknowledge all those who contributed their time and feedback. We thank Aleksandra Turek for her research assistance and help with preparation of the manuscript. Dan Nexon would like to thank Maia Gemmill for sharing her insights and subject matter expertise; Paul Musgrave and Abraham Newman for feedback and inspiration on a variety of aspects of the argument; Megan Stewart for not just assisting with research into conceptual issues related to goods and goods ecologies, but also for many formative discussions about the politics of goods provision; and Steven Ward, who was a crucial intellectual collaborator on the theoretical arguments presented in Chapter 2 – and for allowing us to reproduce them there. And we are thankful to John Haslam and the two reviewers at Cambridge University Press for their insightful comments and guidance.

Finally, the editors dedicate this volume to Iver B. Neumann – pioneering scholar, coauthor, mentor, and friend.

Abbreviations

ACD	Asian Cooperation Dialogue
ADB	Asian Development Bank
AFRICOM	United States Africa Command
AIIB	Asian Infrastructure Investment Bank
ALBA	Bolivarian Alliance for the Peoples of Our America
AOA	Articles of Agreement
APEC	Asia-Pacific Economic Cooperation
ASEAN	Association of Southeast Asian Nations
AU	African Union
bcm	billion cubic meter
BRI	Belt and Road Initiative
BRICS	Brazil, Russia, India, China, and South Africa
CA–CELAC	China–CELAC Forum
CASCF	China–Arab States Cooperation Forum
CDB	China Development Bank
CELAC	Community of Latin American and Caribbean States
CFR	Council on Foreign Relations
China–CEE	China–Central Eastern Europe (17+1)
CICA	Conference on Interaction and Confidence Building Measures in Asia
CIS	Commonwealth of Independent States
CIS-EMO	CIS Election Monitoring Organization
CNPC	China National Petroleum Corporation
COMECON	Council for Mutual Economic Assistance
CPAC	Conservative Political Action Conference
CPIs	country performance indices
CSTO	Collective Security Treaty Organization
CTBTO	Comprehensive Test Ban Treaty Organization
DAC	Development Assistance Committee
DNC	Democratic National Committee

EAEU	Eurasian Economic Union
EBRD	European Bank for Reconstruction and Development
ECOWAS	Economic Community of West African States
EDBI	Ease of Doing Business Index
EEA	European Economic Area
EFTA	European Free Trade Association
EIC	British East India Company
EODE	Eurasian Observatory for Democracy and Elections
EPA	EU Eastern Partnership Agreement
EU	European Union
EUI	Economic Intelligence Unit
FARC	Revolutionary Armed Forces of Colombia
FOCAC	Forum on China–Africa Cooperation
FTA	free trade agreement
FVEY	Five Eyes
G7	Group of Seven
G-20	Group of Twenty
GATT	General Agreement on Tariffs and Trade
GCC	Gulf Cooperation Council
GCI	Global Competitiveness Index
GDP	gross domestic product
GII	Gender Inequality Index
GONGO	government-organized non-governmental organizations
GOP	Grand Old Party, Republican Party
GPIs	global performance indices
GWOT	Global War on Terror
IAEA	International Atomic Energy Agency
IBRD	International Bank for Reconstruction and Development
ICANN	Internet Corporation for Assigned Names and Numbers
ICC	International Criminal Court
IFI	international financial institution
IGO	intergovernmental organization
IMF	International Monetary Fund
IRA	Internet Research Agency (Russia)
IRI	International Republican Institute

JCPOA	Joint Comprehensive Plan of Action (the Iran nuclear deal – the nonproliferation deal concluded with Iran in 2015)
K2	Karshi-Khanabad
Komsomol	All-Union Leninist Young Communist League
LGBTQ	lesbian, gay, bisexual, transgender, and queer
LMC	Lancang-Mekon Cooperation Forum
LTTE	Liberation Tigers of Tamil Eelam
MDB	multilateral development bank
MFA	Ministry of Foreign Affairs
MIST	Mexico, Indonesia, South Korea, Turkey
MoU	memorandum of understanding
NATO	North Atlantic Treaty Organization
NDB	New Development Bank
NDI	National Democratic Institute
NGO	nongovernmental organization
non-DAC	non-Development Assistance Committee member lenders
NRA	National Rifle Association
NUPI	Norwegian Institute of International Affairs
ODA	Official Development Assistance
ODIHR	Office for Democratic Institutions and Human Rights
OECD	Organisation for Economic Co-operation and Development
OECD-DAC	Organisation for Economic Co-Operation and Development – Development Assistance Committee
OPEC	Organization of the Petroleum Exporting Countries
OSCE	Organization for Security and Co-operation in Europe
PESCO	Permanent Structured Cooperation
PRC	People's Republic of China
QCCM	Quadrilateral Cooperation and Coordination Mechanism
R2P	Responsibility to Protect
RATS	Regional Anti-Terror Structure
RCEP	Regional Comprehensive Economic Partnership
RMB	renminbi
RRO	ranking and rating organization
SCO	Shanghai Cooperation Organization
START	Strategic Arms Reduction Treaty

List of Abbreviations

SWIFT	Society of Worldwide Interbank Financial Telecommunications
TAN	transnational activist network
TPP	Trans-Pacific Partnership
UN	United Nations
UNESCO	United Nations Educational, Scientific, and Cultural Organization
UNGAR	United Nations Global Assessment Report
UNHRC	United Nations Human Rights Council
UNSC	United Nations Security Council
USAID	United States Agency for International Development
USSR	Union of Soviet Socialist Republics
WCF	World Congress of Families
WTO	World Trade Organization

1 | Goods Substitution and the Logics of International Order Transformation

DANIEL H. NEXON, ALEXANDER COOLEY, AND MORTEN SKUMSRUD ANDERSEN

One of the most venerable traditions in our field holds that the history of world politics is driven by the rise and decline of hegemonic powers. That is, it argues that international systems remain stable so long as a single political community – usually an empire of one kind or another, but sometimes a city-state, a nomadic confederation, or a sovereign state – achieves unmatchable economic and military capabilities. Those superior capabilities allow it to shape its international system according to its ideological, religious, or more parochial interests. The Romans laid down their law, their roads, and their aqueducts (see, for example, Eckstein 2006; Ward-Perkins 2005); the Ming constructed a series of hierarchical relations with its neighbors that followed, in various ways, Confucian principles (see Lee 2016a, 2016b; Zhang 2015); the British opened markets, suppressed piracy, and built a global system of colonies, protectorates, and other subordinate polities (see Darwin 2009).

This hegemonic order, however, comes under strain when the leading power enters into absolute or relative decline. This is inevitable. Nothing lasts forever. Political and economic systems decay. Other polities experience faster economic growth, or benefit from new military and social technologies. As the hegemon weakens, it finds it increasingly difficult to maintain its preferred order. Newly empowered – or, at least, newly emboldened – polities face a choice: They can opt for the *status quo* and underwrite the order or even help the hegemon maintain its position; or they can decide to *revise* the order to better reflect their own interests, even to the point of going to war to force the issue.

Hegemons themselves must also make decisions. They can retrench, effectively conceding hegemony in at least some regions. The United Kingdom famously got out of the way for the United States in North America at the turn of the twentieth century (see Schake 2017).

Hegemons can otherwise accommodate rising powers, negotiating adjustments in the rules, norms, and arrangements of international politics. Or they can stand their ground, and even go to war, to maintain their position and their preferred international order.

Of course, the choices made by incumbent hegemons and rising powers during these *power transitions* often result from multiple interactions, claims, and counterclaims. But the important thing is that, in many of these frameworks, hegemonic wars drive major transformations in international order. The victors of those wars reshape international order. If neither side emerges from the war in a position to exert international leadership, the order atrophies or breaks down until the cycle begins again.[1]

Contemporary observers believe, for good reason, that we are currently experiencing a power transition, with the center of international power shifting from "the West" to Asia in general, and from the United States to China in particular. They worry, again for good reason, about the possibility of hegemonic conflict between the United States and China (see Allison 2017). And they are starting to focus on the processes and mechanisms that shape international order, especially during power transitions.

This volume looks closely at a major class of those mechanisms. It argues, among other things, that they can significantly erode, and perhaps transform, international orders, even in the absence of a hegemonic war. Consider four vignettes from the last decade.

First, on November 21, 2013, Ukrainian President Viktor Yanukovych announced that his government was abandoning its Association Agreement with the European Union (EU) in favor of closer economic cooperation with the Russian Federation. As the *New York Times* reported, the announcement was "a victory for President Vladimir V. Putin of Russia," who "had maneuvered forcefully to derail the plans, which he regarded as a serious threat, an economic version of the West's effort to build military power by expanding" the North Atlantic Treaty Organization (NATO) "eastward."[2] Russia revealed

---

[1] This summary is drawn, variously, from (Gilpin 1981, 1988; Goddard 2018a, 2018b; Grunberg 1990; Keohane 1980; Kugler and Organski 1989; Lemke 2002; Ikenberry and Nexon 2019; Nexon and Neumann 2018).

[2] www.nytimes.com/2013/11/22/world/europe/ukraine-refuses-to-free-ex-leader-raising-concerns-over-eu-talks.html?pagewanted=all&_r=0. Similar pressure by Russia forced Armenia to abandon its talks with the Europeans.

that it would provide Ukraine with discounted Russian gas and purchase up to $10 billion of Ukrainian government bonds.[3] Moscow's foreign economic pressure and assistance spurred the rise of the Ukraine Maidan movement that ultimately led Yanukovych to flee the country on February 14. In response, Russia invaded and annexed Crimea; it also deployed well-rehearsed tactics in support of separatists in Ukraine's eastern provinces (see Charap and Colton 2018; Menon and Rumer 2015). Relations between the United States and Russia nosedived. The United States and Europe instituted economic sanctions against Russia, while NATO bolstered its presence in its Eastern member states. Some commentators declared the start of a new "Cold War" (Dilanian 2016). Russian efforts to help elect Donald Trump were motivated, in part, by the hope of easing US and European sanctions.

Second, in June 2017, the government of Greece blocked an EU statement at the United Nations (UN) criticizing China's human rights record. According to leading human rights watchdogs, this marked the first time that the EU had failed to make a statement about China's practices at the UN human rights body. While the Greek Foreign Ministry explained its decision to block the statement as avoiding "unconstructive criticism of China," most analysts observed that Athens was heavily influenced by receiving recent investment from Beijing, especially in upgrading the port of Piraeus, which had made cash-strapped Greece a critical European gateway for China's signature Belt and Road Initiative (BRI).[4]

Third, on June 9, 2019, protestors in the post-Soviet Central Asian state of Kazakhstan took to the streets to protest widespread accusations of election fraud that appeared to bolster the victory of President-elect Kassym-Jomart Tokayev, the hand-chosen successor to President Nursultan Nazarbayev who had ruled Kazakhstan since the country's independence. Allegations of voter fraud and ballot stuffing were supported by eye-witness accounts, social media postings, and, perhaps most significantly, harsh criticism from the international election observation mission of the Organization for Security and Co-operation in Europe's (OSCE) Office of Democratic Initiatives and Human Rights, which, having monitored nearly all

---

[3] www.bbc.com/news/world-europe-25411118.
[4] Robin Emmott and Angeliki Koutantou (2017). "Greece Blocks EU Statement on China Human Rights at U.N." *Reuters* June 18. www.reuters.com/article/us-eu-un-rights/greece-blocks-eu-statement-on-china-human-rights-at-u-n-idUSKBN1990FP.

national elections in the post-Communist space since the Soviet collapse, is considered the most credible international organization among Western states and democratic watchdogs.⁵ Nevertheless, Tokayev himself readily dismissed the Office for Democratic Institutions and Human Rights' (ODIHR) critical assessment, calling it "just one of the international organizations" monitoring the vote and stating "we should not focus on the assessment of this organization."⁶ Indeed, the Kazakh government had invited observers from twenty-two different organizations to monitor the election and all but the ODHIR had delivered supportive assessments of what had been an obviously flawed election.⁷

Fourth, in March 2020, Serbian President Aleksandar Vučić issued a broadside against the EU while "praising China for its willingness to assist with the [COVID-19] pandemic." In the early days of the pandemic, a number of European politicians also thanked China for delivering medical equipment – although China would soon lose some of that goodwill as some of that equipment proved to be faulty (Cooley and Nexon 2020b).

While China made a major show of providing international medical assistance to countries across the world, the United States failed to play its traditional leadership role. As Kurt M. Campbell and Rush Doshi (2020) noted Chinese Premiere Xi Jinping "understands that providing global goods can burnish a rising power's leadership credentials. He has spent the last several years pushing [for China to take a greater role in promoting] reforms to 'global governance', and the coronavirus offers an opportunity to put that theory into action." Indeed, many analysts have argued that if the United States follows through on the Trump administration's withdrawal from the WHO, then that "would either advantage China, which recently announced to member states that it would contribute $2 billion to fight the pandemic, or, worse,

---

⁵ The ODHIR report commented, "significant irregularities were observed on election day, including cases of ballot box stuffing, and a disregard of counting procedures meant that an honest count could not be guaranteed, as required by OSCE commitments. There were widespread detentions of peaceful protesters on election day in major cities." www.osce.org/odihr/elections/kazakhstan/422510?download=true.
⁶ Tamara Vaal and Mariya Gordeyeva, "Nazarbayev's Hand-picked Successor Tokayev Elected Kazakh President," *Reuters* June 10, 2019.
⁷ https://astanatimes.com/2019/05/kazakhstan-accredits-22-long-term-odihr-observers-for-june-9-presidential-election/.

embolden it to create a competing health organization, leveraging its position astride the global medical supply chain" (Edson 2020; see also Cooley and Nexon 2020c).

What do these examples have in common? They all involve power politics surrounding *international goods substitution*. In the first, competition among potential goods providers led to military conflict and significantly altered the tenor of relations between Russia and the West. In the second, China's provision of economic goods provided a mechanism for shaping outcomes in the EU and countering liberal norms at the UN. In the third, a government was able to blunt what should have been a clear signal of fraudulent elections by turning to alternative suppliers of election monitors. And, in the fourth, China stepped in to provide international goods in an effort to blunt criticism over its handling of the COVID-19 pandemic and enhance its international influence, especially in the domain of global public health.

The politics of goods substitution take place whenever states or other actors consider adjusting, or actually do adjust, "their portfolio of security, economic, cultural, or other goods." They do so when they, for whatever reason, "find the quality or quantity of a good wanting" and thus "have incentives to expand or change their stock of that good." They can pursue goods substitution by seeking "new arrangements from a current external supplier," attempting "to expand their own production of that good," looking for new external suppliers, or some combination of all three (Cooley, Nexon, and Ward 2019, 704).

As the examples we opened with suggest, the dynamics of goods substitution operate in a wide variety of settings: from inflection points in the relations between great powers to the efforts of weak authoritarian regimes to retain their hold on power. Indeed, recent commentary on Chinese goods provision is correct: The politics of goods substitution can play an important role in shaping the fate of international orders, leading states, and rising powers. Even the simple availability of new providers can help alter international orders by providing states with exit options and thus with greater leverage in their existing relationships. Hegemonic orders, in particular, depend on the effects of a "patronage monopoly" enjoyed by a dominant actor by itself or in conjunction with weaker allies (Cooley and Nexon 2020a, chapters 2–3).

This volume offers a framework for the politics of goods substitution and explores its dynamics in a number of empirical settings. We do not pretend that our framework or arguments are entirely novel; we draw heavily upon existing work across a number of different domains. Discussions of goods substitution run throughout international relations scholarship, albeit often implicitly. Variations on the argument exist, for example, in the literature on soft balancing (see Chan 2017; Pape 2005; Paul 2005); work on forum shopping and regime complexity (see Alter and Meunier 2009; Busch 2007; Drezner 2009); analysis of the impact of the rise of China on global order (Bader 2015; Barma et al. 2009; Cooley 2012; Kastner 2014); findings that competition leads donors to receive fewer policy concessions in exchange for more aid (Bueno de Mesquita and Smith 2016; Dunning 2004); the politics of strategic hedging (Koga 2018; Tessman and Wolfe 2011); and, most notably, in understandings of alliances as mechanisms for the joint production of security (see Cornes and Sandler 1996; Murdoch 1995; Oneal 1990; Sandler and Hartley 2001). Thus, we develop a *synthetic* approach: a framework that emphasizes the *common logics* that operate across different behaviors in the realms of, for example, military security, political economy, and cultural politics (see Barkin 2010; Goddard and Nexon 2016).

In this introductory chapter, we begin with core concepts. We review the major categories of goods: private, public, common-pool, and club. We also discuss the concept of good specificity – essentially, the number of possible suppliers – which matters to the politics of substitution. We then turn toward a discussion of how this volume defines and understands international order. In particular, we argue that an important feature of international order is its "goods ecology" – that is, patterns in the production, supply, quality, and nature of international goods.

The next major section elaborates the logic of goods substitution, and serves as the common framework for the chapters in this volume. We discuss top-down – that is, from great and regional powers – and bottom-up – that is, from weaker states and other actors – drivers of goods substitution, and distinguish between intrinsic and extrinsic reasons why recipients of patronage might seek to alter their portfolios.

We then take a slight detour. Most, but not all, of the goods discussed in this volume are the "objects" or "things" of so-called "rationalist" approaches to international politics, such as military assistance and development projects. But many of the goods in international politics are cultural or symbolic in character. Others – from security commitments to roles in international organizations – might be best understood as having performative dimensions. One of the classic "goods" in hegemonic-order theories, for example, is status or prestige, which is hardly an objective thing (see Duque 2018; Gilpin 1981; Goddard 2018a, 2018b; Ikenberry and Nexon 2019; Larson, Paul, and Wohlforth 2011; Larson and Shevchenko 2010; Volgy and Mayhall 1995; Ward 2017). We therefore discuss this dimension of goods and, although it is not a focus of this volume, how approaches that focus on social fields dovetail nicely with the study of goods substitution.

We conclude by laying out the plan of the volume and the contents of each of the chapters.

Core Concepts

Goods and Assets

Goods are anything, whether tangible or intangible, that provide a benefit and have an exchange value. Although the distinction does not concern us much here, any good that can generate future value is an *asset*. Examples include broad categories of goods, such as military security and economic wealth. They also include a long list of more particular goods, including aircraft carriers, nuclear weapons, military bases, hard-currency reserves, fisheries, rivers, voting rights on the United Nations Security Council (UNSC), and the possession of sacred spaces, such as Jerusalem or Mecca.

An important dimension along which goods differ is excludability: the degree to which a "potential user or beneficiary" can be prevented from benefitting from a good. Another is rivalry: the degree to which a good is "not diminished by consumption or use" (Krahmann 2008, 383). Different categories of goods vary in their position along these dimensions:

- *Public goods* are nonrivalrous and nonexcludable. A classic example is a lighthouse. The owner of a lighthouse cannot prevent a ship from seeing its signal, and thus benefitting from its navigational assistance. Moreover, the lighthouse "has the same utility irrespective of whether it guides one or one hundred ships" (Krahmann 2005, 383–84; see also Olson 1973). In world politics, the suppression of piracy provides an example of a public good. So long as shipping

lanes remain open to everyone, stopping piracy benefits all those engaged in maritime trade and does so irrespective of the number of ships passing through.
- *Private goods* are both excludable and rivalrous. Bilateral economic assistance and arms transfers are, in the main, examples of international private goods. While some third parties might indirectly benefit, the direct benefits go only to the recipient state, whose use of the good reduces its value for others.
- *Common pool goods* are "non-excludable, but rival; everybody has free access to them, but the more people use them the less there is for others" (Krahmann 2008, 384; see also Ostrom, Gardner, and Walker 1994).
- *Club goods* are excludable but nonrivalrous. Collective security arrangements, such as NATO, provide security as a club good. Only member states directly benefit from the promise of mutual defense, but the addition of more members does not, at least in principle, reduce the value of the good (Krahmann 2008, 384; see also Cornes and Sandler 1996).

These categories are ideal typical; real goods combine their features in various ways. For example, to the extent that NATO depresses security rivalries among member states and makes relations in much of Europe more peaceful, it may have spillover effects on the international conflict environment that operate more like a public good. At the same time, the value of NATO's security guarantee probably varies with respect to the number of member states. If NATO had included only the United States, Canada, and Belgium during the Cold War it would have been much less effective at deterring the Soviet Union. But, at some point, NATO might become too large and its benefits decline. Indeed, some believe that the addition of new members after the Cold War diluted the credibility and effectiveness of the alliance (see Sandler and Tschirhart 1997).[8]

Goods vary in other ways that matter for the politics of substitution: their relative *specificity*, which refers to the number of providers that can supply the same good (see Lake 1999, 2001). Gibraltar was a highly specific asset for modern European geopolitics, as it occupied

---

[8] In general, the cases discussed in this volume tend to fall more toward club and private goods than public or common ones, but some do have significant attributes of public goods.

a chokepoint between the Atlantic and the Mediterranean. The Dardanelles provide the only way to sail ships from the Black Sea to the Mediterranean, which made their control a major concern for much of European history. Petroleum and natural gas reserves are *relatively* specific assets, in that there are multiple oil and gas fields across the globe.

These examples suggest that the specificity of assets is a function of their "natural" distribution. This is true to some degree, but a lot of other factors can affect the specificity of an asset. For example, natural gas matters as a source of energy; the development of viable alternatives makes *that energy* a less specific asset even though natural gas deposits remain no more or less specific. As we discuss below, in unipolar systems only the dominant power can provide credible security guarantees, giving it the possession of a highly specific asset. But as new great powers emerge, credible security guarantees become a less specific asset.

International Order

At heart, "international order" refers to relatively stable patterns of relations and practices in world politics (compare Allan, Vucetic, and Hopf 2018, 845; Goddard 2018a, 765). These patterns result from many different processes, such as coercion, negotiation, contention, and resistance. But, regardless of which mechanisms dominate in a particular time or place, international orders emerge from the behavior of states, international institutions, transnational movements, and other important actors in international politics.

This is an extremely broad definition. Scholars usually describe international orders with respect to narrower characteristics. There are a lot of different analytical approaches to thinking about international order, including in terms of social network structures (see Duque 2018; McConaughey, Musgrave, and Nexon 2018; Oatley et al. 2013) or nested social fields (see Go 2008; Go and Krause 2016; Musgrave and Nexon 2018; Nexon and Neumann 2018). But the most common approach focuses on related concepts as rules, norms, values, and social purpose (see Bull 1977, 8; Finnemore 1996; Reus-Smit 1997). For example, Ikenberry (2011, 12–13) argues that "international order is manifest in the settled rules and arrangements between states that define and guide their interaction." Thus, what makes an order "liberal" is the prevalence of governing liberal norms about trade, political rights, and the like.

Another way to think about international order is as a *goods ecology* – defined by patterns in the production, supply, quality, and nature of international goods. States and other actors deliberately provide international goods. But those goods also emerge from their coordinated and uncoordinated activities. States are positioned within that ecology into various niches, with implications for the opportunities and constraints that they face.

The idea that the distribution and quality of goods may, in effect, be "tossed up" by the behavior of states might seem strange. But we already assume something like it in common ways of discussing international politics. For example, when we speak of states facing a difficult or challenging "strategic environment," we reference the quality of its security goods as, at least in part, such an emergent property of its security ecology (Cooley, Nexon, and Ward 2019, 16).[9] This logic extends to other categories of goods. For example, trade regimes not only affect economic goods among their members, but can also shape their quality and quantity for nonmembers (see Carrère 2006).

Conceptualizing at least one of the dimensions of international order as a goods ecology accords with important understandings of what defines a state as *revisionist* or oriented toward the *status quo* (compare Goddard 2018a; Rynning and Ringsmose 2008; Schweller 1996). These are crucial concepts in security studies and hegemonic-order theories, but they often remain ambiguous: The "most common approaches to revisionism place it on one side of a one-dimensional continuum" that is "defined by the costs that a state will bear to alter,

---

[9] Work on alliances and the joint production of security goods points to how the intentional provision of a good may shift the overall security ecology. Mutually Assured Destruction forms of nuclear deterrence, for example, created "public benefits" for NATO and therefore encouraged free riding across security contributions (Sandler and Hartley 2001, 879). More generally NATO's overall production of security to its members – as a club good – impacts the overall security landscape in the region. Moscow appears to perceive it as diminishing the quality of its own security, despite protestations that NATO expansion enhances Russian security by eliminating the pernicious effects of a "power vacuum" in Eastern and Central Europe. A similar disagreement persists with respect to the effects of American security provision in East Asia. Along related lines, Krebs (1999) argues that NATO's provision of security to Greece and Turkey against the Soviet Union altered their security ecologies in ways that exacerbated their rivalry.

Figure 1.1 Dimensions of international order

or defend the status quo" (Cooley, Nexon, and Ward 2019, 4). But what does it mean to alter the status quo?

As Davidson (2006, 14) argues, revisionist states "seek to change the distribution of goods" such as "territory, status, markets" and other club and private goods. More generally, revisionists might object not simply to the *distribution* of goods – their place in the prevailing goods ecology – but to the *form* that those goods take. In these respects, the international goods ecology is analytically distinct from governing rules, norms, and arrangements, even though the two interact closely and shape one another. Norms that favor multilateralism will affect the mixture of public, private, and club goods in some arenas – as well as pushing toward clubs of more than two. If great powers eschew providing public-like goods, it is hard to believe that prevailing norms and rules will ultimately remain intact. For example, China's seeming willingness to abide by Western best practices of governance and transparency in respect of its Asian Infrastructure Investment Bank is important, but if Beijing chooses to route twenty times as much spending via its more opaque Belt and Road initiatives to individual governments, then development financing will no longer retain its predominantly multilateral character.

This matters because, as Ward (2013, 2017) argues, revisionism is not simply a matter of degree. There is a qualitative difference between "*distributive* dissatisfaction – the desire to acquire more of some resources, such as military power or economic influence – and *normative* dissatisfaction – unhappiness with the rules, norms, and institutions that legitimize the existing distribution of resources" (Cooley, Nexon, and Ward 2019, 5). Ward (2017, 11) distinguishes among "distributive" revisionists, who want to alter the distribution of goods in the prevailing ecology; "normative" revisionists, who are generally okay with the distribution of goods but would like to see different norms and rules; and "radical" revisionists who combine "policies aimed at satisfying distributive ambitions with those aimed at rejecting or overthrowing status quo norms, rules, and institutions." The relationship between the two dimensions of international order suggests that these types of revisionism not only bleed into one another (as we would expect from ideal types), but also that many efforts to alter one will change the other, even unintentionally. Cooley and Nexon elaborate on these issues in Chapter 2.

Finally, one of the more important features of goods ecologies concerns the distribution of military capabilities. Whether a system is unipolar (has one great power), bipolar (has two great powers), or multipolar (has three or more great powers) can clearly be conceptualized in terms of international goods ecologies. This highlights the frequent interdependency of different domains of international goods ecologies. It also matters because dissatisfaction with the distribution of military goods lies at the heart of many venerable concepts in the study of world politics, such as balancing – that is, forming alliances or expanding military capability in order to correct a security deficit (Cooley, Nexon, and Ward 2019; see also Haas 2003; Nexon 2009; Walt 1985).

Goods Substitution and International Order

The politics of international goods substitution involve circumstances in which states or other actors consider adjusting, or actually do adjust, their portfolio of security, economic, cultural, or other goods, assets, or capital.[10] Actors "substitute" through a variety of mechanisms: producing the good themselves, jointly producing it with other actors, or contracting for its provision with a third party. In turn, different mechanisms of goods substitution have differential impacts on international order.

---

[10] As noted earlier, we use these terms interchangeably.

If an actor supplies goods in a way consistent with the existing rules and norms that govern relations among states, it usually reinforces international order. This is what we would expect from status quo-oriented actors, but we also may see distributive revisionists at least attempting to maintain the prevailing international architecture. So, for example, if a regime accepts development aid in a way that requires it to better conform with prevailing standards of regime transparency or market relations, say from another Organisation for Economic Co-operation and Development (OECD) provider with similar oversight, then goods substitution works to uphold prevailing international order. We would expect normative and radical revisionists to substitute for that aid in a manner that allows the recipient to deviate from those rules and norms. Doing so potentially chips away at the order – or contributes to the building of an alternative order. Deviation by small or weak states, if permitted or unsanctioned, can, in turn, provide powerful demonstration effects to counterparts to do the same.

Before proceeding, we should stress that the term "substitution" can sometimes be slightly misleading. Actors can alter their portfolio by adding new providers without eliminating existing ones. But even the simple addition of providers has potential implications for international order. Thus, in the next subsection, we distinguish between major categories of substitution. After doing so, we turn to drivers of goods substitution.

Logics of Substitution

Actors pursue the alteration of their portfolios of specific kinds of goods, assets, and capital for a variety of different reasons. These reduce to a few ideal-typical logics: *addition*, in which actors simply want more of a good; *exiting*, in which they abandon a current provider for a new source; *hedging*, in which actors aim to guard against future changes in the goods ecology; and *leverage*, in which actors would prefer not to end their relationship with current providers but seek to secure a better deal.

At the most basic level, when they engage in the politics of goods substitution regimes secure a new supplier for a good currently provided either by another actor – such as a state or an international institution – or the international order itself. In some cases, the provision and use of the relevant good simply takes an additive form: The consumer gains additional providers of a similar good, such as foreign aid or security assistance for the purchases of military hardware. States routinely seek multiple providers of economic assistance, development aid, trade deals, or military hardware simply to increase the quantity of relevant goods.

At the other extreme, actors abandon incumbent providers – say an external patron or a joint-production arrangement – for another, such as when clients switch to different security partners or decide to produce the good entirely indigenously. In the "Diplomatic Revolution of 1756," Austria abandoned its alliance with England in favor of one with France, in large part to counter the growing threat posed by Prussia and reacquire lost territory (see McGill 1971; Sofka 2001). A series of disagreements, including ideological ones, led China to exit, albeit in steps, from its alliance with the Soviet Union – along with its economic and security system – and attempt to build an alternative order (see Lüthi 2010).

Somewhere in between these extremes we find hedging. Most international relations scholars define hedging as adopting a mixture of cooperative and competitive behaviors; states deal with uncertainty by "hedging their bets" and holding open the option of more conflictual or more cooperative behavior in the future (Korolev 2016, 376–77; see also Goh 2006, 2013; Medeiros 2005). Koga (2018, 638) defines hedging as "a state behavior that attempts to maintain strategic ambiguity to reduce or avoid the risks and uncertainties of negative consequences produced by balancing or bandwagoning alone."

In our view, hedging is a more general strategy of seeking to guard against future changes in *any* aspect of a goods ecology, whether the withdrawal of development assistance, termination of an alliance, downgrading of diplomatic precedence, or the imposition of unwanted conditions by a provider of a good (compare Tessman and Wolfe 2011, 216).[11] In the area of symbolic politics, for example, we find repressive regimes inviting external election observers from authoritarian states to validate a problematic or fraudulent election. The aim is to hedge against a probable critical assessment from a more impartial body, such as the OSCE, as in the example of the Kazakh President in our

---

[11] Their understanding is discussed in greater detail in Chapter 2.

opening anecdote, by muddying the waters (Walker and Cooley 2013). Because the immediate aim of hedging is greater autonomy, our understanding is closer to what some scholars of security call "leash slipping" (Walt 2009, 107).

Another reason to diversify suppliers is to make them compete against one another – that is, to leverage the threat of exit to secure better deals. For example, during the Operation Enduring Freedom military campaign, the government of the small Central Asian state of Kyrgyzstan repeatedly sought to extract additional rents from the United States for use of the Manas Transit Center, an air base near its capital city of Bishkek that US military planners used for aerial resupply and to stage US personnel in and out of Afghanistan (Gates 2014, 194–95). These efforts sometimes involved turning to Moscow as a potential alternative provider of loans and economic aid, as Kyrgyz President Kurmanbek Bakiyev did in early 2009. Although Bishkek succeeded in increasing rents from the United States, it ultimately only closed the base when the lease expired in 2014 (Cooley and Nexon 2013).[12] The implicit or explicit threat of exit likely accounts for why the United States had to "pay more and got less by way of security concessions from recipients" once the Soviet Union "became a significant aid player" (Bueno de Mesquita and Smith 2016, 413) and why conditional development aid became more effective after the end of the Cold War, when liberal democratic lenders were the only game in town (Dunning 2004).

Top-Down Drivers of Goods Substitution

There are a number of top-down (often supply-side) factors that make the politics of goods substitution more likely. Many of these reduce to the substitutability of the good, which is generally a function of the *number of providers willing and able to supply a comparable good*. Some goods, as we noted earlier are, by their nature or circumstances, highly specific. Holding a highly specific asset places an actor, *ceteris paribus*, in an advantageous position when it comes to manipulating the politics of goods substitution to maximize its own interests. But as

---

[12] Olga Dzyubenko, "U.S. Vacates Base in Central Asia as Russia's Clout Rises," *Reuters* June 3, 2014.

asset specificity declines, and the possibilities of substitution increase, bargaining leverage can ultimately flip to the consumer.

To take an example familiar to scholars of international security (which we touched on earlier), in strictly unipolar systems only a single political community can provide truly effective security guarantees, because no possible combination of other actors can overcome its military preeminence (Wohlforth 1999). In multipolar systems, however, more polities can extend credible security guarantees. This increases the number of possible balancing configurations – that is, the substitutability of security (see Kim 2016, chapter 3). During the Cold War, the United States used its provision of various club goods as a way to coerce allies into dollarization and other economic arrangements preferred by Washington (Norrlof 2010, 2014). In theory, the advanced industrial democracies and other second-tier powers could exit, but the Soviet Union generally could not offer a better bargain, and shifting to indigenous production risked coercion from both superpowers.

The number of actors capable of providing the good represents something akin to a structural feature of international politics – at least in the sense that realists discuss the distribution of power. But the domains are obviously much greater than military capabilities, including the distribution of energy resources, mechanisms for conferring status and other forms of symbolic capital (Towns 2009), and the size of domestic markets (Drezner 2014, chapter 5). Across different kinds of goods, relevant variation concerns whether a provider enjoys a monopolistic position, multiple providers engage in oligopolistic collusion, and whether the capability to provide the relevant asset is dispersed such that conditions increasingly resemble market competition (see Waltz 1979).

But even when multiple actors could, in principle, act as alternative suppliers of a good, they may choose not to do so. Moreover, existing suppliers may discontinue the relationship, as Trump routinely suggested that the United States might do with respect to security guarantees to many of its allies. They may also act in coordinated ways to limit the bargaining leverage of consumers – in other words, engage, as noted above, in oligopolistic or duopolistic collusion. In practice, these arrangements may prove messy. For example, Washington and Moscow colluded to reduce the spread of nuclear weapons during much of the Cold War (see Colgan and Miller 2019). But the system proved leaky, as both Washington and Moscow provided technical assistance to some states, looked the other way when second-tier nuclear powers transferred sensitive assistance, and so on (Kroenig 2010). However, the more hierarchical control is established by a provider over another actor, the more it deprives that actor of the ability to seek alternatives (Lake 1996, 2001). Thus, as the politics of goods substitution increases, providers have incentives to turn to various kinds of coercive domination to maintain their relationships (see MacDonald 2009). It therefore may contribute to the formation of regional hegemonic "subsystems" within the broader international order.

Bottom-Up Drivers of Goods Substitution

Top-down factors intersect with demand-side drivers of goods substitution. On the demand side, actors are more likely to seek alternative provision when they worry about *intrinsic* aspects of a good, *extrinsic* factors associated with it, or both.

Intrinsic factors refer to how actors will prove more inclined to engage in the politics of goods substitution when they find the good inadequate to meet their needs. They may, for example, worry about the reliability of a security guarantee. The "price" of the good may be too high in terms of associated conditions and quid pro quos – such as requirements to implement specific political reforms or human rights safeguards, provide military access without retaining sufficient legal jurisdiction over foreign personnel, or accept undesired nongovernmental contractors. In the wake of the Vietnam War, in 1976 the Thai government effectively refused to extend basing rights for a residual US force as it proved unwilling to grant the US side exclusive criminal jurisdiction over its personnel in a peacetime setting (Randolph 1986, 189–92).

Actors will also prove more likely to seek alternative providers when they worry about *extrinsic* downsides. Examples of such downsides include: first, the legitimacy or audience costs of associating with a specific foreign regime; and, second, the risks of increasing dependency on a state with which they are likely to have policy disagreements in the future. This second concern seems to have been one motivation for Duterte to seek security assets and cooperation from Russia and China. In the study of alliance politics, we refer to this kind of behavior, depending on the specifics, as "hedging" or "leash slipping" (Goh 2006; Medeiros 2005; Walt 2009; Weitsman 2004, 20). In a general sense, these considerations involve negative externalities associated with existing public, club, and private goods.

Consider economic assistance. Regimes may simply view the amount of a current package as insufficient to meet their needs, but they might also consider the quality subpar. While regimes would often prefer to simply aggregate economic assistance, political factors may force them to choose among packages – that is, substitute one for another. Leaders in recipient states sometimes welcome, for example, loan conditionality as an excuse to forward their own domestic policy preferences (see Vreeland 2003). But they may also see specific conditions as posing unacceptable risks – whether to their ideological goals or to their domestic political survival.

Regimes often prefer fungible forms of assistance that allow them to pursue their own political agendas (see Bermeo 2016). Sometimes such risks stem not from the explicit terms of the good, but from negative externalities. For example, as noted in the opening section of this chapter, for Yanukovych to proceed with the European Union Association Agreement a number of negative externalities were entailed: those associated with poisoning relations with Russia, politically empowering imprisoned political rival Yulia Tymoshenko, and antagonizing specific domestic interest groups with close economic ties to Russia (Menon and Rumer 2015, 53–81).

For example, in June 2011 officials in the post-Mubarak government announced that Egypt would not borrow from the US -influenced International Monetary Fund (IMF) or World Bank, insisting that Qatar would provide $500 million in unconditional budget support that would allow Cairo to maintain its broad array of social subsidies.[13] More Qatari financing for the Egyptian budget and central bank in January 2013 helped Morsi to maintain his holdout.[14] However, in March 2013, after providing $5 billion in total support, Qatar indicated that it would no longer offer assistance to Cairo without an IMF deal, joining the EU and United States in insisting on the IMF's seal of approval as a prerequisite for further financing.[15] With no

---

[13] Edmund Blair, "Egypt Says Will Not Need IMF, World Bank Funds," *Reuters* June 25, 2011.
[14] Andrew Bowman, "Egypt: IMF Pledges Support As Qatar Doubles up," *Financial Times* January 8, 2013.
[15] Heba Saleh, "Egypt Weigh IMF Austerity burden," *Financial Times* March 11, 2013.

alternative financing options, Cairo returned to the negotiating table; but after Morsi's ouster in a military coup in July 2013, new President Abdel Fattah al-Sisi secured pledges for an additional $12 billion from the United Arab Emirates, Saudi Arabia, and Kuwait to stave off immediate economic crisis and strengthen his leverage with the fund.[16] In the overall ecology of international order, these Gulf states are allies of the United States and, obviously, less powerful. However, they acted – intentionally or not – as alternative patrons to the Egyptian government, simultaneously propping up successive regimes and diminishing the influence and leverage of US led international financial institutions.

In sum, the salience of the politics of goods substitution depends on supply-side and demand-side factors. There are at least three conditions that make the dynamics of goods substitution increasingly important for international order and international power politics:

- the number of possible providers increases – that is, more states or other actors can provide relevant goods to others or produce relevant goods themselves;
- a growing subset of these possible providers hold revisionist dispositions;
- states and other "consumers" become increasingly worried about the intrinsic or extrinsic costs associated with existing arrangements.

Of course, these drivers may be at least partially endogenous to one another. For example, the number of potential providers affects the possibilities for states to exit from an existing relationship, and is therefore likely to shape their perceived opportunity costs when it comes to staying put. Also, one or more existing suppliers may become inclined to renegotiate the terms of their provision of international goods on less favorable terms – in some cases, because existing providers themselves want to revise the system. This can simultaneously trigger demand and supply for goods substitution, unless the revisionist provider enjoys a monopoly on goods provision.

---

[16] Max Reibman, "The IMF in Egypt, Act Two," Carnegie Endowment for International Peace April 24, 2014. http://carnegieendowment.org/sada/?fa=55425

The Social Construction of Goods

The framework developed above will strike some readers as problematic, insofar as it conceptualizes international goods as material "things" whose value is related, more or less, to their objective characteristics. They might point out that, in fact, some of the goods relevant to international politics are not objects at all, but, rather, the ability to engage in certain kinds of valuable *performances*. Both the five permanent[17] and ten rotating members of the UNSC translate their social position – and the voting rights it confers – into geostrategic advantages of various kinds. Indeed, a number of studies find that rotating members of the UNSC tend to see increases in the amount of foreign assistance they receive from donors (Vreeland and Dreher 2014). Even many physical goods that matter in world politics – from weapons systems to an advantageous position along a trade route – clearly derive their exchange value, at least in part, from social or cultural processes.

The study of goods substitution does not *require* attention to ways in which international goods are socially constructed, but scholars *can* focus on the symbolic, social, and performative character of international goods. Such perspectives, which show up in various ways in this volume, enrich our understanding of its dynamics.

Here, Pierre Bourdieu's notions of *capital* and *fields* would seem to dovetail nicely with the broader goods substitution framework.[18] For Bourdieu (2011, 81) *capital* is "accumulated labor" that can be instantiated either in physical objects, such as diamonds or missiles, or "incorporated" as embodied dispositions, skills, and capabilities – such as comporting oneself as a skilled diplomat or a military demonstrating superior performance on the battlefield (see Adler-Nissen and Pouliot 2014; Pouliot 2016). In other words, capital is an alternative term for goods that highlights the notion that goods can manifest in performances.

The best known typology of capital involves Bourdieu's broad tripartite distinction between economic capital, social capital, and cultural capital, although he also added new kinds as fitted his empirical concerns, such as "academic capital." Broader forms of capital have subtypes, or subspecies – such as derivatives, stocks, and cash for

---

[17] The P5: China, France, Russia, the United Kingdom, and the United States.
[18] The discussion in this section draws directly from Musgrave and Nexon (2018) and indirectly from Nexon and Neumann (2018).

economic capital – whose value varies in time and space. Although we can understand the relationships produced by fields and the allocation of capital in general terms, the social fields that define any particular kind of capital are historically and socially contingent.

As Adler-Nissen (2008, 668) argues, "a field is a historically derived system of shared meanings, which define agency and make action intelligible and the agents in a field develop a sense of the social game. The stratification of a field is based on different forms of capital … and the efficacy of the capital depends on the contexts where it is used." Agents behave strategically with respect to the socially constituted field in which they operate. Savage, Warde, and Devine (2005, 39) suggest that fields each have "their own 'stakes' around which contestants struggle and jostle for position … agents are conditioned in their strategic behavior by their location in the competitive, game-playing character of the field." They "compete, collude, negotiate, and contest for position" (Savage, Warde, and Devine 2005, 39). Thus, "field is an inclusive concept orienting analysts to both objective positions and cultural meaning, to both objective positions and cultural stances" (Go and Krause 2016, 9).

International relations scholars generally assume, reasonably, that in an overarching field of interstate relations (the "international system") military and economic resources serve as critical field-relevant capital. But those are not the only possible metrics. Towns (2009) shows that actors can also differentiate themselves through "standards of civilization" marked, for instance, by the socio-political position of women. Similarly, racial hierarchies in world politics reflect the construction of membership in different "racial groups" as field-relevant capital for states and other actors (Vitalis 2015; Vucetic 2011). The possession of colonies – and the performance of imperial management – became important capital in the field of great-power competition during the nineteenth century (Barnhart 2016).

The concept of "symbolic capital" captures how some objects or performances become particularly valuable in specific fields. That is, specific goods become invested with particular symbolic significance. As Zhang (2004, 7) argues, "objective capital can be expressed and represented through symbolic capital, as it will always have a symbolic form." But "symbolic capital can exist independently of objective capital: for instance, the word 'progress' may carry symbolic capital, but by itself it has no form of objective capital" (Zhang 2004, 7).

The possession of colonies was once symbolically important as a marker of great-power status. Rulers valued them in ways unrelated to their straightforward economic or military potential. Aircraft carriers have similarly become a prestige good, in no small measure because of their symbolic association with great-power status in the post-1945 period (see Eyre and Suchman 1996; Gilady 2018). In the early 1960s, President Kennedy committed the United States to putting a man on the moon despite seeing the project as enormously wasteful in military and economic terms. He did so because he believed that the United States needed to achieve a "first" in space exploration. An extremely high-profile first could serve as a crucial symbolic good in the broader field of science and technology. Many observers, and Kennedy himself, thought that Washington needed to outcompete the Soviet Union in that arena in order to demonstrate the superiority of the American political and economic system, and therefore the attractiveness of the United States as an alliance partner (Musgrave and Nexon 2018).

While this kind of approach does not receive much attention in this volume, many of the contributors are important players in the elaboration of practice and field-theoretic accounts of world politics. Readers will find traces of these concepts in some of the chapters. We offer it here not only to stress that "goods" can be performative in character, but how more social-constructionist frameworks can potentially shed light on the contestation and evolution of international order as a goods ecology.

Plan of the Volume

Having walked through the logic of goods substitution in this introductory chapter, in Chapter 2, "Goods Substitution and Counter-Hegemonic Strategies," *Alexander Cooley* and *Daniel Nexon* expand upon the insights about asset substitution to recast the debate on revisionism and status quo orientations. They argue that instead of operating with types of state intentions – on a continuum from "revisionist" to "status quo" powers – we should rather focus on the broader strategic environment in which power political maneuvers take place. This is an international goods ecology comprising the different types of goods and their distribution. The key advantage of studying power politics as operating within such a goods ecology is that order itself then becomes something different from polarity or hegemony. In other words, the international order itself becomes an arena for power political struggles, and it is possible to distinguish between challenges to the power position of the hegemon and challenges to the architecture of the international order. Cooley and Nexon therefore develop an alternate typology of how international orders are challenged to show how acts of substitution – to the extent that they alter the efficacy of mechanisms for maintaining order or create qualitative shifts in international goods ecologies – are *themselves* potentially order transforming.

They argue that US-led hegemonic order may be undermined before any overt challenge to the power position of the Unites States emerges. The main benefit of studying the logic of goods substitution is that it gives us a tool to assess how seemingly unimportant acts of substitution, bit by bit and regardless of a lack of revisionist intent, can shape and transform the international order. The politics of goods substitution can unravel hegemony *even* when military goods play a minor role, and some of these dynamics are the by-product of policy decisions made with comparatively little in the way of revisionist aims. Moreover, Cooley and Nexon contend that processes of goods substitution can hollow out hegemonic orders slowly and incrementally; it may not be clear that the order is transforming until the process is far advanced and there is an undergrowth of power political phenomena that has escaped the attention of traditional theories of international relations.

This theme, naturally, is taken up in the other chapters of the volume. In Chapter 3, "International Rankings As Normative Goods: Hegemony and the Quest for Social Status," *Bahar Rumelili* and *Ann Towns* make the case that assets and goods are not only tangible things, like military hardware or trade goods, but may also be normative in nature. They emphasize the centrality of international symbolic and normative goods in maintaining or challenging hegemony. International orders, they argue, may be characterized by different systems of supply of normative goods and status. Rumelili and Towns contend that when stabilized and widely shared, norms can fruitfully be addressed as goods in an international goods ecology. These normative goods, they argue, are characterized by specific patterns of supply, demand, and distribution; they are produced in certain forms and quantities by ranking and rating organizations, and obtained and used as social assets by states in particular ways.

One central case of how norms become stabilized in this way is through international ratings and indices. Thus, Rumelili and Towns analyze the critical role played by ranking and rating organizations and the country performance indices (CPIs) they produce in transforming norms into a set of normative goods. CPIs clarify and specify what states need to do to achieve status. They provide esteem and moral value in three ways: They supply public and comparative information, which constructs moral hierarchies; they define norms by assigning moral value to specific indicators; and they give moral status to states through the ranking systems they employ. States may acquire normative goods to challenge the dominant position of the United States, or they may challenge the existing set of normative goods to undermine the liberal normative order that undergirds US hegemony. Conceiving norms as goods alerts us to a distinct terrain where hegemony is challenged in a bottom-up and gradual fashion, over and through putatively technical measures and standards.

One major agent of change in the international order is China, and the classical debate about its role concerns whether it is surging as a global revisionist challenger to the United States, or if it is gradually being integrated into the liberal world order. In Chapter 4, "China and the Asian Infrastructure Investment Bank: Undermining Hegemony through Goods Substitution?," *Julia Bader* shows how China has begun to take a more active and assertive role in international public goods provision and that the results are more varied than the duality of revisionism versus status quo orientations would have it.

Bader addresses a recurring point in the volume, namely that China as goods supplier is increasingly identifying gaps in the existing international order and starting to fill them without necessarily challenging the United States directly. She shows how the case of China's Asian Infrastructure Investment Bank (AIIB) initiative turned out to be a successful example of goods substitution.

The AIIB was initiated as a counter-hegemonic attempt targeted at the architecture of international finance and at US dominance therein. However, as more European democracies somewhat unexpectedly joined the Bank – against the wishes of the United States – the institution gradually transformed into an integrated part of the existing international financial architecture. While the initiative's effects in terms of deconcentrating power were limited, Bader argues that although it largely conformed to the norms and standards of international development banks, China was successful in making all founding members subscribe to the principles of nonconditionality and noninterference, principles that largely deviate from current practices in development financing. In particular, by targeting infrastructure financing – a real gap in existing goods provision by the United States and the US led order – the AIIB was, and is still, an attractive initiative for prospective lenders and borrowers alike. The United States failed in its attempt to prevent others from joining the initiative, but, more importantly, through the initiative China could disclose discrepancies between US claims of world leadership and actual attempts to fulfill this role. Regarding the demand-side dynamics of goods substitution, the case of the AIIB illustrates how opportunistic hedging and uncoordinated herding by third states may inadvertently undermine the existing order. By analyzing such opportunistic hedging by European states against the wishes of the United States, Bader shows how the framework of international goods provision, involving producers and consumers alike, directs our attention to nonhegemonic actors as crucial but often overlooked players.

In his study of intensifying goods substitution in post-Soviet Central Asia in Chapter 5, "The Silk Road to Goods Substitution: Central Asia and the Rise of New Post-Western International Orders," *Alexander Cooley* details how countries in the region use the competing and overlapping infrastructure of external powers to consolidate their own domestic political standing. In the 2000s, after 9/11 and a string of "Color Revolutions," Russia and China established themselves as alternative providers of goods in a region hitherto seen as countries in "democratic transition" under US influence. Consequently, with alternative goods providers available, Central Asian countries themselves leveraged their relationship with the West to achieve political and economic aims and to push back against criticism about human rights abuses and authoritarian policies.

Cooley's example of how Russia deploys and supports alternative election observers to post-Soviet countries drives home the point that the rise of alternative providers and goods substitution has undermined US hegemony and eroded the policies, norms, and institutions of the US-led liberal international order. As the chapter demonstrates, these dynamics escalated very quickly in a region, originally categorized as "post-Communist," at the outer boundary of the US-led Western sphere of influence. As such, it also serves as a reminder that goods substitution could abruptly trigger similar dynamics in other, comparable regions such as Latin America or the Arctic, which are indeed the subjects of the two succeeding chapters.

An essential component of making the study of "revisionist" states more dynamic and multilayered is demonstrating how the intentions of providers and the effects of goods substitution on order and hegemony may be independent of each other.

In Chapter 6, "Goods Substitution in the USA's Back Yard: Colombia's Diversification Strategies under Conditions of Hierarchy," *Morten Skumsrud Andersen* takes a closer look at the role of Chinese asset substitution in Colombia. Goods substitution dynamics are evident in states that have recently opposed US hegemony, such as Venezuela and Ecuador, particularly through loans-for-oil deals. However, the case of Colombia – one of the United States' closest allies in the region – shows how asset substitution dynamics may come to operate under conditions of hierarchy.

Andersen argues that Colombia does not seek to challenge the United States directly. Rather, Colombia is consistently seeking to *diversify* its ties with the United States, thereby increasing its leverage and autonomy and hedging its bets from *within* a hierarchical arrangement. Colombia is a "least likely" case for a theory of goods substitution, and there is limited evidence of actual Chinese goods substitution in Colombia. Yet, China's increasingly central role in a global goods ecology gives a new context in which Colombian hedging strategies are used to threaten goods substitution. The chapter therefore shows that goods substitution mechanisms may have an effect even in the absence of any actual goods substitution. The mere threat of exiting or hedging strategies has the potential of effecting policy change, particularly when combined with domestic political context – a diversification of ties interacts with domestic and international politics, with one area having possible unintended effects on the other.

This strategy of increasing leverage with one provider by invoking alternative sources of a good receives sustained attention in Chapter 7, "Goods Substitution at High Latitude: Undermining Hegemony from below in the North Atlantic." Here, *Rebecca Adler-Nissen, Benjamin de Carvalho, and Halvard Leira* underline how a potential for goods substitution may foment a strategy of playing the big powers against one another. Client states are using the threat of exit to gain leverage, and to renegotiate deals.

The authors suggest that there are signs of decline of US hegemony in the North Atlantic, and an increased potential for goods substitution by Russia and China. However, the potential for goods substitution has not been initiated by Russia and China offering what the United States or the West have ceased to offer. Rather, the authors suggest, alternative goods provision has been sought out from below, by polities with complex post-colonial and hegemonic relationships with a variety of states. These polities, the chapter shows, are experimenting with new ways of playing the United States, Russia, and China against each other. Greenland, Iceland, and the Faroes exploit their strategic positions in a variety of ways to push great powers to compete in offering a variety of public and private goods.

Indeed, these northern polities have effectively found cracks in the liberal order where they can thrive economically, strategically, and culturally. The authors point out how within a logic of international goods substitution client states may be using the threat of substitution as strategic leverage, which may drive the hegemon to renegotiate. Client leverage will be the highest they argue, when the client can easily switch goods provider, but where the hegemon cannot easily find an alternative client. Although there is little concrete good substitution in this area as yet, local politicians are clearly seeking to diversify their portfolio of goods providers and use the possibility of having alternative providers as leverage towards the West. Undermining hegemony is in this case a form of collateral damage in the wake of seeking economic improvement, political independence, and increased status.

The two chapters on Latin America and the North Atlantic, respectively, highlight how demand-side factors may matter more than the intentions of alternative goods providers. For instance, both in Iceland and in Colombia – two countries that many would instantly categorize as closely aligned to US interests – the mere existence of alternative goods providers such as Russia and China have been used to increase leverage and hedging strategies in their foreign policies.

In both Chapter 6 and Chapter 7, we see how the US led international order and the relationships and alliances in which it consists may prove more fragile than we think. Goods substitution is not only a matter of great powers competing over influence over small states; these client states could aim to "force the hand of an unwilling hegemon" by exploiting exactly this competition for the provision of goods. That is, demand-side factors are important even in the absence of actual goods substitution, and client states can exploit the competition over goods provision to strengthen their bargaining position.

In the concluding chapter, "Reflections on the Volume," *Ole Jacob Sending and Iver B. Neumann* sum up this volume's contribution to the discipline of International Relations and the study of international order, and suggest how the goods substitution framework may be extended in future research. Moving beyond a contractual view of goods substitution, they emphasize how identity would play a central role in goods ecologies, particularly in instances where a goods recipient uses its own resources to *coproduce* the goods with the provider as a means of gaining recognition and relevance. In turn, the quality and perceptions of goods and assets are also likely to play a part in a global goods ecology.

2 Goods Substitution and Counter-Hegemonic Strategies

ALEXANDER COOLEY AND DANIEL H. NEXON

Traditional hegemonic-order theories see much of the history of world politics as dominated by the rise and decline of leading powers: those with sufficient military and economic capital to order relations among other political communities.[1] As noted in Chapter 1, these hegemons structure the architecture of international order in ways consistent with their interests and values. At their most powerful, hegemons provide stability in the form of economic order and the absence of system-wide wars. When they go into decline, the international system faces the risk of a "hegemonic" or "power-transition" war.

The degree of risk depends on whether the incumbent is willing and able to accommodate the interests of the rising powers. If the rising powers are generally disposed toward the status quo, then they are easy to accommodate; they might either help the hegemon maintain its position or form a cartel to support the existing order. If they are revisionist, however, the incumbent power might find itself unwilling or unable to accommodate them. Indeed, Ward (2013, 2017) argues that radical revisionists present the greatest risk of major conflict, and that states move from distributional to radical revisionist when they come to believe that their more moderate aims cannot be accommodated within the existing normative order (see also Davidson 2006; Goddard 2018a; Schweller 1996).

If the rising challenger does signal serious revisionist intent, the incumbent hegemon, fearing it will be overtaken, might launch a preventive war to prevent a further shift in the global balance of power. Alternatively, the rising challenger might decide that it has achieved sufficient capabilities to challenge the hegemon. Three possible results follow: the victorious hegemon has a free hand to conserve

---

[1] For overviews and key works, see (DiCicco and Levy 1999; Edelstein 2017; Gilpin 1981, 1988; Ikenberry 2001; Ikenberry and Nexon 2019; Lake 1993; Lemke 2002; Organski and Kugler 1980).

or alter the original order; the victorious challenger becomes the new hegemon; or, regardless of who wins, no one has the capacity to engage in hegemonic ordering. The system descends into multipolar competition.

In most hegemonic-order approaches, the major driver of change is uneven economic growth. Some second-tier power will inevitably experience faster growth than the hegemon, which will eventually shift the balance of power in its favor. The relative decline of the hegemon is sometimes exacerbated by strategic overextension: the tendency for dominant actors to try to conquer or dominate more than they can afford – and to drain their domestic economies in an attempt to maintain military dominance in the face of that overextension. This is the typical explanation given for the decline of the Spanish Monarchy. It fought wars on too many fronts and destroyed its productive base in the process (Kennedy 1987, chapter 2).

In these accounts, the current international order is the product of three major hegemonic cycles. During the nineteenth century the British Empire emerged as the first global hegemon. London conceded dominance of North America to the United States, thereby heading off conflict. But it could not accommodate Germany. Indeed, World War I and World War II were both variations on power transition wars, and the United States emerged from the rubble as the new global hegemon. It was soon challenged by the Soviet Union, but its decline and then collapse in 1991 left the United States in a new position of dominance. Washington pursued global hegemony by, for example, expanding the North Atlantic Treaty Organization (NATO) and supporting new rounds of trade liberalization. American leaders adopted a policy of trying to preserve the "unipolar moment" by maintaining military superiority and deterring potential challengers from even trying (see Ikenberry 2001, 2011; Schweller and Wohlforth 2000).

Of course, the general consensus is that the world is experiencing a new power transition, with China rising and the United States in relative decline (Ikenberry and Nexon 2019, 395–96). Analysts debate whether or not accommodation is possible, or whether the world now faces the risk of, if not war, serious conflict (see, for example, Allison 2017; Buzan 2010). Observers point to China's growing global presence, including in the form of the Belt and Road Initiative (BRI) or its formation of new development banks, as a threat to the so-called liberal order. China's model of authoritarian capitalism, and its apparent interest in exporting that model, raises particular concerns (see, for example, Dollar 2015; Goh 2013; Kurlantzick 2007; Walker 2018; Walker and Ludwig 2017; Woods 2008).

Many of the chapters in this volume deal with these questions, but this chapter focuses specifically on what the goods substitution framework means for our understanding of hegemony and hegemonic orders.

First, we discuss why the politics of goods substitution becomes increasingly salient during power transitions. The reasons, which we elaborate in the next section, follow directly from the logic of the framework. The most important are that: power transitions increase the number of suppliers; and if those suppliers are revisionist, they will prove attractive alternatives to weaker powers – especially those that dislike aspects of the current international architecture or goods ecology.

Second, we focus on the different power-political *reasons* why actors may engage in goods substitution. We argue that there are four ideal-typical aims of goods substitution in hegemonic orders. These are similar to, but distinct from, Ward's (2013, 2017) four kinds of revisionism. That framework distinguishes between international order and the goods ecology in order to explain general state strategies. In contrast, we focus on whether states *use* goods substitution to try to alter the distribution of power in the system, the architecture of the order, or both.

This produces four ideal-typical aims: *status quo*, *reformist*, *positionalist*, and *revolutionary* (Cooley, Nexon, and Ward 2019). In the context of the use of goods substitution in the American led international order, these correspond to attempts to secure policy adjustments (*counter-policy*), to change international architecture but not challenge American primacy (*counter-order*), to change the distribution of power but not the architecture (*anti-unipolarity*), and *counter-hegemonic* challenges that seek to overturn both. These distinctions highlight important aspects of the politics of order and hegemony, and also how the practical effects of certain kinds of goods substitution efforts can extend beyond their intended purposes.

We illustrate the utility of the approach through two sets of cases. The first explores the different motivations of Russia and China – Moscow's more counter-hegemonic agenda and Beijing's more counter-ordering priorities – in crafting regional integration, norm diffusion, and statements via the Shanghai Cooperation Organization (SCO), often viewed as Central Asia's most robust post-Western institution. The second focuses on the cases of Ecuador and Turkmenistan, two states that received energy-backed loans from China during the 2008 financial crisis, which allowed these regimes to bypass borrowing from traditional Western-controlled financers in favor of Beijing's bilateral patronage.

US Hegemony and Goods Substitution

Traditional hegemonic-order theorists say very little explicitly about goods substitution, yet it plays a central role in their accounts of hegemony. "Hegemonic stability theory", Webb and Krasner (1989, 183–84) note, "argues that international economic openness and stability is most likely when there is a single dominant state." Following Kindleberger, it holds "that international economic stability is a public, or collective, good, since all countries benefit from it regardless of whether or not they contribute to its production" (Webb and Krasner 1989, 183–84).

Broader variants of the approach contend that hegemons not only provide public goods in the form of open trade regimes, but that they also net stabilize international security. Hegemons allow many states to reduce their military spending and otherwise adopt policies made possible by a less war-prone international environment. Lake (2009, 139–43) estimates that, overall, increasingly closer membership in the American security order leads to dramatic reductions in the amount that states must divert to defense. The American presence in Western Europe almost certainly created, at a minimum, a permissive security environment for efforts at European integration.

Of course, most of the security goods facilitated, orchestrated, or directly provided by the United States are *not* genuinely public in character. In NATO, Washington initiated – and underwrites – the joint production of member security as a club good (Sandler and Hartley 2001). In itself, the US–Japan bilateral alliance is closer to an exchange of private goods (or a "club of two"). In such cases, as we noted in Chapter 1, the security architecture creates spillover effects that benefit some third-party states. Of course, these alliances may also worsen the security environment for *other* third parties, thus diminishing the value of their overall security portfolio.

The close relationship between, on the one hand, hegemonic orders and, on the other, the texture and distribution of goods, extends beyond the security and economic domains. The allocation of status resolves as the allocation of symbolic goods; systems of social ranking influenced by hegemonic powers reflect goods hierarchies. In practice, hegemons often shape what particular goods *matter* for international standing – from membership in international organizations, to the performance of specific norms and values, to the possession of specific weapons systems – and they also enjoy some ability to allocate those goods. In field-theoretic terms, this amounts to "meta-capital." The hegemon's concentration of military and economic power allows it to influence the exchange value of field-relevant capital, make some forms of capital newly field relevant, and even create (or help create) new international fields (Musgrave and Nexon 2018; Nexon and Neumann 2018).

It isn't just that hegemons shape both the architecture and goods ecology of international order by providing various substantive kinds of goods (such as military goods) or the degree to which those goods take the form of public-like, club, and private goods. The very *mechanisms* by which hegemons order international politics center around goods provision. Much of the way that hegemons make and enforce international rules and norms is through offering carrots or threatening sticks. The instruments at stake quite literally are assets and other goods – whether military, economic, social, or cultural. International organizations operate in the same way, such as when the International Monetary Fund (IMF) grants assistance conditional on alterations in a state's economic policies. Whether in the form of conditions, specific quid pro quos, or implicit contracts, the production and supply of goods provides an infrastructure for maintaining or transforming international order.

Power Transitions and Goods Substitution

In international systems with multiple great powers, the politics of goods substitution is a fundamental feature of power politics. Unless dominant actors form an effective cartel when it comes to the provision of goods, clients play patrons off against one another, while great powers compete to shape the goods ecology. In hegemonic systems the dominant power is, more or less, the only game in town. It enjoys a patronage monopoly. If acting in concert with second-tier powers that support the same general order – as the United States did during its period of supposed "unipolarity" – the hegemon is first among equals in a cartel or oligopoly.

This means that, as a practical matter, the dynamics of goods substitution become crucial during power transitions, including the one we are currently experiencing. The goods ecology comes under strain during power transitions precisely because new actors emerge with the ability to provide, say, economic, security, and diplomatic goods. Dominant actors may be less able, or less willing, to provide those goods themselves. Even if dominant actors remain committed to supplying public, private, and club goods, the greater availability of alternative suppliers – of exit options – affects the calculations of other states.

In their discussion of "strategic hedging," Tessman and Wolfe (2011) make precisely this point. They argue that power transitions create incentives for second-tier states to substitute their own provision of "public goods and subsidies" for those provided by the hegemon. Some do so because they worry that "the leading state ... may choose to reduce or eliminate some or all of the public goods and subsidies it provides" (Tessman and Wolfe 2011, 219–20). Others do so because they worry that the hegemon will weaponize its goods provision against them by, for example, using the threat of exclusion as a coercive instrument.

Moreover, the proliferation of alternative patrons and providers also undercuts the mechanisms that hegemons use to uphold generalized international architecture. For example, the Trump administration threatened to curtail foreign aid from countries that do not vote consistently with the United States at the United Nations or, in the case of the Central American states, send a disproportionate number of migrants. But the important difference between now and the 1990s is that these same countries can now contemplate replacing US funding with alternative regional or global patrons. As weaker states enjoy growing opportunities to exercise leverage and exit, those carrots and sticks decline in effectiveness. Because of its effect on the goods ecology, even hedging by status quo powers can trigger all of these dynamics.

Beyond "Hard Balancing" and "Soft Balancing"

Realist and realist-inflected scholarship has developed a tendency to refer to all power-political efforts that involve nonmilitary instruments as "soft balancing," with the idea that these efforts use tools of "soft power" rather than "hard power" (see, in general, Chan 2017; Friedman and Long 2015; He 2008; He and Feng 2008; Kelley 2005; Paul 2004, 2005;

Pape 2005; for criticisms, see Brooks and Wohlforth 2005b; Lieber and Alexander 2005).

Of course, not all uses of military or nonmilitary statecraft are, as original formulations of the concept emphasized, examples of something that we might call "balancing" – that is, efforts to correct an unfavorable distribution of capabilities or, in the more restricted sense, prevent or undermine hegemony. But, as we argued in Chapter 1, from a goods substitution perspective even traditional "hard" balancing is a subset of the broader category.

Thinking in terms of goods substitution should sensitize us to the importance of drawing a clear distinction between the *logics*, *instruments*, and *objectives* of any particular power-political maneuver. States routinely draw from a toolkit of different forms of capital – military, economic, diplomatic, cultural, institutional, and so on – to influence the behavior of other actors in international politics. They deploy these instruments in ways that likely reflect a limited number of logics, such as: first, "integration," which includes internal military mobilization and the pooling of military capabilities in alliances, as well as efforts to "bind" actors in ways that limit their autonomy; and, second, "fragmentation," which includes wedge strategies aimed at breaking apart domestic or international coalitions (Goddard and Nexon 2016, 7–9; see also Crawford 2011; Goddard 2018b; Goddard, MacDonald, and Nexon 2019).

Goods substitution is something of a metalogic, one that can be used in ways consistent with more specific strategies within the two categories of "soft" and "hard" balancing. But rather than privilege military-security goods as somehow "harder" or more "material" than diplomatic capital, economic capital, or other goods and performances, we should recognize that a whole range of instruments can potentially shape international politics – let alone the fate of power transitions. Indeed, processes of goods substitution that look nothing like military balancing may "hollow out" hegemonic orders: first, by stripping the leading power of the mechanisms necessary to uphold its order and, second, by altering the distribution of military capabilities through a variety of processes independent of balancing or even warfare.

In the next section, we discuss two major objectives with respect to the character of international systems that may be at stake in goods substitution: shifting the distribution of power and altering the architecture of international order.

Goods Substitution As Statecraft: The Different Aims of Goods Substitution in Hegemonic Orders

Debates over the stability of hegemonic systems tend to focus on the attractiveness of the order and the willingness of incumbent powers to accommodate rising ones. The same argument, when approached through the lens of balance-of-power theories, pivots around *the stability of unipolar systems*. Traditional balance-of-power theorists believe the natural equilibrium of international politics involves two or more great powers forming a rough balance of capabilities. States, empires, and other political communities that strive for hegemony should encourage counterbalancing coalitions. These threaten the autonomy, if not the outright survival, of other great powers (see Hui 2004, 2005; Ikenberry 2002; Kauffman, Little, and Wohlforth 2007; Layne 1993, 2006; Nexon 2009; Schweller 2006; Waltz 1979, 2000).

By the late 1990s, however, the United States did not appear to be provoking a counterbalancing coalition – even though classic balance-of-power theory suggests that unipolar systems represent an intolerable condition for second-tier powers. In an influential article, Wohlforth (1999) argued that unipolar systems *are* stable from a balance-of-power perspective, because no conceivable coalition of second-tier powers can actually form effective counterbalancing coalitions. Efforts at balancing – whether through domestic military buildups or the formation of alliances – would be impossible to hide and thus too likely to incur the wrath of the leading state. Thus, unipolar systems end through processes of uneven growth and relative decline, not through counter-hegemonic balancing (see Brooks and Wohlforth 2005a, 2008; Ikenberry 2002).

In important respects, these debates never really were that distinct, so it is not surprising that they quickly converged. But the two frameworks highlight an important distinction: between the architecture of international order and the distribution of power (see Ikenberry 2002; Ikenberry and Nexon 2019; Nexon 2009). As our discussion of revisionism in Chapter 1 highlights, it is possible to object to aspects of the architecture of international order without challenging the distribution of military capabilities. It is also possible for states to want to alter the distribution of capabilities but accept prevailing rules, norms, and values.

As the two authors of this chapter, joined by Steven Ward, have argued elsewhere, this suggests disaggregating revisionism along these

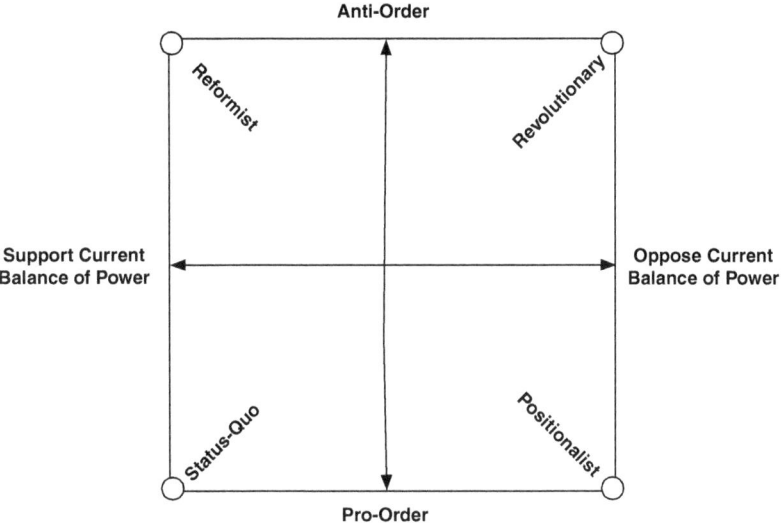

Figure 2.1 Revisionism, an alternative typology
(Source: Cooley, Nexon, and Ward 2019, 696)

two axes (Cooley, Nexon, and Ward 2019).[2] The result is four ideal-typical orientations: *status quo*, *reformist*, *positionalist*, and *revolutionary* (see Figure 2.1). An important advantage of this framework is that it allows analysts to think more systematically about *revisionist hegemons* – particularly at times when the US government has sought to alter the very order that it played an outsized role in constructing (see Lissner and Rapp-Hooper 2018a, 2018b; Schake 2018).

Revolutionary

We borrow this label from Kissinger's notion of a "revolutionary power." As he notes, "Whenever there exists a power which considers the international order or the manner of legitimizing it oppressive, relations between it and other powers will be revolutionary. In such cases, it is not the adjustment of differences within a given which will be at issue, but the system itself" (Kissinger 2017, 2). Revolutionary states

---

[2] The discussion in this subsection draws heavily on that article. We thank Steven Ward for giving us permission to use it, and stress that he is essentially a coauthor for this part of the chapter.

are akin to Ward's (2017, chapter 1) category of "radical" revisionism. In this approach, the ideal-typical revolutionary state (or actor) is similar to a radical revisionist, but defined as a state that simultaneously challenges the balance of military capabilities and the architecture of international order.

Real-world actors may combine relatively high levels of both orientations without reaching something close to the ideal-typical limit; we should expect to see substantial variation in the intensity and mix of revolutionary orientations. Regardless, for revolutionary actors the distinction between the distribution of capabilities and international architecture tends to collapse. It is not just that they reject both, but that as they become more revisionist, they increasingly see the two as inseparable. In this sense, the category is well-trodden in prevailing approaches – that is, those that aggregate both objects of dissatisfaction into a single category of "revisionism." In hegemonic systems, power-political activities of revolutionary revisionists will tend to be comprehensively *counter-hegemonic*, and they will deploy strategies of goods substitution with the aim of undermining the entire hegemonic order.

Positionalist

Ideal-typical positionalists are satisfied with prevailing rules, norms, and institutions but *not* the existing balance of power. This differs from Joseph Grieco's (1993) description of states as "defensive positionalists" by assumption: the idea that states always worry about maintaining their relative position and therefore will avoid pareto-improving cooperation when it leaves them relatively worse off than their partners. Indeed, realists tend to divide on whether states generally embrace "offensive positionalism" – seek to maximize their relative power – or "defensive positionalism" – seek to maintain their relative power (see Peou 2002; Schimmelfennig 1998, 6–7; also Lynn-Jones 1995).

In unidimensional accounts, states that seek to alter the distribution of power out of, for example, parochial security concerns – to correct a perceived security deficit – are usually coded as status quo states or mildly revisionist ones. But this masks variation between revolutionary actors who seek to alter the distribution of power as part of an effort to change other elements of order, and positionalist actors who may aim to alter the distribution of power to maintain the broader order.

Thus, in hegemonic systems, a hegemon that turns against its own order may, in principle, provoke other status quo states to increase their own capabilities in order to check those efforts, or to decouple their security from the hegemon in order to be able to resist its counter-order activities. Schweller and Pu (2011, 45) argue that "under unipolarity ... balancing becomes the very definition of revisionism; the goal of restoring a global balance of power requires the overthrow of the existing unipolar structure." But this only holds if we fail to disaggregate order and the distribution of military capabilities. Rising challengers, therefore, need not "delegitimize the hegemon's global authority and order" to provoke balancing; balancing can derive from the legitimacy of the order and the hegemon's loss of authority by adopting a more reformist orientation. (Schweller and Pu 2011, 55)

For instance, if the United States continues down the path of trying to revise the international order along less liberal lines and to raise doubts about the NATO alliance, major European powers might move towards "decoupling": engaging in (military) goods substitution that would allow them to preserve aspects of international order without help from the United States, or even to help them function as an effective counterweight against Washington's efforts. This is *counter-unipolarity* goods substitution, but not counter-order substitution.

Reformist

Goods substitution efforts in hegemonic systems that follow reformist logics are best understood as counter-order, but not counter-unipolarity or counter-hegemonic. Even though they are satisfied with the prevailing distribution of military capabilities, ideal-typical reformist states may desire deep changes in the architecture of international order.

How is this possible? Consider three scenarios.

First, states may seek changes in areas of international order besides the distribution of capabilities for purely domestic reasons. For example, the international economic order may look unfavorable to politically ascendant economic sectors or interests; or a newly empowered coalition may dislike the international order for ideological reasons (Chapman, McDonald, and Moser 2015; Owen 2012; Philpott 2001).

Second, reformist efforts may be aimed at maintaining the current distribution of power. For example, actors might seek to engineer elements of international order in ways that forestall potential future adverse shifts in the distribution of capabilities.

Third, states might seek changes in various elements of international order to reduce existing, or potential, threats resulting from the current distribution of power. For example, in hegemonic systems second-tier powers may see a growing threat of predation from the dominant power. Thus, they may want to alter the order – by, say, promoting institutional or normative constraints on military intervention – so as to restrain the dominant power. Similar logics might hold in systems with great power concerts or other arrangements.

In the real world, of course, we will not find purely reformist states. Most reform-oriented actors will have at least some discomfort with the prevailing distribution of power or trajectories of change in military capabilities. Even domestic motivations for changing or conserving international order, including ideological ones, seldom develop in isolation from changing relative capabilities (Gunitsky 2017).

To the extent that the United States, whether during the Bush or Trump administrations, can be classified as a "revisionist hegemon," we suspect that dissatisfaction with institutional, normative, or international economic elements of order are more important than dissatisfaction with the distribution of power. Hegemons generally want to conserve a distribution of power that favors them, and thus seek to reform international order in ways that, at least in part, their leadership believes will accomplish this task.

The reformist character of the Bush administration, in particular, probably helps explain the lack of traditional counterbalancing among America's great power allies. The United States was not taking steps that risked significantly altering the place of its second-tier partners in the global distribution of power. The Trump administration's revisionist bent – while driven by different dynamics and carrying different kinds of dangers for other actors – is similarly aimed, at least with respect to American allies, less at altering the distribution of capabilities than at rejecting core elements of liberal international order (Cooley and Nexon 2020a, Chapter 7; see also Lissner and Rapp-Hooper 2018a, 2018b; Norrlof 2018; Schake 2019; Stokes 2018).

Status Quo

Status quo orientations do not differ in this framework from any other. They match Ward's (2017) conception and more traditional ones (see Davidson 2006; Goddard 2018a). Status quo-oriented goods substitution is best understood as counter-policy in character; that is, actors pursue it for more parochial or limited interests.

When states substitute goods formerly provided by a hegemon, they do so not out of a desire to alter the order or affect the distribution of power, but to pressure the leading state to adopt different policies *within* the contours of the existing architecture. For example, they may care about, *as they see it*, small differences in the distribution of nonmilitary goods.

Here we need, once again, to emphasize the ideal-typical character of these distinctions. In hegemonic systems, no efforts to substitute goods provided by the hegemon will ever be *purely* status quo in orientation. But they may still fall well below the threshold of what participants would recognize as counter-order, counter-unipolar, or counter-hegemonic steps.

Intentions and Effects

Standard stories about the emergence of challengers during power transitions identify causal processes in which positionalist or reformist states become increasingly revolutionary. Reformist states come to view the existing hegemon as a barrier to their preferred international order. Positionalist states increasingly see the international order as incompatible with their preferred distribution of capabilities (see Goddard 2018a; Ward 2013, 2017).

But actors may engage in the politics of goods substitution for reasons other than the *effects* of their actions. As we have noted a few times in this chapter, engaging in goods substitution for even status quo aims can still undermine hegemonic powers by depriving them of a mechanism they previously used to uphold their order, their power-political position, or both. Conflict and bargaining over policies, orders, and the distribution of capabilities may lead actors to alter their aims. Efforts that begin as counter-order may serve, down the road, counter-hegemonic purposes. This recognition appears to have driven the belated, and apparently ineffectual, decision of the Obama

Administration to oppose the Asian Infrastructure Investment Bank (AIIB).

Indeed, reformist hegemons can trigger action–reaction cycles where the efforts taken by states that want to preserve the international order become increasingly positionalist, prompting more aggressive action by the leading power, and thus resulting in the unravelling of the hegemonic order – including elements of its architecture that states wanted to preserve in the first place. Similarly, reformist hegemons can create openings for rising powers by, first, allowing those powers to position themselves as defenders of the existing architecture or, second, taking away reasons for more status quo powers to prefer its leadership over that of the rising power. For example, to the degree that the Trump administration, or its successors, make good on its antipathy toward elements of liberal order, it will likely qualitatively alter the international goods ecology by diminishing the value of multilateral mechanisms, commitments, and democratic norms. A likely result, as Bader points out in Chapter 4, is that China will accelerate its efforts to fill "identified gaps" in the international order and assume international leadership roles over selective sectors. But this is a very different logic than to code Chinese intentions as order enhancing or order diminishing.

Regional and Global Hegemony

The previous discussion, as well as the typology, largely assumes that we are talking about a single international system with a single distribution of capabilities. But the world has seen only one example of truly global hegemony: the United States after the collapse of the Soviet Union. There is a reasonable case that the United Kingdom operated as a global hegemon for part of the nineteenth century. The same holds of the United States after World War II.[3]

Both Britain and the post-war United States faced challengers capable of giving them a run for their money. Those rivals often carved out regional subsystems in which they established hegemonic dominance. For instance, if we read the Cold War as a case of a hegemon – the United States – facing off against a challenger – the Soviet Union – then

---

[3] One reason why we have so few cases of global hegemony is that, until around two centuries ago, technologies of governance – including transportation and

there is no question that the USSR exercised hegemony over Eastern Europe, where it controlled an informal empire. In some respects, the Soviet Union itself amounted to a successor to prior iterations of Russian-centered imperial hegemony that ultimately spanned Eurasia from the Baltic to the Pacific (see Beissinger 2002; Bunce 1985; Motyl 2001; Wendt and Friedheim 1995).

Introducing regional hegemons – or bids for hegemony – into the mix complicates matters, because it introduces the possibility that actors have different orientations toward prevailing international conditions in different regions and at different aggregations of international subsystems. Russian leaders almost certainly saw their 2008 intervention in Georgia and their 2014 intervention in Ukraine as upholding their claims to regional leadership – to their historical sphere of privileged influence – even as the United States and its allies saw them as evidence of revisionism toward broader international order. Moreover, both were caught up in wider concerns about American support for democracy promotion and support for uprisings against incumbent regimes, both of which we typically associate with revolutionary revisionism (for a nuanced discussion, see Toal 2017).

Attention to the interaction among different regional orders – hegemonic or otherwise – and among regional and global or other aggregate orders also matters in the context of the politics of goods substitution (see Mastanduno 2019). The reasons why are very familiar to scholars of international security. States and other actors may align with extra-regional powers to oppose or sustain regional orders. The United States currently backs a coalition including Israel and the Kingdom of Saudi Arabia against Iran; Saudi Arabia and Iran are locked in a struggle for hegemony in the wider Middle East; and Russia backs a coalition including Iran, the Syrian government, and Hezbollah (Byman 2019; Ghoble 2019). At the same time, dispositions toward global order may drive actors to seek goods substitution from would-be regional hegemons, thus facilitating bids for regional dominance. Finally, once we think about international order as a composite not only of regional orders but also of issue areas, then we open up the possibility of more complicated – but also more interesting – interactions.

> communication – were simply incapable of supporting global dominance. For more on this, see Buzan and Little 2000; Kauffman, Little, and Wohlforth 2007; Hui 2004, 2005; Lee 2016a, 2016b; Phillips 2013.

An Example: The Rise of the BRICS

While Figure 2.1 made no assumptions about the prevailing distribution of power, Figure 2.2 applies the general typology to a system characterized by a single hegemonic power – in this case, the United States. But it also does so in the context of international political contention that implicates the United States. Thus, "revolutionary" aims resolve as "counter-hegemonic" as they seek to undermine the position of the incumbent superpower and change the prevailing order. "Positionalist" aims are specifically "anti-unipolar" as they attempt to forward a more bipolar or multipolar world but not an alteration in order. "Reformist" goals remain "counter-order." And we term "counter-policy" those efforts to thwart the United States on some

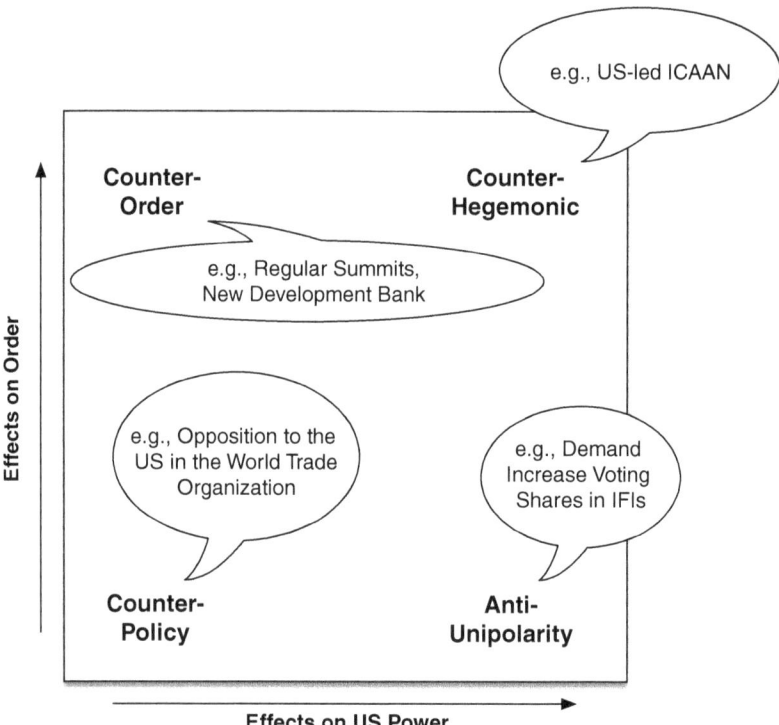

Figure 2.2 Implications for power-political maneuvers on US-led order: The example of the BRICS

issue that, nevertheless, neither aim to challenge its preponderance of power nor the existing order.

The rise of the BRICS (Brazil, Russia, India, China, and South Africa) and expressions by its members of broader dissatisfaction with the nature of Western-controlled international financial institutions illustrate the different types of contentious challenges. Jim O'Neill, Head of Global Economic Research at Goldman Sachs, coined the BRIC acronym in a seminal 2001 paper that argued that four emerging powers (Brazil, China, Russia, and India) were increasing their share of the world economy and that their interests remained ill-represented by existing major international economic institutions such as the G7 (O'Neill 2001). The first annual BRIC summit was held in Russia in 2009; the group expanded to include South Africa in 2010. Since then, the group has held annual summits that have engaged with a range of international economic and global governance issues, while analysts and scholars have debated the extent of the group's revisionist agenda and actual cooperative accomplishments. Using our analytical space, we can more precisely map the various challenges that the BRICS, as an organization, might bring against US-led economic institutions and practices; indeed, we can place BRICS activities into all four quadrants, suggesting the organization represents a complex and multifaceted challenge to the US-led liberal hegemonic order.

In the counter-policy ("status quo") space – the southwest quadrant – BRICS members might act more out of opposition to a specific US proposal or institutional priority without any broader aim. This might, in practice, involve collectively expressing their voice within a global governance negotiation as a community. In 2011, Brazil, China, Russia and India abstained on United Nations Security Council (UNSC) Resolution 1973, which authorized the implementation of a no-fly zone and the sanctioning of Libya under the Responsibility to Protect (R2P) principle. Soon after, they criticized Western military actions as violating the spirit of the vote (Steunkel 2020, 142–43). In the economic realm, the BRICS maintain an informal conference within the World Trade Organization (WTO) that seeks policy coordination and consensus, while membership in BRICS offers an informal bargaining coalition that can, in theory, be leveraged across other negotiations in global fora. Even across issue areas like climate change and food security, where member states initially lacked consensus, the BRICS managed to carve out consensus areas so as to project a committed community (Brütsch and Papa 2013). Critical BRICS summit statements – such as against the Washington Consensus and in support for Syria's sovereignty and territorial integrity – have also countered the Western consensus on prevailing economic and security matters.

Moving rightwards towards the anti-unipolarity ("positionalist") quadrant (the southeast), BRICS members might also seek to challenge the decision-making power or rules of an existing organization primarily to erode the power of the United States rather than to alter broader international order. For example, in 2009 the BRICS acted as a bargaining coalition to lobby the International Monetary Fund (IMF) and World Bank to reallocate voting shares away from Western Europe and to emerging countries, in exchange for increasing their contributions to the international financial institutions (IFIs). China also used the BRICS to successfully sideline Washington's criticism of Beijing's currency policies within the IMF (Armijo and Roberts 2014).

The northeastern cell represents overtly counter-hegemonic (or revolutionary) aims, where BRICS members both promote their own institutions and exit from – or attempt to otherwise delegitimize – the institutions of the liberal order. To take a high-profile example, all BRICS members expressed strong support for removing internet governance from the US-based Internet Corporation for Assigned Names and Numbers (ICAAN), which until 2016 operated under the auspices of the US Department of Commerce, and replace it with a new international regulatory framework and institution. Tellingly, however, the coalition members disagreed on what type of institution should actually replace ICAAN. While China and Russia backed asserting individual national sovereignty over internet governance, India, Brazil, and South Africa advocated establishing a new multilateral organization to replace the US-based body (Ebert and Maurer 2013). The BRICS also served as a source of legitimacy and international support for specific Russian actions after it annexed Crimea in 2014; Oliver Steunkel (2020, 162–63) points out that the group effectively blocked an Australian proposal to bar Russia from the G20 summit; all the foreign ministries of the BRICS refrained from criticizing Russia in public and, at the United Nations, abstained from voting for UN resolution 68/262 that affirmed Ukraine's sovereignty over the peninsula.

An Example: The Rise of the BRICS

Finally, the northwestern quadrant represents the counter-order (reformist) challenge, where the BRICS establish new institutions designed to run in parallel with the American-led order, but maintain their membership of the Western-led bodies as well. This fairly accurately describes how the celebrated annual BRICS summits have sought to expand the area of coordination and discussion. At the 2014 summit, the BRICS announced the establishment of the New Development Bank (NDB), a new IFI intended to fund infrastructure projects in the developing world. Tellingly, as with the AIIB, Beijing emphasized that the NDB was intended to complement, not substitute for, established IFIs (Chin 2014).

Returning to the case of the AIIB, this map also suggests that even if the AIIB, like the NDB, represents an attempt at (partial) exit from the World Bank component of the Bretton Woods system, it carries possible unintended implications for American hegemony. European states are not likely signing on to the project in order to counter US power and influence – let alone the international order – but Washington's failed attempt to pressurize them to eschew participation reflects concern about just such effects. Consider also how IMF conditionality during the 1998 East Asian financial crisis prompted the Malaysian government to eschew IMF assistance altogether. In the wake of the crisis, East Asian regimes substituted via their own recognizance – by amassing large foreign exchange reserves – and ramped up efforts to engage in club goods substitution through collective action. Here the concerns are not simply those of policy autonomy, but of regime stability: East Asian governments believe that acceding to IMF conditionality creates unacceptable risks to their political survival.

This behavior is itself a good example of *counter-order* asset substitution that does not *directly* challenge the position of the unipolar power nor seek to alter its policies. Indeed, to the extent that it supported inexpensive US borrowing, it might have provided a medium-term benefit to American military superiority (Oatley 2015). Nonetheless, these actions may also have downstream ramifications for the ability of the United States to pursue its preferred polices, and even for its power and influence. At the very least, they attenuate Washington's ability to aggressively push Washington-consensus international economic policies.

China and Goods Substitution

We initially probe some of the practical consequences of the logic of goods substitution, and their potential to move countries across different international orientations, by examining two different cases of Chinese policies and their unintended regional effects. This serves as a complement to Chapter 4 which provides a more extensive overview of the range of issues and sectors where China is actively engaging in international asset substitution: regional forums, trade and investment agreements, and diplomatic forums.

Theoretically, we wish to highlight that much of the debate about China's growing international economic role fails to distinguish, on the one hand, among revisionist, positionalist, and reformist dimensions of activity and, on the other, between the aims of policies and their effects. Popular works tend to focus on China's growing soft economic power and how that may translate, eventually, to positionalist and reformist outcomes (Halper 2010; Jacques 2009). Others focus more narrowly on assessing evidence of actual counter-hegemonic capabilities and activity.[4] Similarly, the emerging debate on the potential counter-order effects of Chinese economic activity center on its aid and investment policies, particularly whether China acts as a "rogue donor" that indiscriminately feeds corruption and human rights violations in recipients (Naim 2007; Woods 2008). Even sober and dat-rich assessments of China's role in areas such as Africa tend to focus on Beijing's economic intentions and local developmental outcomes (Brautigam 2009), rather than the systemic externalities that might result from how elites in target states wield such flows for their own purposes. In sum, any discussion or attempt to grasp the analytical significance of whether China is promoting goods substitution must consider the diversity of China's foreign economic activities, as well as distinguish among the logics of reformist, positionalist, and revisionist aims.

Our illustrative cases show the interplay of these international goods substitution dynamics across two areas of foreign policy engagement of the People's Republic of China (PRC): the evolution of the Shanghai

---

[4] For example, Beckley (2012) dismisses claims of China's future rise by examining a range of leading indicators of globalization where the United States still maintains a clear advantage. Similarly, Drezner's (2009) analysis of China's role as a creditor during the 2008 financial crisis concludes that Beijing proved unwilling and unable to use its financial power to compel US decisions.

Cooperation Organization (SCO) and China's loans-for-energy deals with developing countries. These cases illustrate both the analytical dimensions of our four-cornered property space and the empirical importance of related policy drivers. The SCO has spawned a near cottage industry of analysis – much of it focused on whether it is fostering a counter-hegemonic Sino–Russian alliance (Allison 2004; Cohen 2006). No such alliance has, of course, materialized; in fact, our case demonstrates critical strategic disagreements between Moscow and Beijing that have undermined the SCO's overall effectiveness as a facilitator of collective action and provider of international goods. While Beijing would like the institution to serve as a "reformist" source of collective goods and regional integration in Central Asia, Moscow treats the organization as a revisionist vehicle to denounce major foreign policy decisions of the West. This lingering tension between its major patrons over the exact role and revisionist purpose of the organization is critical for understanding its institutional development and regional impact.

Our second set of cases examines the loans-for-energy agreements that China concluded during the great financial crisis with Ecuador and Turkmenistan. Analysts usually treat these as some combination of attempts to secure vital energy supplies and growing Chinese influence in the developing world. The case studies – originally considered simple acts of status quo investments, albeit counter-cyclical – show that these Chinese energy loans also produced counter-order implications: They shielded the government in Quito from the adverse economic impact of defaulting on its international bond payments; and they enabled Ashgabat to cope with a financial crisis without turning to commercial lenders or IFIs. In fact, it remains unclear whether or not Beijing sought to counteract principles of liberal order – even though its loans had that effect. This suggests that demand-side factors can matter more than the intentions of providers of alternative public and private goods. It reinforces the possibility that revisionist and reformist suppliers are unnecessary to hollow out hegemonic orders.

Sino–Russian Revisionist Outlooks and the Shanghai Cooperation Organization

The rise and evolution of the SCO over the last decade illustrates a range of strategic aims of goods substitution, as well as how one member, Russia, has attempted to shift the organization from its "reformist" origins to a clear global "revisionist" stance. The SCO's founding membership in June 2001 included Russia, China, Kazakhstan, Kyrgyzstan, Uzbekistan, and Tajikistan; it was joined by the admission of India and Pakistan in 2017. The group was a formal successor to the Shanghai Five group, a forum that during the 1990s successfully negotiated the old disputed Soviet–Chinese border in Central Asia. Initially formed as a new-style security organization, SCO defines its organizational mission as combating "three evils" in the region: terrorism, separatism, and extremism (Aris 2009). Though Beijing presents the organization as multilateral in character, regional players generally perceive it as a Chinese-driven initiative. Indeed, many view it as providing multilateral cover for China's bilateral security and economic policies in Central Asia (Cooley 2012; Kassenova 2009). The SCO's "three evils" doctrine draws directly from Chinese domestic concerns about Uighur separatism in its Western province of Xinjiang. Beijing views promoting regional economic development and infrastructure in neighboring Central Asia as critical to stabilizing its Western province (Clarke 2011; Laruelle and Peyrouse 2012).

In keeping with its status as an organization founded to deal with regional and transnational security threats, the SCO conducts biennial military exercises within the region – referred to as "Peace Missions." These concern some Western observers in that they offer platforms for Sino–Russian military cooperation. In 2004, the SCO opened a permanent Regional Anti-Terror Structure (RATS) in Tashkent, Uzbekistan. RATS has facilitated internal security cooperation among its member states – including maintaining a unified blacklist of regional security threats, exchanging data, and sanctioning extraordinary renditions and the transferring of suspects among members (Cooley 2013; Human Rights in China 2011). Its representatives report directly to their respective Interior Ministries rather than to the Secretary General in Beijing. More broadly, cooperation by the group's internal security services – including the signing of a Counterterrorism Treaty that allows for close cooperation, data sharing, and common blacklisting of political opponents – has been extensive. However, it has also drawn criticism from human rights organizations for undermining international human rights norms and creating new forms of regional law, in the name of security, to insulate regimes from their human rights commitments (Cooley and Schaaf 2017).

Beijing has sought to expand the SCO's regional agenda to include economic cooperation. At various points, Beijing has introduced plans to promote free trade, establish a regional development bank, and form a regional business council. The SCO also sponsors election monitoring missions in the region. It should come as little surprise that these missions are far less critical about the quality of elections than their Western counterparts.[5] The SCO also funds educational exchanges and state-sponsored youth networking projects.

So how should we understand the challenge posed by the SCO and its varied portfolio of activities? Some commentators, especially in the United States, point to the organization's possible counter-hegemonic or revisionist aspirations. The most common concern was that the SCO might form the nucleus of a counter-NATO bloc (Cohen 2006). The SCO's own foundational documents are littered with invocations of the importance of "non-interference" in the domestic affairs of other states – the so-called "Shanghai Spirit" (Ambrosio 2008). The same documents reject "unilateralism" and call for the promotion of the "democratization of international relations," a reference to the rejection of US-led order in the region. The group's counter-hegemonic potential received international attention when, at its 2005 summit in Astana, it issued a joint declaration calling for the establishment of a timetable for the removal of foreign military bases in the Central Asian region. Just a few days later, the government of Uzbekistan expelled the United States from its airbase at Karshi-Khanabad (K2). Some officials, including the US Secretary of Defense Donald Rumsfeld, publicly blamed Russian and Chinese pressure on Uzbekistan for the eviction. In fact, Tashkent had already planned the eviction in light of intensifying US criticisms over the Uzbek security service's bloody crackdown in the city of Andijon (Cooley 2012, 38–40).

Moscow – especially during the period 2007–8 – was comfortable with promoting the SCO as a counter-hegemonic group. This stance mirrored Moscow's more aggressive public positioning of Russia as a revisionist power intent on unravelling the American-led liberal international order. The Russian leadership went so far as to push for Iranian membership in the organization. However, Beijing proved

---

[5] Indeed, the election-monitoring activities of the SCO constitute a clear example of goods substitution designed to enhance regime security. The verdict of election observers played a key role in the so-called "Color Revolutions" – a lesson regional authoritarian regimes took to heart.

increasingly reluctant to follow this agenda, particularly in light of negative Western reaction to the Astana basing declaration. China also adamantly refused Russia's request following the 2008 Russia–Georgia War to use the 2008 SCO summit to consider recognition of the independence of Abkhazia and South Ossetia (Cooley 2009).

China's preference has been to play down Western fears about the organization's possible counter-hegemonic role and push, instead, for the forum to become the primary vehicle for goods provision within Central Asia. However, it is exactly Beijing's reformist aspirations for the SCO that has led Moscow to privately oppose recent regional initiatives and to undermine their implementation. Russia considers Central Asia to be part of its privileged sphere of influence and is reluctant to endorse any economic architecture that would cede the role to Beijing and compete with Russian-led regional organizations – such as the Eurasian Economic Union. For example, during the financial crisis Beijing approached Moscow in fall 2008 with a proposal to establish a $10 billion "anti-crisis" fund, designed to finance regional infrastructure projects (Cooley 2009). Moscow initially refused, choosing to focus, instead, on developing its own anti-crisis emergency packages to Belarus and Kyrgyzstan.[6]

In spring 2009, Chinese officials once again proposed the creation of the emergency fund, this time suggesting that Moscow and Beijing each contribute $5 billion of its capital and jointly decide its projects. Moscow once again refused and frustrated Chinese officials put the plan on hold. Prior to the 2012 summit, another Beijing-led effort for an SCO regional development bank failed to materialize due to Russian foot-dragging. China announced at the Beijing summit that it would fund $10 billion worth of new infrastructure projects anyway, in keeping with its practice of framing many of its bilateral development and assistance projects as SCO initiatives.[7] The formal expansion of the group's membership in 2017 to include India and Pakistan appears to have been an admission that its economic agenda, from the Chinese

---

[6] Each of these approaches carried a political condition that the target countries considered, but ultimately did not enact. For Belarus, the loan was tied to its recognition of the declarations of independence of Abkhazia and South Ossetia following the 2008 Russia–Georgia War. For Kyrgyzstan, a $2 billion emergency package was conditional on Bishkek closing the US air base at Manas.

[7] Alexander Cooley, "In Central Asia, Public Cooperation and Private Rivalry," *New York Times* June 8, 2012.

perspective, will be carried out by other instruments. As Bader (Chapter 4) details, the rise of the Belt and Road project, the AIIB, and the NDB all offer Beijing alternative vehicles from which to invest in the region, build infrastructure, and promote connectivity with Western China.

In sum, Russia views the SCO as more counter-hegemonic than reformist, while China views the group as more reformist – serving as a vehicle for the provision of regional club and public goods – than revisionist. Despite these problems, Western commentaries about the SCO's regional role are often eager to emphasize its dynamic role as a goods provider. Strikingly, a group of prominent Western scholars have even called on the EU and NATO to drop any normative reservations they might have about engaging with the SCO in order to avoid losing influence in Central Asia (e.g., Antonenko 2007; Bailes 2007). This suggests a further twist to our analytical distinctions: that despite the SCO's meager accomplishments in actually institutionalizing counter-order in the economic sphere, it has nevertheless prompted calls for Western engagement and policy accommodation through its exaggerated reputation as a regional powerhouse.

Such perceptions are shared by other world leaders. In January 2013, Turkish Prime Minister Recep Tayyip Erdogan caused a diplomatic sensation when he openly called for Turkey to give up on its EU aspirations and enter the organization as a full member (it was granted Dialogue Partner status in 2012).[8] The Turkish leader gave no specific indications of how joining the SCO would enhance Turkish national interests, but the declaration was broadly interpreted as a signal to both the Turkish public and the EU that Turkey was now a major emerging power and would not subject itself to a protracted membership negotiation with Brussels. Whatever the "real" accomplishments of the SCO, it has clearly succeeded in projecting itself as a regional bloc, engaging in an array of security, economic, and social activities, that

---

[8] Erdogan was reported as saying: "When things go so poorly, you inevitably, as the prime minister of 75 million people, seek other paths. That's why I recently said to Mr. [Vladimir] Putin: 'Take us into the Shanghai Five; do it, and we will say farewell to the EU, leave it altogether. Why all this stalling?'... The Shanghai Five is better and more powerful and we have common values with them." Yigal Schliefer, "With EU Talks Stalled, Erdogan Suggests Ankara May Join SCO" *Eurasianet* January 28, 2013.

proudly functions as a non-Western forum for Eurasian governance and cooperation.

China's Loans-for-Energy Initiatives

Our second example focuses on the broader international impact of a range of loans-for-energy deals concluded by China with six states in Latin America and Eurasia – Brazil, Venezuela, Ecuador, Russia, Turkmenistan, and Kazakhstan – in 2009–10 during the global financial downturn. These loans have totaled $75 billion and have involved granting packages to target countries in exchange for energy supplies to Chinese companies.[9] The China Development Bank (CDB) has served as an institutional lynchpin for these deals, and has linked China's foreign policy goals and strategic aims with the commercial interests of Chinese energy companies (Downs 2011).[10] The foreign policy goals combine loans to targets and oil sales. The CDB provides the target country with a loan that can be used not only for development, but also for direct budget support. Chinese energy companies buy the pledged energy from the target state at world-market prices. They then deposit the proceeds directly into the target state's CDB account until the recipient pays the loan's principal and interest (Sanderson and Forsythe 2012).

The global financial crisis proved to be an inflection point in China's overseas lending and investment. A *Financial Times* research report estimates that, in 2009–10, China signed loans with developing countries worth at least $110 billion. Two-thirds were in the form of loans-for-oil agreements,[11] a sum that exceeded the World Bank's record $100 billion in crisis lending from mid-2008 to 2010.[12] China's lending occurred at a time when many international companies were scaling back or cancelling investments; no other financial institutions were willing to provide such large sums. Although Chinese energy packages were intended to invest in these countries and lock in their energy

---

[9] Downs (2011) excludes Kazakhstan's $10 billion deal from her inventory, bringing her figure of total Chinese energy-backed loans to $65 billion during 2009–10.

[10] The CBD is one of only two banks, along with China's Central Bank, to hold a Ministerial-level rank.

[11] "China's Lending Hits New Heights," *Financial Times* January 17, 2011.

[12] "China's Lending Hits New Heights," *Financial Times* January 17, 2011.

supply, Beijing's provision of loans-for-energy packages during the global economic downturn also played the classic hegemonic function (see Kindleberger 1973), of a last resort lender and counter-cyclical provider of development assistance.

China's Partnership with Ecuador

In December 2008, Ecuadorian President Rafael Correa announced that the Andean country would default on $3.2 billion of bonds due in 2012 and 2025. He argued that the debt was accumulated by a previous regime and therefore the Ecuadorian people had no obligation to service it. Earlier that year, Correa had used the same logic to justify not renewing the lease, set to expire in 2009, of a US military base in the coastal town of Manta. Part of a populist campaign message in the run-up to his reelection, Correa claimed that – as the lease was signed by an unrepresentative government and not ratified by congress – the basing agreement lacked legal standing (Bitar 2015, 112–14). Ecuador's default, championed by the president, the first in Latin America since Argentina defaulted in 2001, effectively froze the country out of international capital markets and any possible IFI support. The magnitude of the debt was not, by normal standards, particularly burdensome; defaulted interest payments have been estimated at just $400 million. Indeed, the following year, Quito repurchased 91 percent of the debt at 35 cents on the dollar, achieving a voluntary restructuring rate well beyond its 75 percent target.[13]

Correa publicly did not make the connection between his decision to default and the availability of Chinese financing. But in the post-default period Chinese loans provided short-term financing for Ecuador's severe budget shortfalls. Ecuador received its first loan-for-oil payment in July 2009: $1 billion secured with 69 million barrels of oil at an effective interest rate of 7.25 percent. In 2010, the CDB disbursed another $1 billion, followed by an additional $2 billion in 2011 – all secured with oil.[14] In 2012, Beijing provided $1 billion to help plug Quito's more than $4 billion deficit. In December 2012, China extended yet another $2 billion loan to help make up a projected

---

[13] "Ecuador's Winning Strategy," *The Economist* June 17, 2009.
[14] The 2011 loan was secured by a pledge to sell 39,000 barrels per day to PetroChina for two years. See Mercedes Alvaro, "China, Ecuador Sign $2 billion deal," *Wall Street Journal* June 28, 2011.

$6 billion budget shortfall in 2013.[15] Since its default, Ecuador has received $7.25 billion in oil export backed loans from China; CDB loans have allowed it to avoid a credit squeeze, "despite its status as a serial defaulter."[16] As a result, it appears that China has purchased a significant majority of Ecuador's oil production in the post-default period. In 2012, Quito sent 80 percent of its oil exports to China, with the same percentage projected for 2013.[17] Overall, a 2015 *New York Times* report estimated that, in total, "State-owned Chinese banks have already put nearly $11 billion into the country, and the Ecuadorean government is asking for more."[18]

China's high-profile partnership with Ecuador has spawned a number of studies assessing the possible reformist effects of the PRC's investment activities in Latin America. One analysis found that, since 2005, Chinese loans to the region have surpassed $75 billion dollars. In 2010 alone, Chinese commitments to Latin America totaled $37 billion, exceeding the combined value of lending from the World Bank, Inter-American Development and the United States Export-Import Bank (Gallagher, Irwin, and Koleski 2012, 1).

China's Partnership with Turkmenistan

Beijing also used the economic downturn to secure long-sought energy supplies from Russia (a $25 billion deal with Russian oil giant Rosneft) and Central Asia. The most important of these Central Asian agreements was reached with politically insular Turkmenistan – known both for its significant energy reserves, especially natural gas, and its reclusive politics and colorful dictators, as well as a long-standing policy of foreign policy "neutrality."[19] Within the space of months, China's investments and energy deals quickly and dramatically reoriented Ashgabat from the Russian sphere of influence – including reliance on Gazprom to export its supplies – to its current status as a Chinese economic client.

---

[15] Nathan Gill, "Ecuador to Use $2 Billion China Loan to Fund Budget Deficit," *Bloomberg* December 12, 2012.
[16] "China–Ecuador: The Love-In Continues," *Financial Times* February 12, 2012.
[17] "Ecuador, China Development Bank Sign $2 billion Loan Agreement," *Wall Street Journal* January 31, 2013.
[18] "China's Global Ambitions, Cash and Strings Attached," *New York Times* July 24, 2015.
[19] Turkmenistan is not a member of the Russian-led Commonwealth of Independent States (CIS) or the SCO.

Since 2006, the China National Petroleum Corporation (CNPC) had been constructing a major new gas pipeline originating in Turkmenistan to bring Central Asian gas east to China. The China–Central Asia pipeline represented the first significant export pipeline to break Russia's gas export infrastructure and offer an alternative market for Central Asia's producers. The pipeline's capacity has been revised upwards from 30 billion cubic meters (bcm) in 2006 to 40 bcm (Lines A+B), and then to 55 bcm per year following the completion of a third spur (Line C) in 2014; an additional line D, designed to access gas fields in Tajikistan and traverse Kyrgyzstan, was announced in 2016, possibly increasing capacity to about 80–85 bcm.[20]

During the pipeline's construction, CNPC seemingly capitalized on its high-level access to Turkmen officials and in 2007 concluded Turkmenistan's first foreign production sharing agreement for the Bagtyarlyk (South Yolotan) field. While precise information on export volumes is scant, at a conference in 2016 Deng Menmin, General Manager for CNPC International Turkmenistan, stated that as of May 2016 Turkmenistan had exported a total of 138.6 bcm to China; he reported 2015 export volumes at 29 bcm and estimated 2016 export volumes at 35 bcm.[21] This is a substantial volume given that Turkmen total output (including domestic consumption) in 2015 was estimated at 83.8 bcm, while exports to Russia accounted for just 5 bcm.[22] Overall, Turkmenistan has substituted dependence on Russia and its export infrastructure with Chinese patronage.

But beyond providing critical investment, CNPC's interest in Turkmen gas also provided the Central Asian state with emergency counter-cyclical lending of the last resort. The global financial crisis confronted Ashgabat with two simultaneous financial challenges: first, collapsing demand for gas in Europe, which led Gazprom to halt purchases even though it had just signed a long-term supply deal with Turkmenistan; then, in April 2009, an explosion ruptured the main

---

[20] As detailed on CNPC's website, "Flow of Natural Gas from Central Asia," www.cnpc.com.cn/en/FlowofnaturalgasfromCentralAsia/Flowofnaturalgasfrom CentralAsia2.shtml.

[21] "China Keeps Turkmen Galkynysh in Reserve," *Natural Gas Europe*, May 30, 2016, www.naturalgaseurope.com/china-quiet-on-galkynysh-field-29846.

[22] "Turkmenistan: The Diversification of the Gas Export Market," *Natural Gas Europe*, December 16, 2015.

Turkmen–Russia pipeline connector.[23] The explosion plunged Russian–Turkmen relations into crisis; it also blew a massive hole in the government's budget. Analysts have estimated lost gas-sale revenues at $1 billion per month (Cooley 2012, 67–68). With Ashgabat in financial turmoil, Beijing moved in quickly to support the Turkmen economy. Its loans were secured with new natural gas commitments and new contracts for Chinese companies.

Just a few weeks after the pipeline incident in early April 2009, the CDB extended a $4 billion credit to Turkmenistan. In December 2009, CNPC acquired a service contract for Turkmenistan's sought after South Yolotan (Galkynysh) field – estimated as the world's second largest natural gas field. In March 2011, the CDB extended yet another $4 billion credit to Ashgabat. The exact purpose of the loan remains unclear, but it is to be paid off over ten years with a pledge of even more natural gas to the China–Central Asia pipeline.

US companies and officials note that such loans-for-energy deals place the United States and other Western companies at a clear disadvantage in their efforts to court Turkmenistan, precisely because of the additional goods provided by these packages. Special Envoy of the US Secretary of State for Eurasian Energy, Ambassador Richard Morningstar, stated in July 2009: "It's easy for Turkmenistan to make a deal with China, when China comes in and says, 'Hey, we're going to write a check for X amount of money, we're going to build a pipeline.' That's not a hard deal to accept, and we [US] can't compete in that way."[24] More broadly, China's forays into Turkmenistan also indicate a reformist goods substitution effect. Beijing's emergency financial support in 2009 kept the Turkmen economy afloat. The terms of the 2011 loan to Ashgabat were reportedly more favorable than a competing offer from German banks, while a turn to IFIs would likely have required an opening of the Turkmen economy to bring it more in line with liberal economic norms.[25] Overall, Turkmenistan has

---

[23] Turkmenistan claims the rupture resulted from Russia suddenly reducing the volume of Turkmen gas in the pipeline. It remains unclear if Russia deliberately orchestrated the rupture.

[24] M. K. Bhadrakumar, "China Resets Terms of Engagement in Central Asia," *Asia Times* December 24, 2009.

[25] "Second Pipeline, Loan to Keep China Tops in Turkmenistan," *International Oil Daily* October 8, 2010.

now become an indebted client of Beijing, with the new export pipeline locking in the Central Asian country as a Chinese supplier for decades.

A decade following these initial loans, the examples of both Ecuador and Turkmenistan draw attention to a further possible unintended consequence: that the inability of debtors to repay these loans will force them to support China's international agendas or strategic priorities in spheres unrelated to the purpose of the original loan deals. During its rise as a provider of overseas aid in Africa, China has written off some outstanding debts, but these have been relatively small sums from its poorest recipients.[26] However, China's rapid and substantial expansion in Eurasia and Latin America combined with declining commodity prices has left it exposed to large-scale defaults. A *Financial Times* report has estimated that, as of 2015, large outstanding debtors to China included Venezuela ($56 billion), Argentina ($19 billion), Myanmar ($20 billion), and Russia ($30 billion), as well as Ecuador ($5.3 billion) and Sri Lanka ($1.5 billion).[27] If Chinese officials are not willing to write off such sums – which are significantly greater than the few billion written off in Africa – then Beijing may well demand greater equity stakes in these countries' strategic assets or greater support for Chinese foreign policy positions at international governance bodies such as the UN. Once again, what may appear as simple investment, when viewed through the framework of asset substitution, may have broader counter-order effects.

Conclusion

Our approach to the logic of asset substitution explores how seemingly unimportant acts of substitution by non-Western patrons – in the economic, security, and symbolic realms – can both shape the international order and also transform the texture or ecology of the international order itself. Attention to the relationship among hegemony, international order, and goods substitution suggests multiple pathways through which dominant powers themselves may alter international order. In this chapter we identified four types of "revisionist" dispositions, ranging from status quo to positionalist, to reformist, and

---

[26] According to Brautigam (2009, 127–30) in its first debt-forgiveness pledge in 2000, China cancelled $1.2 billion and, after several more rounds, in June 2008 Premier Wen Jiabao announced that Beijing had cancelled a total of $3.6 billion.

[27] "China: With Friends Like These," *Financial Times* March 17, 2015.

outright revisionism – that aims to erode both US power and its hegemonic order. Rather than think of revisionism as a continuum or privileged hard power by regarding instances of substitution as "soft-balancing," we show how our four ideal-typical forms are applicable to a much wider array of international actors and organizations involved in international politics. In turn, thinking more broadly about the components of hegemonic order and the hidden mechanisms that may contribute to its transformation or, in certain cases, enduring resilience, yields a more dynamic understanding of how international orders transform that does not involve hegemonic war and that privileges the agency and regime calculations of even the smallest and supposedly inconsequential states in the international system. As the subsequent chapters will reveal, studying states such as Colombia, Kyrgyzstan, and Iceland is not just instructive – their actions, cumulatively, actively shape the international goods ecology and the very nature of the international order.

One of the more significant implications of our approach is that the sequencing and logic of the current erosion of American order may not feature overt challenges to Washington. Rather, states and regions may selectively disengage with the hegemonic order and substitute goods from alternative providers. The Trump administration's symbolic disengagement from various areas of global governance, such as climate change or cybersecurity, certainly has highlighted and heightened perceptions of a growing global leadership vacuum. But our analysis also suggests less recognizable ways in which the liberal order might be undermined, namely, by states invoking exit options to minimize Western political criticism or conditions. As many of the chapters in this volume show, this now describes the diminished state of Western influence across Russia and Eurasia, Latin America, and Africa, and even across the North Atlantic and Western organizations such as the Organization for Security and Co-operation in Europe (OSCE), especially when compared to US standing in the region during the 1990s.

Finally, as Chapter 8 will explore further, a shift toward more realpolitik and transactional goods provision might insulate the United States from defections by regimes, once thought of as democratic allies, and now experiencing autocratic consolidation – such as Duterte in the Philippines, Orban in Hungary, or Erdogan in Turkey – that want to avoid the extrinsic political and normative pressures generated by overt dependence on the United States. But we see

Conclusion

significant risks from rearranging the order from within, especially in terms of altering the ecology of the international order so that actors, institutions, and norms – once afforded special status by Washington and its allies – no longer carry the same geopolitical weight. These aspects of liberal order have, in many respects, provided Washington with an exorbitant geostrategic privilege: an infrastructure that maximizes its diplomatic, economic, and military capital (see Henke 2017; Kreiger, Souma, and Nexon 2015). Ongoing Russian efforts to boost illiberal leaders and political parties in Western democracies that oppose Euro–Atlantic institutions wager that the dynamics of good substitution – driven by those states themselves – can profoundly alter international order and power. In the context of present trends, the American-led hegemonic order may be hollowed out long before, or even in the absence of, any direct challenge to the power position of the United States.

3 | International Rankings As Normative Goods: Hegemony and the Quest for Social Status

BAHAR RUMELILI AND ANN TOWNS

The aim of this chapter is to draw attention to the centrality of international symbolic and normative goods in maintaining or challenging hegemony. The notion of normative "goods," to be wielded and substituted akin to military and economic goods, may be provocative to conventional and critical scholars alike. Realist international relations scholars generally find symbolic and normative politics trivial in power politics (e.g., Mearsheimer 1994), whereas critical scholars might object that as norms are intersubjective and constantly in motion, they are ill conceived as a stable "good" (e.g., Laffey and Weldes 1997). We contend that when stabilized and widely shared, norms can be fruitfully addressed using "goods" as a heuristic device. In this respect, we point to the critical roles played by ranking and rating organizations (RROs) and the global performance indices (GPIs) they produce in transforming norms into a set of normative goods. These normative goods, in the form of indices, scores, and rankings, have become important social assets for states to pursue and achieve high status. There are now hundreds of such rankings and most states pay close attention to the status they are attributed in them. High rankings in indices on, say, gender equality or environmental sustainability allow states to emerge as authorities on these issues, to take on leadership roles, and to enjoy the esteem that comes with fulfilling standards. These dynamics have not escaped power contenders such as Russia and China, as they have begun to actively contest indices where they are poorly ranked and attempt to produce alternatives.

Attention to norms in international power politics is of course not new. A long tradition in international relations theory asserts a close link between great powers and the definition, diffusion, and enforcement of international norms. Starting with E. H. Carr's scathing critique that attempts to morally outlaw war following WWI only served the interests of victor powers, realists have argued in various ways that the dominant norms of the international system reflect the interests of great powers (e.g., Ikenberry and Kupchan 1990). On the other hand, liberals have stressed that the ability to shape moral standards enables dominant states to rule by consent. In a recent formulation of this argument, Ikenberry (2011) contends that the United States has led the formation of a distinctive type of international order in the post-WWII period, in which liberal principles of open markets, cooperative security, international institutions, democratic community, shared sovereignty, and rule of law were fused with American power. The allegedly open and rule-based character of this liberal international order allowed the United States to rule largely by consent. A host of constructivist scholars have also pointed to the critical role great powers play in triggering normative diffusion (e.g., Klotz 1993; Thomas 2001).

In recent years, however, norms have become grounds for challenging US hegemony. The US position on high-profile issues such as the violation of basic rights in Guantánamo Bay, the withdrawal from the Kyoto protocol, and the decision not to join the International Criminal Court, have repeatedly drawn criticism from liberal international norm advocates. The recent flurry of normative developments in the liberal international order has been realized not through the leadership of the United States, but by other liberal state and nonstate actors and, in several cases, as in the establishment of the International Criminal Court, despite opposition from the United States (Bower 2017). The weakening of US moral leadership has opened up space for lesser powers such as the EU to claim the status of being the "normative power" in international relations (Manners 2002).

As other liberal states have started to challenge US hegemony by assuming roles and positions of moral leadership in the liberal international order, some of the so-called rising powers and non-Western states have begun to use norms to oppose the power dynamics inherent in contemporary liberal order. This opposition has taken many forms. For example, until recently, Turkey sought to counter the reluctance of the EU to admit it to its membership, by using the EU's normative standards and exposing its double standards (Rumelili 2007). Russia has selectively reinterpreted the norm of Responsibility to Protect in order to justify its invasion of Ukraine (Kurowska 2014). Some African countries have actively resisted the diffusion of lesbian, gay, bisexual, transgender, and queer (LGBTQ) norms by criminalizing homosexuality altogether, and challenged the universalistic claims of liberal values by championing alternatives, such as African values (Symons and Altman 2015).

In this chapter, we contend that when stabilized in rankings and performance indicators, norms are converted into goods, and come to constitute critical elements of the international goods ecology, described by Cooley and Nexon in Chapter 2, on which hegemony rests. Focusing on normative goods, in this fashion, furthers our understanding of how hegemony may be maintained and challenged through norms. In the last couple of decades, a plethora of international governmental and nongovernmental organizations have transformed a large set of international political, economic, and social norms into normative goods, by converting intersubjective understandings about shared principles into standardized measures and rank positions. We argue that these normative goods are characterized by specific patterns of supply, demand, and distribution; they are produced in certain forms and quantities by RROs, and obtained and used as social assets by states in particular ways. These patterns, which make up the international normative goods ecology, structure the normative status competition between the United States, other liberal states, and rising powers, by shaping the conditions under which high normative status may be obtained. The international normative goods ecology, as such, constitutes a distinct terrain for challenging hegemony in a bottom-up and gradual fashion, over and through technical measures and standards.

Within this international normative goods ecology, it is possible to talk about two specific kinds of challenges to hegemony. On the one hand, states committed to liberal norms challenge the United States' dominant position in the liberal international order by acquiring normative goods, in the form of rank positions that surpass the United States in GPIs in various liberal normative issue areas. They actively use the GPIs to buttress their claims to normative leadership, and to brand themselves as normatively superior. On the other hand, power contenders such as Russia and China can seek to undermine the liberal normative order that undergirds US hegemony by challenging the existing set of normative goods, undermining their authority, and providing substitute normative goods in the form of alternative norms, indices, and rankings.

The aim of this chapter is to dig deeper into the question of normative goods, how they function in the international goods ecology that is the subject of this book, and how states maneuver normative goods in their quest for status. The first section develops the argument that international norms generate the normative goods of social status and esteem by serving as the foundation for moral hierarchies, and that these normative goods constitute integral parts of the international goods ecology. The second section then turns to GPIs as an overlooked but crucial provider of normative goods in international order. We claim that GPIs provide esteem and moral value in three ways. First of all, GPIs perform a crucial supply role by generating regular, public, and comparative information which facilitates the construction of explicit and shared moral hierarchies. Second, GPIs play a definitional role by assigning moral value to specific indicators that end up concretizing the more abstract norms they are intended to measure. Third, GPIs play a distributive role in allocating moral status to states through the ranking systems they employ. Through the ways in which they provide, produce, and distribute normative goods, the GPIs affect the distribution of esteem among states, and shape the strategies that states employ in pursuit of higher status.

The third section then turns to the ways in which states respond to the distribution of esteem by GPIs. Building on the existing literature on status seeking in international relations, we show through a number of illustrations how states combine strategies of mobility, competition, and creativity in their actual pursuits of normative status. We also note the extent and the ways in which these strategies rely on goods substitution, paving the way for the bit-by-bit undermining of the liberal normative order. In conclusion, we underscore that the proliferation of indices, when coupled with status-seeking dynamics in the context of the declining leadership of the United States, has opened up space for lesser powers to carve away at the social status of the United States.

The Nature of International Normative Goods

To understand how norms can come to function as a good, it may be helpful to take a few steps back to address some fundamental theoretical points about norms and how norms attribute status and esteem. Norms, according to the now standard international relations definition, are standards of behavior for a stipulated category of actors

(Katzenstein 1996). Norms are intersubjective, consisting of shared meanings and shared interpretations among actors. As such, they can naturally also be contested. Furthermore, the shared understanding of norms is not necessarily stable, as many norms shift in meaning as they are contextually interpreted (e.g., Towns 2010, Wiener 2008). Norms whose meaning is highly fluid and in movement are difficult to grasp as a "good," as such norms are hardly a stable entity that can be possessed, utilized, and traded by actors akin to military or economic goods. However, when norms are stabilized and enshrined, such as in the GPIs we will discuss below, they are converted into stable measures of normative value and markers of moral esteem. While the norm of "gender equality" as such cannot be provided or possessed by individual actors, the status of being the "top state in gender equality" can. These markers of esteem, we argue, constitute normative goods, which are supplied and distributed by a variety of ranking organizations and obtained and utilized by states. Possession of these markers of esteem enable states to engage in certain kinds of performances, such as the assertion of moral authority in an issue area. And they can be traded upon in ways similar to other goods.

Hence, normative goods consist of status and esteem, the social standing entailed in meeting the social standards set by norms, and their various measures and markers. Even though norms by themselves are not goods, they are closely intertwined with the construction of social status and esteem. Indeed, a central function of norms is to ascribe social value to conformity with behavioral standards. As standards of behavior, norms enable assessment of the extent to which behavior conforms to expectations. The attribution of esteem, then, rest on the assignment of value to certain attributes and acts as worthy of recognition, respect, and distinction. When assessments are made about how well behavior meets standards, social hierarchies are established, ordering states (or other actors) in terms of degree of normative conformity (Towns 2010, 2012, Towns and Rumelili 2017). Meeting standards leads to higher status, esteem, or honor, whereas deviation can entail various degrees of shame, anxiety, or even stigma (on stigma, see Adler-Nissen 2014b and Zarakol 2010).

Norms and their social hierarchies exist in all social settings. Historically, communities and organizations have developed elaborate processes for attributing and distributing esteem and honor to those who fulfill expectations of appropriate and valuable behavior.

Consequently, esteem and honor have been characterized by distinct patterns of supply and distribution in different historical and social/organizational settings (Welsh 2008). In some systems of recognition, social standards are supplied by actors in authority. In others, systems of recognition and distribution of esteem and honor have been more meritocratic, decentralized, and institutionalized (Clark 2016).

In contemporary international society, international norms provide the basis for the distribution of esteem and status (or disregard, contempt, and stigma) among states. Esteem is regularly assigned with status markers such as a "gender equal" society, a "highly competitive" economy, or an "anti-corrupt" or "transparent" government attributed to states that successfully conform with international norms. The attribution of esteem, such as being identified as the most competitive economy in a particular year, being among the ten most gender-equal societies for women, receiving an A1 credit rating or the classification high human development, find widespread publicity in international media, and function as critical assets through which states attract investment and human capital, assume diplomatic agenda-setting capacity, and achieve overall status in international politics. Not fully meeting standards – or not meeting them at all – in turn entails being ascribed a status as inadequate, deficient, or deviant. Being rated as among the ten most oppressive societies for women, receiving a poor credit rating, or being classified as a society with low human development has very different implications – for a state's status and international agenda-setting capacity, for example. States assessed in this way can expect to become the object of all sorts of international interventions, in contrast with states deemed to meet standards. Normative goods, while essentially meaning-laden, are thus not "merely" symbolic in the sense of simply honorific – the esteem or disregard they bestow is intimately tied to and has important bearing on military and economic processes.

If international norms provide the basis for the distribution of esteem in international society, who creates the standards on the basis of which esteem is attributed and shapes how esteem is distributed among states? International orders may be characterized by different systems of supply of normative goods. In an ideal-typical hegemonic order, the materially dominant state has exclusive control over the supply and distribution of esteem. The dominant state defines norms according to its interests and ranks other states accordingly while reserving the top position for itself. The demand for esteem on the part of other states may be high or low depending on the specific benefits attached to being bestowed with high moral status by the hegemon. At the other end of the spectrum, in an ideal-typical liberal-pluralist order, the supply and distribution of moral esteem and status is undertaken by multiple actors, independently of the hegemon. Material capabilities are divorced from moral value and status; hence, the hegemonic state does not necessarily enjoy the top position in international normative hierarchies. States compete for high moral status in order to gain moral authority and influence. The more moral authority matters in international politics, the greater is the demand for moral status.

In recent years, the international normative order has come to more closely resemble the liberal-pluralist ideal type. A wide range of ranking and rating organizations now enjoy the authority to set up concrete behavioral standards for states, regularly assess how well states meet these standards, and then rank them accordingly and help distribute esteem in doing so. As such, they have become the main suppliers of normative goods. Rankings have emerged as a new technology in global governance (Davis et al. 2012), and have largely divorced the distribution of esteem from US hegemonic power. A complex normative goods ecology exists, consisting of multiple indices, measures, scores, and rankings in different normative areas, and sets the terrain for the normative status competition between the United States and its rivals. The United States enjoys esteem only to the extent of its meeting the socially shared standards; it cannot independently alter the standards to its advantage. For example, the United States has no direct power over the British firm Economic Intelligence Unit, whose Democracy Index, which puts strong emphasis on trust in political institutions, demoted the United States to the category of "flawed democracy" in 2017.[1] Thus, within this normative goods ecology, like all others, the hegemonic state finds itself an order-taker.

The normative goods ecology also constitutes an arena for challenging US hegemony. States can acquire the existing set of normative goods – markers of status and esteem – by outperforming the United States on various performance indicators. In fact, the United States is outperformed by other states on virtually all existing GPIs, whether on transparency, innovativeness, democracy, gender equality, or environmental

---

[1] www.cnbc.com/2017/01/25/us-is-no-longer-a-full-democracy-eiu-warns.html.

performance. Another way of challenging US hegemony is by contesting and substituting normative goods, rather than by trying to outperform the United States in given GPIs. Within the existing pluralist normative goods ecology, there is indeed considerable space for various dynamics of goods substitution. State and nonstate actors are free to lead the formulation of new indices, measures, and ranking systems that replace the existing ones, without necessarily contesting the underlying principles of liberal international order. Focusing on normative goods in addition to military and economic ones allows us to pay attention to such lower-key dynamics that may gradually undermine US hegemony.

In sum, measures of normative value and markers of esteem form a critical part of the international goods ecology and function in ways akin to military and economic goods. These normative goods constitute critical assets for states in the pursuit of status and are characterized by specific patterns of supply and distribution. In the next section, we will discuss how GPIs produce and provide these international normative goods. We stress that the ways in which GPIs produce and provide normative goods have distributional consequences, which shape the ways in which states pursue status.

Global Performance Indices and the Production of International Normative Goods

GPIs are cross-national comparative measures of country performance in a given issue area. These indices are premised on a specific set of indicators, and they assign each state a score (an independent numeric measure of performance) and a rank position (an ordinal measure of how well a state is doing in relation to others). Their numbers have indeed exploded since the end of the 1990s. While there were fewer than 20 indices in 1995, as of 2012, Kelley and Simmons (2015a) identified approximately 150 active indices.

A growing literature in international relations has drawn critical attention to the power that GPIs exercise over policymaking. We stress that GPIs are also playing increasingly important roles in the more precise formulation of international norms and the associated provision and distribution of moral status. GPIs do not simply set technical standards; they actively link the standards to existing norms in international society and hence define behavior and actors that meet and/or exceed the standards as normatively valuable and morally superior.

The indicators through which GPIs measure performance stabilize the norms by fixing their behavioral prerequisites, and the scores and rank positions assigned to states distribute esteem. In sum, we contend that GPIs have become the main producers and providers of international normative goods.

Providing Public and Comparable Normative Standards

A first and primary way in which GPIs produce international normative goods is by providing public and comparable normative standards and data to all states. In the absence of such shared standards, there would be no normative good to speak of – status and esteem would be based on implicit and subjective self-assessments of moral superiority and inferiority. GPIs clarify and specify what states need to do to achieve moral status. While there is undoubtedly variation among individual GPIs in terms of the quality, range, and frequency of data they provide and their capacity for impact, they collectively fulfill an important supply function in the international goods ecology. Overall, the GPI collective ascribes moral value and rank to all states on multiple dimensions, makes this information freely available to all actors on a regular basis, and widely publicizes it through international media outlets. Instead of a system of implicit and subjective standards, there is now an abundance of public and comparative information (Kelley and Simmons 2015a). The GPIs construct explicit and shared esteem hierarchies; facilitate comparative judgment by informing states not only of their own positions but also of the ranking of other states; and serve as reference points in pressuring various states on norm adoption and implementation. Even though, at an individual level, the indicators and ranking criteria of some GPIs may be contested by some states, the overall GPI collective strengthens the intersubjective dimension of moral assessments in world politics.

It is worth underlining that the GPI collective provides the normative goods of status and esteem in disaggregated form. Instead of receiving an overall aggregate score and rank, every state is independently assessed and ranked on the basis of multiple norms, by multiple institutions, and according to multiple criteria. This form of goods provision makes it possible for a state to enjoy higher moral status in some norms and indices than in others. For example, while Freedom House positions Russia in the lowest category of nonfree regimes, on an equal footing with China, other democracy indices such as Polity IV or the Economic Intelligence Unit's (EUI) Democracy Index characterize Russia as a hybrid regime and superior to China (Tsygankov and Parker 2015). As we elaborate below, this wealth of indices and indicators encourages various strategic responses on the part of states. States may selectively publicize the indices and measures where they enjoy higher moral status, and at other times they may emphasize the discrepancy between ratings to discredit the GPIs where they are unfavorably ranked.

Finally, the GPI collective is selective in its coverage of norms – not all norms are equally represented in available GPIs, and not all GPIs enjoy equal publicity and impact policy to the same degree. Kelley and Simmons (2015a) find that most of the currently existing GPIs focus on economic, social, development, and governance issues, while there are relatively fewer GPIs analyzing performance in privacy, trade, legal matters, and human rights. This means that certain behaviors and policies are more regularly and intensely monitored and assigned moral value, while others are less so. This selective focus also has implications for the distribution of esteem among states. It means that states are able to acquire disproportionately higher levels of overall esteem if they secure favorable rankings on indices that are well publicized. For example, the high publicity surrounding the annual publication of the Ease of Doing Business Index ensures that Singapore enjoys coverage as the top-performing country in all leading media outlets.

Specifying and Concretizing the Meaning of Norms

A second way in which GPIs provide a normative good is by specifying and concretizing the meaning of norms. In doing so, they play a power-laden definitional role, as they reduce norms to a set of measurable performance outputs, which are at best imperfect equivalents. As Hirai (2017) discusses in the context of the UNDP Human Development Index, indices can never be as broad as the norms they represent, and they reflect choices in the selection of relevant dimensions, in the choice of variables that represent those dimensions, and in the standardization of those variables. While norms distinguish morally acceptable and nonacceptable behavior in general terms, GPIs assign moral value to specific measurable indicators (Kelley and Simmons 2015b). For example, while the norm of gender equality prescribes equality between men and women in general terms, the Gender Inequality Index (GII) assigns moral value to what it defines as measurable indicators of gender equality, such as the maternal mortality ratio, the adolescent birth rate, the share of parliamentary seats held by women, the share of female population with at least some secondary education, and women's participation in the labor force. Thus, measurable indicators take precedence over the principle, drawing its boundaries and shaping its limits.

While indices provide standardized and fixed specifications of the underlying norms, norms are dynamic and contested in nature (Wiener 2008). Norms are in continuous evolution, being reshaped and challenged by differing interpretations adopted by different parties at different points in time. As the underlying norms of existing indices evolve, new indices that better reflect the current interpretations of the norms are often created, and indices become sites of normative contestation. For example, as dominant understandings of development shifted from being predominantly economic to being also inclusive of social and sustainability dimensions, multiple new development indices were developed and proposed. The current Human Development Index is a product of long-lasting and still ongoing contestations over the meaning of development and how it can best be reflected and measured with indicators (Hirai 2017).

Moreover, the choices entailed in the formulation of specific indicators also have repercussions on the distribution of esteem among states. For instance, Permanyer (2013) finds that the GII does not sufficiently separate the effects of low income from gender norms, and consequently penalizes the performance of low-income countries. Bukovansky (2015) similarly finds that the Corruption Perception Index produced by Transparency International defines anti-corruption norms in such a way that it excludes certain types of questionable economic activity primarily occurring in the West and focuses international scrutiny on the forms of corruption generally observed in the developing world.

A related definitional role, which affects the distribution of esteem, manifests itself in the production of composite indicators. Most GPIs package a number of indicators and associate them with a normative purpose (Kelley and Simmons 2015a). For example, the UNDP's Human Development Index combines material development measured in terms of GDP/capita with social development in education and healthcare measures, and assigns normative purpose to this combination in terms of human development. The equal weighting of these dimensions in the calculation of the overall indicator also defines them as equal in importance (Hirai 2017). Arguably, this distorts the distribution of the esteem of high human development in favor of high-income countries, such as Qatar, to the relative detriment of countries like Cuba which maintain high education and healthcare standards in the context of low income levels.

Importantly, while assigning moral value to measurable indicators, GPIs also reflect the normative preferences and material interests of the institutions that choose to compose them. As Bradley (2015) shows in a detailed archival study on the origins of Freedom House's renowned Freedom in the World Index, institutions develop GPIs mainly in order to serve organizational interests, such as enhancing their visibility, reputation, ability to raise funds, and the scope of their activities. As a result, norms are concretized and converted to a set of normative goods in ways that reflect the preferences of organizations that are willing and able to devote institutional resources to the production of GPIs. That does not mean that normative assessments made by different organizations radically differ from one another. As Poe et al. (2001) have demonstrated through a comparison of US State Department and Amnesty International's human rights reports, there is often considerable convergence in assessments made by different organizations. However, overall, the GPI collective tends to reflect the normative preferences of the dominant institutions of the liberal international order. For example, most of the available measures and benchmarks of competitiveness reflect and reproduce neoliberal understandings of states as market actors, in competition with one another to attract competitive enterprises (Fougner 2008). As a result, alternative understandings of competitiveness and economic success do not figure in the normative goods ecology and distribution of esteem among states.

Most GPIs are formally independent from state power. Rather than being produced by dominant states, most GPIs are the product of a variety of intergovernmental and nongovernmental institutions, such as the United Nations, World Bank, and specialist NGOs such as Transparency International. However, it is worth underlining that GPIs are overwhelmingly produced in the West. According to the dataset of Kelley and Simmons (2015a), about half of the GPIs are maintained by institutions headquartered in the United States, one-third are in Europe, and only 5 percent are created and maintained in the Global South. Despite some recent talks, neither Russia nor China have yet succeeded in putting together alternative indices. GPIs thus represent an essentially Western and liberal technology of governance and power.

While it is debatable whether or not the concentration of GPI-producing organizations in the West favors Western countries over non-Western ones in the distribution of esteem, it is also a fact that a select number of Western countries occupy top positions in most of the indices. This has enabled critics of GPIs to discredit them as instruments of Western power. As will be discussed in greater detail in the following section, in reaction to unfavorable ratings non-Western countries such as Russia, China, and Cuba have, on multiple occasions, called into question the political values and biases embedded in indices. Not surprisingly, those that are reliant on US government funding, such as Freedom House (Bradley 2015), have drawn the heaviest criticism. The concentration of the GPI collective in the West drives and justifies various attempts by non-Western countries to challenge the normative goods provided by existing GPIs. Even though their attempts at producing alternative indices have so far remained limited and ineffective, non-Western states have mounted successful challenges to the authority of a number of existing GPIs.

Allocating Moral Status among States

A third and closely related role GPIs play is an allocative role. GPIs not only provide and produce normative goods, but they also allocate them among states through the categorization and ranking systems they employ. All GPIs rank and categorize states into positions of relative moral superiority and inferiority, such that only a limited number of actors are allocated a position of high moral status at a given point in time. Hence, GPIs constitute moral status as a rivalrous good and direct the attention of policymakers to how well a country is doing in relation to others.

GPIs adopt different systems of categorizing and ranking, which generate different distributive effects. One important difference concerns whether the GPI uses a categorical classification (categorizing states into two or more groups) or a continuous ranking which orders countries without classifying them into categories. Another important difference concerns whether the benchmarks are absolute (with set yardsticks against which performance is measured) or relative (with the performance of states only ranked against one another). (On the importance of categorical/continuous and absolute/relative rankings, see Towns and Rumelili 2017.) In addition, some GPIs stigmatize poor performance by generating watch lists or blacklists.

As an illustration, the UNDP Human Development Index classifies countries into the categories of high, medium, and low human development in terms of absolute (set) benchmarks. Countries are classified into three clusters of high human development (with an HDI of 0.800 or above), medium human development (0.500–0.799), and low human development (less than 0.500). In theory, then, any and all countries can be classified as of high human development if they meet the benchmark standards. On the other hand, the Global Competitiveness Index's ranking type is relative and continuous. It does not classify countries into categories of high and low competitiveness, and it does not employ benchmarks in its distinctions between better or worse performers. Instead, in this relative ranking system, a "competitive" economy is one that outperforms others, with the implication that not all countries can be "competitive" at the same time. There is no benchmark standard to be met to be competitive – this standing can only be gained by beating out others.

These different ranking systems matter because they generate different types of social pressures on states, which, in extension, encourage states to take different routes to achieve esteem (Towns and Rumelili 2017). They also matter because they shape how normative esteem is distributed. Relative ranking makes it difficult for states in low-status positions to attain high status. This is because GPIs that employ relative standards of assessment distribute esteem in an inherently competitive manner. They create zero-sum hierarchies wherein the higher moral status of some states *necessarily* entails lower moral status of others. In order to attain high status, low-status states need to outperform the high-status ones, which is highly difficult when all actors are improving their performances in order to maintain and attain higher status. On the other hand, GPIs with absolute standards offer the possibility that every actor can rise to a high moral-status position if the benchmark requirements are met.

Most GPIs employ continuous ranking systems, in order to prod states toward ever better performance. Even categorical indices, such as the Human Development Index, continue to rank countries within and among categories, and provide numeric rank positions for all states. Media reporting surrounding the publication of GPIs also give greater emphasis to these numeric rank positions rather than, say, the overall improvement in scores or the increase in the number of states meeting various benchmarks. Consequently, GPIs end up allocating the normative goods of status and esteem in a manner which makes it more challenging for low-ranked states to rise to positions of higher rank by improving their performance.

In sum, GPIs provide, produce, and allocate normative goods. They provide public information, specify and concretize norms, and help set up explicit social hierarchies where states are ranked vis-à-vis one another. In this section, we underscored that GPIs are not simply value-neutral measures that reflect the actual performance of states. They actively shape the distribution of esteem among states through the particular ways in which they produce normative goods. The GPI collective provides public information about the normative performance of all states in a disaggregated form and in a selective manner. The ways in which GPIs concretize norms fail to fully represent the underlying principles and often reflect the value biases of the organizations that produce them. Most GPIs rank states according to relative criteria, which encourages a zero-sum competition for esteem. All these factors matter in the distribution of esteem; they determine which attributes and policies are considered worthy of esteem, who is deserving of esteem and who gets to be stigmatized, and how esteem can be claimed and obtained.

Naturally, states do not remain passive in the face of these distributions of esteem. As a wealth of prior scholarship has shown, status and esteem matter to states (de Carvalho and Neumann 2014; Larson and Shevchenko 2010; Paul et al. 2014; Suzuki 2008; Wolf 2011). "States are highly interested in acquiring a higher social status" (Suzuki 2008, 49) or at least in simply maintaining the status they occupy (e.g., Wolf 2011). States may furthermore exhibit status anxiety when they experience, or expect to experience, a decline in their status vis-à-vis other states (Onea 2014). Since GPIs shape the distribution of esteem in the ways outlined above, the normative goods provided by GPIs constitute a terrain of status competition. States face the incentive not only to improve their performance to obtain higher scores and rankings, but also to compete over the setting of standards in ways that favorably reflect on their status. Assuming that status in normative hierarchies matters to states, we now turn to the question of how states go about acquiring a higher social status and/or maintaining the status they occupy in and through rankings.

Social Status-Seeking Strategies and Normative Goods Substitution

In the current international order, moral value and status are in high demand. As an aspect of overall status, moral status constitutes an important social asset in international politics. High moral status generates moral authority; it allows states with high moral status to shape the international political agenda on normative issues. High status also allows states to claim the moral high ground as a "good state" (de Carvalho and Neumann 2014), criticize others on their normative failures, and claim the authority to instruct others on how to progress. Thus, as Manners (2002) has underlined in the case of the EU and de Carvalho and Neumann (2014) in the case of small states, moral status can be a source of power for actors that are experiencing status insecurity in material aspects of power.

Conversely, low moral status actors find themselves excluded from and shunned in international fora where normative issues are discussed. They bear the burden of proof in explaining actions that others consider as normative failures. In international society, low moral status is often coupled with stigma and shaming (Adler-Nissen 2014b), which generates ontological insecurity (Zarakol 2011) and status discrepancy on the part of low moral status actors. In cases of serious normative breaches, low status actors may face material repercussions in the form of declined aid and sanctions. As we will discuss below, these social and material pressures drive different types of status-seeking and stigma-management strategies.

How states seek to maintain or increase their social status through various strategies has been examined in a growing body of scholarship on international status-seeking behavior. Two analogous typologies exist in this scholarship that helps categorize states' attempts to maintain or raise their status. One is Larson and Shevchenko's (2010) now widely used typology, which adapts Tajfel and Turner's (1979) established framework in social psychology to power politics. In this framework, mobility, competition, and creativity are identified as the main status-seeking strategies states employ. A *social mobility* strategy includes "emulating the institutions, values, or ideology of dominant states" in order to be admitted to the more "prestigious institutions or clubs [of dominant states]" (Larson and Shevchenko 2010, 71–2). *Social competition* involves a group of states seeking a positive social identity by "trying to equal or surpass the dominant group in the areas on which its claims to superior status rest" (Larson and Shevchenko 2010, 67). With the case of Russian foreign policy in mind, Larson and Shevchenko (2014, 271) argue that states engage in social competition "when they strive to have the most destructive weapons, acquire more clients than the other, display advanced weapons in parades, intervene militarily against a weaker power, prevent the other state from achieving its goals, or act as a spoiler to block collective efforts to restore regional stability." Finally, *social creativity* includes several distinctive strategies: comparing the in-group and out-group on some new dimension, changing the values assigned to the attributes of the group so that comparisons which were previously negative are now perceived as positive, and changing the out-group with which the in-group is compared (Tajfel and Turner 1979, 43). In international relations, this can be done by re-evaluating the meaning of a negative characteristic or finding a new dimension on which their group is superior, outside the area of geopolitical competition (Larson and Shevchenko 2010, 73).

A second status-seeking typology can be found in the stigma-management strategies developed by Adler-Nissen (2014b), drawing on Goffman. This typology specifically focuses on the responses of states that end up at the bottom of normative hierarchies, marked as deviant by the international community. Adler-Nissen (2014b, 153) argues that states may respond to stigma imposition through stigma recognition, rejection, or counter-stigmatization. *Stigma recognition* entails the internalization of the value judgments that mark them as normatively inferior and deviant. Stigma recognizing states apologize for their normative transgressions, and then, in essence, adopt a strategy of social mobility, emulating the behavioral patterns of normatively superior states in an effort to be ultimately accepted by the international community. In contrast, *counter-stigmatization* entails turning the stigma into an emblem of pride and identifying with the group of those stigmatized. Adler-Nissen (2014b) notes that counter-stigmatizing actors establish an alternative "system of honor" and seek esteem and status within it. This is largely akin to a strategy of social creativity, as it entails the construction of an alternative normative domain where superior status may be claimed. Finally, *stigma rejection* occurs when actors marked as deviant deny being any different from those claiming higher moral status. Stigma rejectors recognize the overall value system but reject the imposition of the stigma on the basis of that value system. Stigma rejection largely corresponds to a strategy of social competition because it entails competition for status within the same normative domain.

We find that these typologies do not fully capture the more sophisticated ways in which states pursue normative status in the competitive terrain constituted by GPIs. As we will discuss below, normative status-seeking strategies in GPIs often blur the distinctions between mobility, competition, and creativity on the one hand and stigma recognition, rejection, and counter-stigmatization on the other. Some strategies entail accepting the normative goods provided by GPIs and seeking status within them. Others entail attempts to substitute various aspects of these normative goods, such as the indicators used to concretize and stabilize the norms, the categorization and ranking systems, and ultimately the norms themselves. Below, we adapt the existing typologies of status-seeking to the specific context of normative/moral hierarchies. Through a series of empirical illustrations, we discuss how states combine various strategies in their actual pursuits of normative status. We also note the extent and the ways in which these strategies rely on goods substitution, paving the way for bit-by-bit undermining of the liberal normative order.

Social Mobility

In its pure form, a social mobility strategy in moral hierarchies constituted by GPIs would entail accepting the normative good and the status order it provides and seeking to improve ranking by adopting the requisite policies. It would entail, as an illustration, recognizing that the prevalence of domestic violence is a legitimate ground for a normative hierarchy among states. A lower-ranked state pursuing a strategy of social mobility would also recognize its subordinate positioning as legitimate, and accept the need for improvement (stigma recognition). It might collect statistics on incidences of domestic violence, share that information with others, and learn strategies to combat domestic violence from better-performing states. It would publicize any improvement in its performance to domestic and foreign audiences.

Social mobility is generally the preferred strategy of states that are committed to the normative principles and have the potential to attain high rankings. Higher-ranked states generally accept the normative goods provided by GPIs as fair and legitimate measures of their esteem, and endorse them by publicizing their ranking status in various indices as part of their nation-branding strategies. For instance, while listing "gender equality" as one of the five reasons to work in Sweden, the country's official website underscores that it has never finished lower than fourth in the Gender Gap rankings of the World Economic Forum.[2] The Economic Development Board of Singapore similarly flaunts that the country is the third most competitive economy in the world, and the second in the world for ease of doing business.[3] Slovenia, a country that has made significant strides in gender equality in the past few years, also underlines its high status on its government website.[4]

A very good example of a lower-ranked state pursuing a strategy of mobility is Rwanda in gender equality. While it is one of the poorest countries in the world, Rwanda ranks fifth in the World Economic Forum's Global Gender Gap Index, just below Iceland, Finland, Norway, and Sweden,[5] due to its high level of female participation in the workforce and a gender quota ensuring a high ratio of women parliamentarians. While the post-genocide gender imbalance in Rwanda has been a contributing factor, this success has nevertheless been achieved through the strong commitment that the Rwandan government has made to gender equality, such as by enshrining in the Constitution a 30 percent quota of female representation in government institutions.[6] Another notable case of status mobility is the unprecedentedly rapid rise of Georgia in the World Bank's Ease of Doing Business Index (EDBI) from 100th place in 2006 to the top 20 by 2008 (Scheuth 2011). In this case, government commitment to a successfully targeted strategy formulated in cooperation with the

---

[2] https://sweden.se/society/gender-equality-in-sweden/.
[3] www.edb.gov.sg/en/why-singapore/discover-the-singapore-difference.html.
[4] www.vlada.si/en/media_room/newsletter/slovenia_weekly/news/article/slovenia_ranks_8th_in_closing_gender_gap_58844/.
[5] www.weforum.org/agenda/2017/05/how-rwanda-beats-almost-every-other-country-in-gender-equality/.
[6] www.newtimes.co.rw/section/read/223053/.

United States Agency for International Development (USAID) and World Bank led to the creation of strong regulatory institutions.

As has been underlined by Cooley (2015), lower-ranked states rarely follow mobility strategies in a pure form. This is because GPIs provide an opportunity structure that allows states to introduce elements of competition and creativity into an overall strategy of mobility. Because of the multitude of GPIs, states can strategically improve their performance in select indicators which boost their rankings, without necessarily internalizing the underlying value system. The presence of multiple GPIs in an issue area give states the option to focus on GPIs that use preferred indicators or weigh the same indicators in a more favorable manner. In the case of Georgia, Scheuth (2011) underscores the wide discrepancy between Georgia's rapidly improved ranking in the EDBI and its languishing status in the Global Competitiveness Index (GCI), and shows how this discrepancy is a product of the different ways in which these two indices specify the norm of competitiveness. While the EDBI measures competitiveness on the basis of regulatory rules, the GCI advances a broader conception taking into account "all institutions, policies and factors that affect the level of productivity in a country" (Scheuth 2011, 59). Thus, the presence of different GPIs in the issue area of competitiveness allowed Georgia to strategically target a rapid ascension in one index, which can be effectively used to promote the country as an attractive destination of foreign direct investment, and thereby to also conceal institutional deficiencies that are revealed by the other indices.

The disaggregated structure of the GPI collective also allows states to selectively pursue social mobility in one normative issue area in order to deflect the social pressure and shaming due to poor performance in other issue areas. In the case Rwanda, for example, the stellar performance in gender equality is coupled with an authoritarian government structure ranked as "Not Free" by Freedom House. Debusscher and Ansoms (2013) note that the Rwandan government's target-driven commitment to gender equality pleases the donor community and serves to shield the country from criticism of restrictions of political liberties. Because some GPI indicators are reliant on data provided by governments, they can furthermore tamper with the data in order to attain higher scores. Perhaps the best known example is Greece's manipulation of macroeconomic figures prior to its admission into the Eurozone and in the period leading up to the Eurozone debt crisis in 2010.[7] GPIs also allow states to compare themselves to multiple in- and out-groups, hence giving states the opportunity to publicize their normative status in ways that reflect positively on them. For example, the Economic Development Board of Singapore chooses to compare the country to others in Asia, branding Singapore as the first in Asia in the issues of intellectual property protection and sustainability, while underlining its top global ranking in competitiveness and ease of doing business.[8]

Social Competition

Similarly, social competition in normative hierarchies constituted by GPIs incorporates elements of both stigma rejection and counter-stigmatization (cf. Adler-Nissen 2014b), and it often includes elements of social creativity (see section below). In its pure form, social competition entails the recognition of a norm and the underlying value system of its normative hierarchy while contesting the group's status position within that hierarchy. Low-status states positively identify and cooperate with one another to change the way in which they are ranked. Because social competition essentially entails group-level pursuit of status by low-status states, it relies on the presence of in-group/out-group dynamics within hierarchies. In the context of GPIs, these dynamics may be introduced by the categorical distinctions (e.g., high/medium/low development, free/partly free/not free) employed by GPIs themselves and/or by norm advocating organizations, which use GPI scores and rankings to shame under-performers.

However, even when categorization and stigmatization are not overtly present, lower-ranked states may flag out in-group/out-group dynamics as part of a strategy of social competition. For example, Russian officials have routinely characterized ratings of corruption, political freedoms, and economic development as ideological instruments of a US-dominated Western hegemony (Tsygankov and Parker 2015) and have led a backlash in the post-Soviet region against the ratings of Freedom House, portraying it as serving the Western strategy of regime change in the region (Cooley 2015, 8). In a similar manner, although not formally within a GPI framework, Turkish policymakers

---

[7] www.bbc.com/news/world-europe-16834815.
[8] www.edb.gov.sg/en/why-singapore/discover-the-singapore-difference.html.

routinely attribute the country's low-rated performance on the EU's membership criteria to the historical prejudices of Europeans toward Islam (Morozov and Rumelili 2012).

Social competition in normative hierarchies involves various attempts at *goods substitution*. Negative outcomes may be attributed to the biases of GPIs rather than to characteristics of the state in question. Low-status states may claim that the indicators through which normative performance is assessed are biased, and they collectively pressure the ranking and rating organizations to change their indicators. When China's position on Transparency International's Corruption Perceptions Index dramatically deteriorated in 2014 in the course of a highly publicized anti-corruption drive led by the government, Chinese officials dismissed the value of the index by claiming that it is inconsistent.[9] The World Bank's EDBI has similarly been criticized by China and some other developing countries for failing to take into account local conditions. In response, the World Bank revised its methodology in 2014 to put more emphasis on the "distance to frontier" measure, which indicates how close or far a country is from the best practices in the world.[10] Most recently, the World Bank has accepted accusations of political bias leveled at it by Chilean officials and agreed to correct and recalculate national rankings going back at least four years.[11]

Going beyond these challenges directed at specific indicators, a more ambitious social competition strategy may involve the establishment of an alternative ranking and rating organization, which would develop an alternative index in which low-status states would be more favorably rated. Plans to develop alternatives to the US-based credit rating agencies are already underway, with Russia and China agreeing to set up a joint "apolitical" credit rating agency.[12] Such attempts have not yet succeeded. However, given the mounting criticism of existing indices, efforts to develop such alternatives in other issue areas are likely to accelerate in the future (Cooley 2015). The leading states in this endeavor may prod other low-status states to cease their cooperation with the "biased" GPIs

---

[9] www.cnn.com/2014/12/03/world/asia/china-transparency-international-corruption-2014/index.html
[10] https://gbtimes.com/china-ranks-84th-ease-doing-business.
[11] www.wsj.com/articles/world-bank-unfairly-influenced-its-own-competitiveness-rankings-1515797620
[12] Fojcik, Beata. "Report: Russia, China agree to set up 'apolitical' credit rating agency." *SNL European Financials Daily*. June 4, 2014.

by no longer releasing their data and remaining indifferent to their rankings and ratings, and supporting the "alternative" GPI instead.

Social Creativity

However, low-status states often couple competition with creativity. For instance, as they directly contest the indicators which place them in low-status positions, they may also pursue counter-stigmatization to turn aspects of their low status into an emblem of pride. In its pure form, social creativity in normative hierarchies includes efforts to reinterpret the norm and/or one's status position in the normative hierarchy in ways that allow the actor to gain a higher status position. States can declare norms which position them in low-status positions as not applicable to them; they can *substitute* them with alternative norms, so that they can present their low-status position in the context of one normative framework as high status in an alternative framework. For example, several African states, including Uganda, have turned their anti-homosexual policies into a point of pride, representing themselves as defenders of African values in the context of Western cultural intrusions (Symons and Altman 2015). When faced with criticism about its anti-gay laws, Uganda hardened its stance by criminalizing homosexuality altogether.

Also common are social creativity responses that involve emphasizing achievement in another normative domain or on another criterion than the one in which a state is poorly ranked, making alternative comparisons to buffer a state from devaluation (Adler-Nissen 2014b, 165). For example, Russia's recent attempts to seek higher social status in norms of gender relations have combined social competition and creativity. Liberal interpretations of this norm hold that women and men should be treated equally as individuals with similar rights and responsibilities. Such interpretations have been codified in international law and institutionalized in a range of GPIs, which in turn have ranked a number of West European countries, Slovenia, South Korea, and Singapore highly while ranking states such as Russia much more poorly (e.g., United Nations Development Programme 2016; World Bank Group 2015). For instance, Russia is one of the countries with the highest number of legal bans prohibiting women to enter certain professions (World Bank Group 2015). In the past decade or so, Russia has turned to attempts at goods substitution. First, it sought to substitute liberal interpretations of norms of gender relations premised on equality-as-similarity, with alternative interpretations based on "cultural tradition." Promoting the principle that women should be treated according to traditional values, Russia has increasingly declared loudly that it is outperforming the West in this regard (e.g., Curanovic 2015). Women are treated most appropriately when recognized as fundamentally different from men and when subjected to male authority, Russian officials regularly declare. Indeed, Russia is the world's primary defender of traditional values, Putin has proclaimed, against the West's "genderless and infertile" liberalism (Whitmore 2013).

Russian attempts to promote alternative interpretations of gender norms have been coupled with stigma rejection and counter-stigmatization. When decriminalizing "milder" forms of domestic violence in 2017 within the normative framework of traditional Orthodox family values, United Russia representatives embraced it as a point of pride and distinction from the West. Promoting the new law, one MP stated, "we want to show that Russian deputies will not allow the same excesses present in Western Europe" (BBC 2017). There is now a goods substitution attempt to change the indicators measuring normative superiority in gender relations. In the United Nations, Russia has aligned with the Vatican, the Organization of Islamic States, and a number of other nonstate and state actors in attempts to change international standards to reflect this vision of the appropriate treatment of women (e.g., Stensvold 2017). We expect such attempts to be formalized into an "International Family Prosperity Index" in the not too distant future, akin to the "Family Prosperity Index" created by the American Conservative Union Foundation to rank US states on how well they perform on a number of "family values" standards.

In sum, states adopt and combine various strategic responses as they pursue normative status and esteem in the competitive terrain set by GPIs. Some accept the normative goods in the forms currently provided by existing GPIs, while others set out to contest the existing goods, undermine the authority of various indicators, and substitute them with alternatives. Some low-status states strategically target policy change in areas measured by GPIs, while others convert their low status into an emblem of pride by reinterpreting the norms. Through a number of illustrations, we have shown how these strategic responses present themselves in contemporary international order. In conclusion, we now turn to a brief discussion of the implications of these strategies for maintaining and challenging hegemony through norms.

Conclusion

In this chapter, we have argued that the growing number of indices that comparatively measure the performance of countries in various issue areas convert norms into normative goods, measures, and markers of esteem which are provided to and traded upon by states. As such, they function in similar ways to military and economic goods. These normative goods are characterized by specific patterns of supply, demand, and distribution, which make up the international normative goods ecology. These patterns of normative hierarchy structure the normative status competition between the United States, other liberal states, and rising powers, by shaping the conditions under which high normative status may be obtained. Conceiving of normative goods therefore alerts us to this distinct terrain where hegemony is challenged in a bottom-up and gradual fashion, over and through putatively technical measures and standards.

Competition within and about normative goods constitutes, first of all, yet another way in which US hegemony is challenged in liberal international order. GPIs open up the possibility for states with lesser economic and military capabilities to compete in social status with dominant powers – for example, by including more women in government or having more progressive climate policies. With the United States less committed to a range of liberal principles enshrined in GPIs, there is ample room for lesser powers in material terms to individually compete with and carve away at the social status of the United States.

Second, normative goods constitute a terrain in which to erode the underlying premises of the liberal order itself. Low-status states not only compete with the United States and other leading states of the liberal order by pursuing higher GPI scores and rankings; they also actively contest the authority of specific indices that place them in low-status positions by questioning the appropriateness of various measures and developing alternatives. As we have seen in the contestation of anti-corruption and EDBI indices by China, a pushback is evident even in well-defined rankings and indexes. In some cases, states seek to turn their low status into an emblem of pride, by reinterpreting the norms and proposing alternative normative goods. Russia's push back against gender equality standards is but one illustration.

Given the growing role of GPIs in global governance, we can expect that normative goods will become an even more important part of international goods ecology in the coming years. Scores and rankings in various issue areas will constitute a public and highly publicized arena for status competition, with media outlets covering the annual publication of GPIs and the shifting rankings of states vis-à-vis one another. States willing to compete with dominant powers in normative issue areas will thus find ample opportunities to mark and publicize their high status. With the publication of each GPI report that indicates the declining status of the United States relative to other states, the moral status and leadership of the United States will be eroded.

In the meantime, nonliberal power contenders like Russia and China are likely to lead bottom-up dynamics of goods substitution through questioning the authority of the existing indices and supporting the creation of new ones. It is questionable, however, whether alternative indices can succeed in achieving credibility and eroding the authority of the existing ones. New indices that are openly backed by Russia or China, and that radically contradict the indicators and measures that presently exist, are likely to be perceived as biased and self-serving and will most likely not gain a foothold in the international goods ecology. Subtler interventions in the distribution of esteem through questioning existing measures and proposing alternative indicators are more likely to succeed in the short term.

When Donald Trump became President of the United States in January 2017, it appeared that the greatest challenge to liberal order would end up coming from the hegemon itself. With the election of Joseph Biden in 2020, the United States is likely to try to recover some liberal leadership. However, if the country subsequently elects another conservative and nativist president, the United States may come to lead the production of new normative goods, indices that concretize and measure conservative, nativist, authoritarian, and protectionist values, and rank states on those bases. As the Family Prosperity Index discussed in this chapter illustrates, such revisionist attempts by the United States are also likely to find strong support in Russia and China.

4 | *China and the Asian Infrastructure Investment Bank: Undermining Hegemony through Goods Substitution?*

JULIA BADER

When Britain's Chancellor of the Exchequer, George Osborne, unexpectedly announced the UK's intention to join the China-led Asian Infrastructure Investment Bank (AIIB) in mid-March 2015, an unnerved US official could not hold back his concern 'about a trend [in the UK] toward constant accommodation of China' (Watt et al. 2015). This rare instance of rebuking a close partner in public, however, did not prevent other US allies from following the British example: in a domino-like manner other European states, Australia and South Korea followed suit. By March 2015, fifty-seven countries, including non-Asian and G7 states, had applied for membership of the AIIB (AIIB 2020). Since then, membership has grown to 102 members.

China is increasingly ready and able to openly challenge the hegemonic position of the United States in international relations. Indeed, the academic debate about the rise of China in international relations has long shifted from discussing *whether* China will affect the existing international order to debating about *how* it will do so. That is, the early literature investigating the nature of China's rise in terms of a status quo or revisionist orientation towards the existing international order (Johnston 2003; Legro 2007; Chan 2008; Buzan 2010; Schweller and Pu 2011; Kastner and Saunders 2012; Wuthnow, et al. 2012) is being complemented by examinations of how China uses its economic cloud to effectively influence the policy preferences of others in order to protect its own (foreign) policy interests (Flores-Macías and Kreps 2013; Fuchs and Klann 2013; Kastner 2014; Strüver 2017; Bader 2019).

Yet, the role that China has started to take on in the new millennium goes much further than employing economic statecraft in its bilateral relations (Medeiros and Fravel 2003; Economy 2010). China now sees the UN 'as one of the key venues in which to demonstrate its responsible

Great Power status and its willingness to provide global public goods' so as to gain legitimacy at home and abroad (Foot 2014:1088).[1] Outside of the UN, Xi Jinping's Belt and Road Initiative signals the readiness for leadership of the kind that 'America has not shown since the post-war days of the Marshall Plan' (The Economist 2017). More generally, experts have noted a trend in China's foreign policy towards 're-engineering' – or 'shadow diplomacy' as some have called it – which involves the construction of new, supplementary international platforms and institutions (Heilmann et al. 2014; Wesley 2015). The AIIB is a prime example thereof.

To make sense of China's recent power-political manoeuvres, this chapter builds on the concept of goods substitution and on the categorisation of orientation towards the international system as introduced in the earlier chapters of this book. While I am not intending to reduce the establishment of the AIIB to power-political considerations, I argue that the AIIB was initiated as a counter-hegemonic attempt targeted at the architecture of international finance *and* at US dominance therein. The initiative's effects in terms of deconcentrating power were only limited. But, while largely conforming to the norms and standards of existing international financial institutions (IFIs) and development banks, China was successful in making all founding members subscribe to the principles of non-conditionality and non-interference, which largely deviate from current practices in development finance.

The AIIB serves well as an illustrative case of goods substitution. It was seen primarily as a power-political manoeuvre by policy-makers in the United States who feared that the AIIB would undermine governance conditionality – and hence political influence in lending countries – in the short-term, and hollow out US supremacy in global finance in the long run (Callaghan and Hubbard 2016). Hence, US opposition and its attempts to prevent others from joining the Chinese initiative. In addition, the case of the AIIB sheds light on the demand-side dynamics of goods substitution and illustrates how opportunistic hedging and uncoordinated herding by third states may inadvertently undermine the existing order.

---

[1] For example, China is now the 10th largest contributor of UN Blue Helmet troops and is actively involved in anti-piracy operations in the Gulf of Aden (Pham 2013; United Nations 2020). See Christensen (2015) for a detailed discussion of China's willingness to cooperate with the United States on a variety of issues.

The chapter starts by placing the AIIB initiative in the context of the existing international arrangements which the AIIB sought to substitute. Then, I develop the argument that the AIIB – initially thought of as a revisionist counter-hegemonic initiative – transformed into an integrated part of the existing international financial architecture due to the engagement of Western third states. I conclude by arguing that goods substitution as an analytical lens may advance the study of international relations by placing the mechanisms of power politics at the centre of inquiry, being less obsessed with traditional security concerns and, most importantly, attributing more agency to non-hegemonic actors.

AIIB and the Existing Order in International Finance

When the idea of the AIIB was first raised, in 2013, its nature was still unclear. Initially, it was conceived purely as a commercially guided bank; however, the AIIB has instead become a new multilateral development bank that focuses on infrastructure financing needs in Asia. The bank has a US$100 billion capital stock, with US$20 billion paid-in capital (AIIB 2020). The goods that the AIIB sought to provide was infrastructure financing, but it has, in fact, broadened its financing to the sectors of 'energy and power, transportation and telecommunications, rural infrastructure and agriculture development, water supply and sanitation, environmental protection, and urban development and logistics' (AIIB 2020). Clearly, the envisioned activities of the AIIB fell into the domain of existing IFIs such as the International Monetary Fund (IMF), the World Bank and the Asian Development Bank (ADB). As I will argue in more detail below, these institutions did not satisfy the demand for infrastructure financing. In 2009, the ADB estimated an infrastructure investment need of about US$750 billion annually for the period 2010 to 2020 in Asia alone (Asian Development Bank 2009:5).

The idea of establishing a Chinese infrastructure bank was discussed in 2007, but was not taken up by the Chinese leadership at the time. Pursuing a more ambitious foreign policy agenda than his predecessors, President Xi Jinping raised the idea when he announced the establishment of the AIIB in October 2013 at an Asia-Pacific Economic Cooperation (APEC) meeting (Perlez 2015). Just one year later, twenty-one Asian countries, including all Association of Southeast Asian

Nations (ASEAN) countries (except Indonesia), India, Kazakhstan, Kuwait, Mongolia, Nepal, Bangladesh, Oman, Pakistan, Qatar, Sri Lanka and Uzbekistan signed a Memorandum of Understanding (MoU) to establish the AIIB, headquartered in Beijing (Indonesia followed in November 2014).

In December 2014, New Zealand joined as the first 'Western' founding member. The United States, which had earlier ignored the proposal, openly voiced opposition to a Chinese-led bank, questioning whether it would meet international governance and lending standards. Yet China, determined to establish the AIIB, set a membership application deadline of 31 March 2015. This triggered the United States to start actively dissuading others from joining – in particular, South Korea and Australia, which had both expressed interest in the bank.

However, events took an unexpected turn when, on 12 March 2015, two weeks before the application deadline, the United Kingdom – surprising even the Chinese government – announced its application for founding membership.[2] The United Kingdom's decision was followed by a cascade of membership applications from a dozen other European countries and prompted South Korea and Australia to reconsider their decisions. By the end of March 2015, fifty-seven countries, including the three European G7 states, South Korea and Australia, had applied for membership of the AIIB (AIIB 2020).[3] In late 2015, the Articles of Agreement (AOA) of the AIIB came into force, and in early 2016 the AIIB became operational.

The AIIB's Initial Counter-Hegemonic Intentions

There are several reasons for believing that the AIIB was initially intended as a counter-hegemonic initiative, implying a counter-order and an anti-unipolarity orientation. The most consequential anti-unipolarity aspect of the AIIB was the initial idea to use the bank to further the internationalisation of the renminbi (RMB) with the goal of turning the RMB into a global reserve currency. While a common reserve currency is beneficial for all those participating in international exchange, it comes with significant material benefits for its producer in

---

[2] In fact, Luxembourg had submitted its membership application even ahead of the United Kingdom, but this was not immediately published (Anderlini 2015).
[3] Two more applications, those of North Korea and Taiwan, were rejected.

the form of seignorage and the shifting of the transaction costs of currency exchange to others (Drezner 2010; Cohen 2012). The dollar's status as the global reserve currency facilitates the Unites States' autonomous monetary policies and this allows the projection of power capabilities without material constraints. Given that 'possessing the world's reserve currency is both cause and consequence of US economic hegemony' (Drezner 2010:393), it is not surprising that China is trying to turn the RMB into a global reserve currency by promoting it in international finance and international trade (Cohen 2012).[4] Some Chinese strategists envisioned using the AIIB to further the internationalisation of the RMB (Sun 2015b).

Moreover, initially the AIIB sought to compete with the Japanese dominated ADB and exclude not only the United States, but also other important Asian countries such as Japan, South Korea and India (Arase 2015). In fact, an early discussion with prospective member states about establishing the AIIB took place during ADB's annual meeting in Kazakhstan in May 2014. Sixteen countries reportedly did not attend a dinner scheduled by the ADB, but instead joined a Chinese invitation which left out the United States, Japan and India (Hamanaka 2016:289). China's non-transparency and lack of information about the AIIB has been interpreted as a tactic to keep the United States out of the initiative (Harris 2015; Hamanaka 2016:209). Clearly, the initial attempt was to establish a China-dominated institution; this was reflected in China's prospective capital contribution of up to 50 per cent, implying Chinese veto power over any decisions requiring a simple majority (Sun 2015a).

To the extent that China's discontent with existing international IFIs related to their inability to adjust to shifting weights in global productivity, AIIB's anti-unipolarity orientation overlaps with its counter-order orientation. Emerging economies, and China in particular, have long been under-represented in existing IFIs. In 2010, a reform package was agreed by the IMF's board of governors to increase IMF quotas, and to shift about 6 per cent of quota shares and two seats on the IMF board of executive directors from developed countries to developing

---

[4] To that end, China has set up alternative credit card and rating agencies, promoted Shanghai as a financial centre (Heilmann et al. 2014; Ryan 2015) and established a network of bilateral central bank swap agreements designed to enable the use of the RMB to settle trade in the absence of full currency convertibility (Cohen 2012; Liao and McDowell 2015:405).

and emerging economies. However, these voice reforms (i.e., adjustments to voting power in the IMF), which increased the Chinese representation, were blocked for several years by the US congress which refused to ratify the package (Kawai 2015). Yet, due to various classification issues, high-income countries continue to be represented in the World Bank and the IMF with more than 60 per cent of voting shares, even after the reforms (Vestergaard and Wade 2013).

But AIIB's initial counter-order orientation went beyond voting rights in the Bretton Woods institutions and extended to their norms and practices in international development financing, and even the underlying development paradigm. First, the provision of financing for infrastructure was a result of discontent with existing IFIs. Since the 1980s and 1990s, most established multilateral development banks (MDBs) focused on pro-poor poverty alleviation, especially in health, education and social protection, and on sustainable development (Chin 2014). With about US$15 billion and US$13 billion annually, respectively, the World Bank and ADB's investment in infrastructure in Asia remained far below the estimated needs (Kawai 2015). It became even harder for developing countries to meet their infrastructure financing demands after the global financial crisis. Although the G20 summit in Seoul in 2010 agreed on promoting infrastructure financing in the developing world, this agenda was later obstructed by rich donor countries. According to Chin (2014:369), Chinese officials noted that the World Bank appeared to ignore the G20 Seoul summit agreement and continued to keep its focus on liberalisation and institutional adjustments so as to make developing countries more attractive to private investors, while the G7 did not seem to bother and did not see it as a problem.

Second, the AIIB was also intended to challenge the operational procedures of existing IFIs. In early discussions, the bank was envisioned to be a purely commercially guided investment bank that would yield high profits given the identified infrastructure investment gap (Callaghan and Hubbard 2016). When the AIIB took shape as a new MDB, China had the ambition to deliver infrastructure through the AIIB 'more efficiently and more effectively than the World Bank and ADB' (Sun 2015a:40). For example, to take the bank's final lending decisions, China wanted a technical panel instead of a perceivably wasteful and ineffective full-time resident board, as in many other MDBs (Callaghan and Hubbard 2016). In light of China's controversial track record as a bilateral donor in the infrastructure sector, these ambitions led to concerns that the bank would prioritise quantity, speed or political considerations over quality and environmental or social sustainability (Arase 2015).

While there are clear indications of the AIIB's counter-hegemonic orientation, particularly in the early stages, it is important to note that for China establishing the AIIB made sense for many reasons beyond power politics, and hence the initiative should not be considered only from this perspective. Chinese strategists thought of the AIIB as a response to domestic overcapacities and the flattening of China's economic growth.[5] As part of the Silk Road initiative, the AIIB – with its focus on the development of infrastructure – was initially designed to open up new investment opportunities. And while the initiative coincided with unmet demand for infrastructure financing in Asia, a multilateral financing instrument such as the AIIB – as opposed to a purely Chinese one – would bring with it a variety of strategic advantages for China. For example, it would dilute the perception of creating dependency on China among its neighbours (Callaghan and Hubbard 2016) and de-politicise projects in countries sensitive to Chinese influence because of territorial disputes with China or backlashes against Chinese investment in the past (Hilpert and Wacker 2015; Callaghan and Hubbard 2016).

Anti-Unipolarity, Self-Inflicted Isolation, Strategic Exclusion, Hedging and Herding

China has maintained control over the AIIB and this has ensured that it will remain an Asian-controlled organisation. Inclusive membership was not initially expected and this required adjustments of capital shares and voting rights. In order to accommodate additional members, China reduced its capital share to 30 per cent and adopted a more sophisticated voting rights formula. China still retains veto power on issues that require a supermajority. While these rights are comparatively extensive (Callaghan and Hubbard 2016), some observers

---

[5] Sun notes that 'one of China's most controversial goals in launching AIIB – promoting exports to absorb excess capacity – has gradually disappeared from government statements and media reports' even though there are still expectations by important Chinese constituencies, such as local governments and companies, that China will advantage Chinese bidders in project tenders (Sun 2015a:39–40).

interpret them as being rather symbolic because, in practice, China would only need to employ them when faced with unanimous opposition, a scenario which seems rather unlikely (Sun 2015a). Most importantly, the definition of regional and non-regional members and the limitation of capital subscriptions for non-regional members to a maximum of 25 per cent ensures that the AIIB is controlled by Asian and developing countries.

The proposal to set up the AIIB, in October 2013, was received positively in most parts of Asia that were initially invited by China to join. It fitted nicely with APEC's theme of improving connectivity and it was sensible in economic terms. Many of the prospective member states had large estimated infrastructure investment needs (Kawai 2015:11). Most East Asian states also sought to maintain good relations with both the United States *and* China and given that the United States did not offer any alternative solution to the investment problem, it is not surprising that these Asian countries joined. For them, the AIIB promised to be a source of infrastructure financing that the United States and US-led institutions in the existing international order failed to provide.

One may argue that, with regard to the most important aspect of US hegemony in global finance, the AIIB was not a very successful tool in de-concentrating US power. For the time being, loans provided by the AIIB will be denominated in US dollars, and not in Chinese yuan (Wildau and Mitchell 2016). But even if the AIIB does not challenge the US dollar's status as global reserve currency, the United States has appeared to be a loser in terms of power politics.

In the view of many observers, the United States mishandled the AIIB initiative. It could have made a counter-proposal and promoted an alternative initiative that was easier to control. Through engagement, it could also have influenced the institutional configurations and could even have defeated the whole initiative from within (Hamanaka 2016). Instead, the United States first ignored the initiative and then attempted to limit its scope by raising concerns about the AIIB's capabilities to keep up with the governance standards of existing lending institutions. Officially, American diplomats made support for the AIIB conditional on its standards and transparency; behind the scenes, they tried to convince America's allies, particularly Korea and Australia, not to join.

The United States opposed the AIIB because it viewed the initiative primarily from a geopolitical perspective (Harris 2015; Hamanaka

2016). Ultimately, the United States feared that the AIIB would contribute to the hollowing out of US supremacy in global finance and, in the short term, political influence in lending countries (Callaghan and Hubbard 2016). US rejection was also a reflection of Japan's resistance to the initiative (Harris 2015). Given the existing historically rooted distrust between Japan and China, their overlapping territorial claims in the East China Sea and their competition over leadership in East Asia, Japan was most concerned about the nature of the Chinese initiative. Moreover, being the dominant player in the ADB, Japan feared that the AIIB, as a new institution with lower governance and lending standards, could possibly draw bankable projects away from the ADB, leading to a race-to-the-bottom (Kawai 2015).[6]

Moreover, the Obama administration was occupied with the fight against the Islamic State and the Ukraine crisis and, in any event, did not see a way to stop China from establishing the AIIB (Harris 2015; Hamanaka 2016). Having blocked IMF's capital increase earlier, it was not a viable option for US decision-makers to become a contributor to the AIIB and so exert influence from within (Harris 2015). Indeed, even if the United States had wanted to join, the fact that China had requested a formal founding member application to be part of the negotiations strategically excluded the United States and so obstructed the country's meddling in the founding process (Hamanaka 2016:291). In sum, America's inability to prevent the formation of the AIIB was partly due to self-inflicted isolation, and partly due to the Chinese strategy to exclude the United States from the process.

Chinese commentators interpreted US failure to prevent its close allies from joining as an indication of waning American influence (Thomas and Hutzler 2015). This argument may be most valid with regard to South Korea and Australia, the main targets of both Chinese and US lobbying. Indeed, a Korean official, described the decision in terms of the 'deep dilemma on what strategic choices [Korea] has to make as China challenges the U.S.-led (sic) international order' (cited in Callaghan and Hubbard 2016:13). In Australia too, the decision not to sign the MoU was accompanied by intense domestic debate.

---

[6] While Japan was reportedly offered a junior role in the AIIB (the vice-presidency) in late 2014 (Hamanaka 2016), some observers argue that a high-level invitation, if it was made at all, came too late (Kawai 2015).

The European democracies did not really perceive the issue as a strategic dilemma, and in the absence of that strategic perspective, there was little reason not to join. Earlier attempts to unite the G7 on a common position had failed, because not all members agreed with Japanese and US opposition (Thomas and Hutzler 2015). Germany, France, Italy and the United Kingdom did reportedly discuss a common approach. However, the issue was discussed only informally in the EU; this might have reflected China's strategy of inviting prospective member countries individually (Taylor and James 2015). In any event, this does not suggest a strategic approach towards the issue, but the rather typical inability and unwillingness of many EU member states to formulate a common position due to competing national interests.

Indeed, the United Kingdom's announcement to join came as a surprise, and seemed to be largely driven by narrow self-interest. In his announcement, George Osborne, the United Kingdom's then Chancellor of the Exchequer, related the decision to economic motives to give British companies 'the best opportunity to work and invest in the world's fastest growing markets' (UK.gov. 2015). Reportedly, the United Kingdom asked for the vice-presidency, a seat on the Board of Directors and an AIIB office in London in return for breaking with the United States (Müller 2015). With this move the United Kingdom attempted to outmanoeuvre other financial centres in Europe to strengthen London's position as a financial trading place for the RMB (Taylor and James 2015; Knoerich and Urdinez 2019). Media reports also connected the decision to join the AIIB to the British desire to improve diplomatic relations, which had nosedived after Prime Minister Cameron's meeting with the Dalai Lama in 2012, as well as with much needed investments in the United Kingdom's domestic nuclear power sector (Perlez 2015). Prime Minister Cameron later defended the decision, explaining it in terms of the United Kingdom's 'national interest' (BBC News 2015).

According to European diplomats, the United Kingdom's announcement 'helped to clear the way for other Western economies to follow suit' (Thomas and Hutzler 2015). Yet it appears likely that the European G7 states would have engaged with the AIIB anyway. Germany announced that it was joining the AIIB in parallel with France and Italy two days after the United Kingdom during an official occasion, the First China–Germany High Level Financial Dialogue in Berlin. According to 'a German aide', for Germany the decision to join was 'a no brainer' (Taylor and James 2015). In the final days before the deadline expired, twelve other European countries, the rest of the Brazil, Russia, India, China, and South Africa (BRICS) group, Egypt, Israel and eventually Australia and South Korea applied for founding membership.

Many democratic governments, and specifically the first movers, justified their decision to join as a desire to be able to influence the bank from within (for a systematic analysis see Knoerich and Urdinez 2019). The Western democracies' insistence helped to bring the institution into conformity with the standards of existing IFIs during the negotiation of the AOA. China, on the other hand, was willing to accommodate these preferences and concerns in return for the legitimacy and credibility these countries' participation lent to the bank. New Zealand, the first Western democracy to join, passed information about China's flexibility to other Western democracies (Knoerich and Urdinez 2019). And when China lobbied the United Kingdom to become a member, it promised safeguards over governance and political interference to win over sceptics in the Foreign Office (Anderlini and Stacey 2015). The United Kingdom joined the bank on the condition that China would commit to transparency and governance standards (BBC News 2015).

In addition to engaging with the AIIB in order to influence the initiative, there are indications of strategic hedging among the European early movers. Strategic hedging describes attempts of second-tier states 'to compensate for the potential loss of public goods or direct subsidies that are currently provided by the system leader' when the power position of a unipolar system leader risks being eroded (Tessman and Wolfe 2011:222). The United Kingdom's motivation to join the AIIB to secure Chinese investment in domestic industries has already been mentioned;[7] in their announcement to join, many other states referred to the investment opportunities in a dynamic world region that membership in the AIIB was expected to offer. Journalistic accounts also implied that within the governments of the big European states, financial considerations were judged to be more important than foreign affairs (Anderlini and Stacey 2015; Taylor and James 2015;), which is indicative of the fact that such considerations played a major role.

---

[7] See Harris (2017) for a discussion of the Conservative Party's promotion of Chinese investment to the United Kingdom in order to facilitate a partisan austerity agenda.

If hedging describes the early movers' intentions, herding may characterise those who joined later on. The cascade-like dynamic also suggests that rather than there being just a concern to antagonise the United States, once a critical number of countries had filed their applications, this turned into an issue of antagonizing China. One European diplomat recounted the discussions as about a big train that 'was leaving the station and it was in our interest to jump aboard' (Taylor and James 2015).

If we understand power as the ability to make others do what they would not otherwise have done, US power clearly failed. Arguably, the most important fallout from the AIIB affair for the United States was that it exposed the incongruence between American rhetoric and behaviour and damaged its credibility as a benign leader. Like a quasi-monopolistic supplier who ignores demand-side requests and therefore misses out on the innovative ideas of potential competitors, Washington came painfully to realise that frustration over US obstruction of 'a very mild and reasonable set of reforms in the IMF' (US Treasury Secretary Jack Lew, cited in Taylor and James, 2015) had pushed others to go along with the Chinese alternative. Not by coincidence, the US Congress blockade over ratifying the capital increase for the IMF was removed shortly after the AIIB's inception.

Taming the Tiger: AIIB's Integration into Existing Financial Structures

Compared to the initial proposal and China's underlying motivations, the nature of the AIIB project has changed significantly as it has developed (Sun 2015b). As a result, the AIIB has become much more like a MDB integrated in the current international financial order than a counter-order vehicle against it. AIIB is as much cooperating as it is competing with existing IFIs, and it has adopted many of the current norms and practices.

In contrast to the desire to prioritise the quick delivery of infrastructure over any other considerations, the AIIB has adopted standards that compare to those of existing MDBs. The AIIB promises to be a lean (efficient and highly skilled), clean (ethical and non-corrupt) and green (environmentally friendly) organisation that draws on the experience of existing MDBs and will implement strong policies on governance, accountability, financial, procurement and environmental and social frameworks (Saldinger 2017).

As argued in the section above, the participation of major Western democracies helped to ensure high standards in AIIB's AOA. For example, because they were concerned about transparency, Western countries rejected the Chinese idea of a technical panel instead of a full-time resident board (Callaghan and Hubbard 2016). As a compromise, accountability is secured by a non-resident board that is not involved in day-to-day management. Moreover, based on an Australian proposal, procurement in the AIIB is not limited to member countries (Perlez 2015). Whether the AIIB will keep all these promises remains to be seen but, at this stage, there are no reasons to believe otherwise. To the contrary, failure or misuse of the bank would incur high reputational costs for both China and those countries that have committed to it, so there high stakes in challenging AIIB's legitimacy and credibility.

Although the bank was intended to compete with the Japanese-dominated ADB (Callaghan and Hubbard 2016), China's leaders soon moved away from this vision and stressed its complementary and cooperative character. Indeed, during the AIIB's first months in operation, several MoUs were signed to partner with existing MDBs, including the World Bank, the ADB and the European Bank for Reconstruction and Development. The majority of AIIB's projects are co-financed (AIIB 2020).

In sum, AIIB has become a truly multilateral rather than a purely commercial bank, or a channel for Chinese aid. It is not an instrument to finance political prestige projects or economically unviable undertakings, nor an investment bank yielding high profits. Despite the infrastructure funding gap, the scope of projects and the size of loans are more modest than initially envisioned, while the economic standards for loan provision will be high and comparable to those of existing IFIs (Sun 2015a).

However, through its integration, the AIIB has also helped to reform existing structures. While its operational standards seem to be relatively consistent with the rules, norms and practices of existing Western-dominated MDBs, the AIIB has already visibly impacted on Bretton Woods institutions in several ways, and some remarkable deviations of the AIIB may potentially affect existing MDBs in the long term. On the one hand, as a response to the AIIB, the BRICS' New Development Bank and other new funding schemes, as well as existing development banks, have started to rebalance their portfolios from their heavy focus on pro-poor poverty alleviation, health, education and social protection to include more infrastructure financing (Chin 2014:368). On the other hand, as argued earlier, the mere existence of the AIIB, as a potential substitution to development financing in the framework of the diverse Western-led MDBs, was a boost for overdue voice reforms. With regard to these reactions, one may argue that the establishment of the AIIB has stimulated much needed renewal of IFIs which may, in the long run, strengthen rather than undermine the existing architecture.

Yet, at least in two respects, one can also view the AIIB as a potential vehicle of norm contestation. First, the AIIB deviates in the formula to determine the voting shares of individual members. Unlike other MDB's, the AIIB's allocation of capital subscriptions, and hence voting shares, across countries is determined by GDP. But second, and more importantly, the AIIB clearly questions the interventionism and aid conditionality of the current financial architecture. While Bretton Woods institutions have been a tool to promote democracy and free markets, AIIB's AOA explicitly prohibits interference in the political affairs of any of its member states. It is remarkable that China managed to make all AIIB member states, including its OECD donors, endorse the principles of non-interference and unconditionality (Peng and Tok 2016). Whether this will lead to the lowering of conditionality in Bretton Woods institutions in the long term remains to be seen. However, because it is not in the interests of the AIIB or any of its members to fund economically risky or wasteful projects, one may expect that the bank will simply formulate conditionality in economic terms to minimise the risks that accrue from corruption, bad governance or political instability.

Conclusions

This chapter has used the case of China's AIIB initiative to probe the concept of goods substitution as a power-political tool in international relations. Although the initiative has taken a different shape than initially envisioned, it has turned out to be a highly successful example of goods substitution. Targeting infrastructure financing – a real gap in existing goods provision by the United States and the US-led order – the AIIB remains an attractive initiative for prospective lenders and borrowers alike. The United States clearly failed in its attempt to prevent other states joining the initiative and, more importantly, China has been able to use it to reveal US hypocrisy and discrepancies between US claims of world leadership and actual attempts to fulfil this role.

The AIIB is, in many respects, a particularly illustrative case. Yet, most of China's recent activities, including its outstanding contribution of UN Blue Helmets troops, its engagement in anti-piracy operations in the Gulf of Aden (Pham 2013; United Nations n.d.), One Belt one Road (now the Belt and Road Initiative) and the establishment of it various diplomatic platforms, make formidable sense through the lens of goods substitution. This is not to say that power-political calculations are the sole, or even the most important, driver of Chinese foreign policy; but once these policies are in place, they work as power-political instruments.

Goods substitution as an analytical lens potentially advances the study of international relations in several ways. First, it treats power politics as an object of inquiry in its own right by explicitly focusing on the 'mechanisms, instruments, and logics' by which 'actors enhance their influence in global politics' (Goddard and Nexon 2016:6). Second, it allows for a view of international relations that is more issue specific and less centred on security aspects, and as such it may better reflect the post– Cold War era in which security-driven incentives for cooperation have been weakened (Ikenberry 2009:79). In the case of the AIIB, perceived immediate economic opportunities overruled potential long-term security concerns– if they existed at all – at least in European countries.

Third, because goods provision involves both producers and consumers, it directs more attention towards non-hegemonic actors as important but often overlooked players.[8] The implications of the creation of the AIIB for both the balance of power and US-led international order would have been much less significant without second-tier states hedging and smaller states herding behaviours. Paradoxically, the participation of major Western democracies helped to integrate the AIIB into the existing architecture of international finance by ensuring that it adopted existing rules and norms; at the same time, it may unintentionally have contributed to the hollowing out of existing norms in the long term by

---

[8] In Organski's power transition theory, for example, there is no role for second-tier states, because it is assumed that an established place in the existing international hierarchy of power is sufficient to tie 'the weak and satisfied' to the hegemon (Organski 1958:329).

Conclusions

endorsing the principles of non-interference and unconditionality, which have been lambasted for undermining the position of Bretton Woods institutions. But the concept of goods substitution does not only explicitly invite the inclusion of non-hegemonic actors; it is also consistent with a variety of behaviours of such actors.

In economics, competition is usually seen as positive as it creates important stimuli for innovation and efficiency – especially when it challenges existing monopolies. How well (monopolistic) businesses can weather exposure to competition or changes in circumstances crucially depends on their ability to innovate their products, respond to consumer demands and compete on prices. Analogously, the rise of China may be seen as a healthy correction to the current hegemon and the existing international order rather than a replacement. While much depends on US reaction to the rise of China, empirical evidence suggests that China's goods substitution offers both challenges and opportunities for international relations.

5 | *The Silk Road to Goods Substitution: Central Asia and the Rise of New Post-Western International Orders*

ALEXANDER COOLEY

Unlike Latin America or the North Atlantic, Central Asia was not historically an integral part of the US-led hegemonic order. In fact, the contemporary region was created by the collapse of the Soviet Union in 1991, which yielded five new independent states – Kazakhstan, Kyrgyzstan, Tajikistan, Turkmenistan and Uzbekistan. Importantly, independence was initially "unwanted," as the Central Asian states did not incubate potent national independence movements as witnessed in the Baltic states or the Caucasus. As Soviet republics, these regimes, which had grown dependent on Moscow's fiscal subsidies and enjoyed considerable local political autonomy to build their patronage machines, suddenly found themselves having to forge new independent governing institutions in the wake of the Soviet collapse (Olcott 1996).[1]

In terms of foreign relations, the 1990s were dominated by post-Soviet extrication and shallow integration into the US-led liberal order and global governance. Post-Soviet extrication necessitated building or repurposing new governing bureaucracies, independent foreign policies and security services, as well as managing the physical legacies of fragmented Soviet military and industrial complexes. Economically, a centrally planned system that had been coordinated and managed by Moscow for Soviet central needs was rapidly dismantled, with each of the states needing to take responsibility for their own economic affairs and the pressing problem of facilitating the tradition to a market-based system (Pomfret 1995). The energy-rich Central Asian states – Kazakhstan and Turkmenistan – were optimistic that

---

[1] On pathways of late-Soviet elite transition and local Communist Party dynamics, see McGlinchey (2011).

104

they could take advantage of their natural endowments in oil and gas as a basis of national prosperity, but they lacked the necessary investment and infrastructure to get their energy to markets. Uzbekistan, the most populous country at the heart of the region, became increasingly autarkic and inward looking, while Kyrgyzstan and civil-war ravaged Tajikistan turned to external lenders and humanitarian providers to assist with the devastating economic and social hardships of the transition.

Regional order and cooperation – once based on Soviet-era rules, coordination and norms – was weakened further as individual countries delineated and even militarized national borders and introduced national currencies without warning. Regional trade ground to a halt as a result of nonfunctioning payments systems and a lack of foreign reserves. Although a decade later Moscow would assert itself as the region's historical great power and security guarantor, in the 1990s Russia was relatively disengaged, busy coping with its own tumultuous economic and political transition. Its preferred Soviet successor forum, the Commonwealth of Independent States (CIS), was more an attempt to preserve ties from the past than to form a new basis of regional cooperation. And although the Central Asian region was designated as "post-Communist," it lacked the linkages to the West that characterized East-Central Europe and, importantly, the pull of the EU or NATO as potentially anchoring institutions (Kopstein and Reilly 2000; Way and Levitsky 2007).

Almost by default then, the vacuum left by the Soviet collapse was mostly filled by the institutions, rules and norms of the US-led hegemonic order. However, their institutionalization and influence in the region were relatively weak, and the region, at the margins of global liberalism, appeared open to engaging with almost any external actors with an interest and the means to provide material support (see Adamson 2005).[2] In the political sphere, the Central Asian states joined regional organizations such as the Organization for Security and Co-operation in Europe (OSCE) that embodied the US-led order and institutionally espoused liberal values (Fawn 2013). In economics, officials had no alternative but to engage with Western-led international financial institutions such as the World Bank, International

---

[2] Adamson makes the apt point that many outside groups viewed Central Asia in the 1990s as a tabula rasa for projecting influence.

Monetary Fund (IMF) and European Bank for Reconstruction and Development (EBRD) and they integrated themselves into global networks of Central Banking that encouraged central bank independence and noninterference.[3] The United States and the EU sent teams of consultants and other technical assistance providers to advise on these institutional reforms.[4] And in terms of norms and values, even as all the Central Asian regimes took steps to consolidate power and create single party and family-based regimes, they acknowledged the legitimacy of liberal norms by signing international human rights treaties, accepting the presence of foreign-funded NGOs and civil society and inviting international election observers to monitor national elections.[5] By the end of the 1990s, Central Asian governments had stalled in most areas of political and economic reform, but remained engaged with the international community primarily to secure much-needed financing, investment and political legitimacy.

Dramatic events in the early 2000s rapidly brought this era of isolation to a halt and accelerated "asset substitution" across the region in the areas of security, economy and political governance. Indeed, Central Asia represents a textbook example of these dynamics as Russia and China – emerging and competing regional powers –not only established themselves as alternative providers of assets and public goods, but drove the Central Asian states to push back against the political and economic conditions, criticism and demands made by the United States, EU and other Western-led international organizations.

The rest of this chapter recounts this rapid process of reordering across the region away from loose association with the US-led liberal order to post-liberal alternatives, mostly led by Russia and China. Across nearly all major issue domains – including security, economics and political norms – elements of the US-led liberal international order, once paramount, are still present, but they are no longer the main source of ordering. Central Asian rulers now routinely invoke the importance of new economic patrons, cultural systems and norms to

---

[3] On the IMF's role in Central Asia, see Broome (2010). On the influential and tight transnational networks of Central Bankers, see Johnson (2016).
[4] On the ineffectiveness of Western technical assistance in promoting reforms in Central Asia, see Cooley and Ron (2002).
[5] In the phrasing of Beth Simmons (2009), the Central Asian states could be considered insincere signers of human rights treaties, doing so to avoid the international spotlight as nonconforming states.

justify their authoritarian practices, while their membership in new institutions and regional governance projects has effectively ensured Russian and Chinese tutelage.

Security: The Eagle Lands, Competes and Departs

The 9/11 terrorist attacks proved to be an important inflection point in Central Asian international relations as the region shed its marginalized status. The aftermath of the events of 9/11 not only thrust the Central Asian states into the frontlines of the US-led Global War on Terror (GWOT); they also prompted Russia and China to accelerate their own regional engagement and security initiatives. In 1999, Vladimir Putin had ascended to power advocating for great security cooperation in the post–Soviet Union to combat regional terrorism, and post-2001 these efforts were channeled into creating new formal organizations like the Collective Security Treaty Organization (CSTO). China's reengagement with Central Asia through the Shanghai Forum of the 1990s led to the establishment of the Shanghai Cooperation Organization (SCO) in June 2001, a regional security organization, without Western members or geopolitical agendas, comprised of China, Russia, Kazakhstan, Kyrgyzstan, Uzbekistan and Tajikistan. From a relative backwater in the 1990s, Central Asia – over the course of just a few months – was suddenly a strategic frontline for Washington, Moscow and Beijing.[6]

The immediate concern for US planners was to set up a network of logistical bases and supply routes to support Operation Enduring Freedom in Afghanistan. In October 2001 US officials secured access to the Soviet-era Karshi-Khanabad (K2) airfield in southern Uzbekistan, with the Uzbek government consenting to the base's use for supply efforts, but not actual combat operations. Two months later, US planners obtained the use of an additional site - the Manas civilian airport, on the outskirts of Bishkek, the capital of Kyrgyzstan, which had just been renovated with an upgraded runway that could accommodate the loads of heavy military transport and refueling aircraft. Initially, these countries charged minimal "rent," though the agreements included a number of transit, parking and landing fees that were intended to placate airport authorities and their government

---

[6] These events are recounted in greater detail in Cooley (2012).

connections. US officials also secured refueling rights and the use of airspace across the region, even stationing a small refueling contingent in Turkmenistan's capital, Ashgabat airport (Tynan 2009). The year 2002 also saw a large spike in US economic and security assistance to the region (at least $476 in security assistance) – with Uzbekistan receiving the lion's share (Kucera 2012: 8). US aid appears to have been concentrated on training and equipping Central Asian state special forces, while Central Asian governments appeared disinterested in reforming their defense institutions or improving oversight and governance (Kucera 2012: 8).

In theory, US planners had hoped that securing military access, coupled with more security engagement and foreign aid, would also nudge the Central Asian states to commit to implementing political reforms. For example, in March 2002 Presidents George W. Bush and Islam Karimov of Uzbekistan signed a cooperation framework agreement outlining aspects of security cooperation in which Uzbekistan also pledged to pursue political and economic reforms, as well as respect human rights and an open media environment. However, the opposite subsequently transpired as the Central Asian states used their new partnership with the United States to justify their increased authoritarian crackdown, while using the Pentagon's need for access to push back against State Department and NGO-led criticisms of their governance.

The situation's contradictions reached a peak in 2005 when, in the wake of other post-Soviet revolutions, Kyrgyz President Askar Akayev was ousted from office in March amid allegations of base-related corruption and embezzlement from logistics contracts. His successor Kurmanbek Bakiyev ran on a "Kyrgyz sovereignty" campaign that advocated charging the United States one hundred times more than its current fees in rent ($200 million).[7] Just two months later, with the Uzbek government distrustful of the regional trend of street protests and regime challenges, Uzbek interior forces ruthlessly cracked down on a street protest in the eastern city of Andijon, killing between 180 and up to 600 protestors (Denber and Levine 2005). The US reaction to the so-called "Andijon massacre" was mixed; the State Department and Congress condemned the Uzbek government and demanded an international investigation into the events, while the Pentagon – fearing

---

[7] See Cooley (2012: chapter 3).

loss of basing rights – remained conspicuously silent. Eventually, US officials imposed a ban on military aid to the country, with Uzbek authorities imposing greater restrictions on operations at K2.

In July 2005, the Uzbek government formally evicted the United States from K2, effectively leaving Manas as the only operational US military base in the region. The terms of the Kyrgyz deal were also subject to intense negotiations, as Bakiyev demanded increased rent and quid pro quo from the United States throughout 2005 and 2006. More broadly, however, the clear tension that had emerged between ensuring military access and not condoning the corruption and authoritarian excesses of the Central Asian regimes provided new openings for Moscow and Beijing to curry favor with the Central Asian regimes in their bids to deepen their own security partnerships.

Great Power Response and Competitive Regional Securitization

Both Russia and China soon took important steps to build up their own security infrastructures to counter those of the United States. In 2002, Russia formalized the CSTO, an organization roughly modeled on NATO. In 2003, Moscow announced the establishment of a formal CSTO military base in Kyrgyzstan at Kant, just a few kilometers away from the coalition facility at Manas, making Kyrgyzstan the only country in the world to formally host both Russian and US-led foreign military bases. In 2004, Russia concluded an agreement that formalized its basing presence in neighboring Tajikistan, including the 5,000-person facility of the 201st Motorized Rifle Division in the capital of Dushanbe and the Nurek space observation center, in exchange for $300 million in Russian debt relief.[8]

China also channeled the events of 9/11 to serve its security priorities, especially in its restive province of Xinjiang. Almost immediately following the events of 9/11, Beijing seized upon the announcement of the US GWOT to implicate Uighur separatists and social movements in Xinjiang as Al-Qaeda affiliates.[9]

In the summer of 2005, just weeks after the Andijon crackdown, the SCO was further thrust into the international spotlight as a possible "anti-NATO" security organization when, at its annual summit in

---

[8] "Russia Opens Permanent Tajikistan Base," *New York Times* October 18, 2004.
[9] See especially Clarke (2010).

Astana, it issued a declaration that foreign military bases in the region had served their purpose and should be placed on a timetable for removal.[10] Just days later, Uzbek authorities formally notified US officials that they were terminating the authorization of the US presence at K2. US officials and media accounts portrayed the decision as a Russian- and Chinese-backed campaign to pressure Uzbekistan, though it appears that President Karimov had already taken the decision to evict US troops and was looking for regional support. While the US State Department and the EU denounced Tashkent for its crackdown in Andijon and imposed sanctions, Moscow and Beijing strongly backed the actions of the Uzbek President. In any event, after the base was closed in fall 2005, Uzbekistan seemingly concluded its geopolitical reorientation by joining the Russian-led CSTO in what was widely viewed as realignment away from the United States (Fumagalli 2007). The international consensus that allowed for the campaign against Afghanistan, had given way to regional concerns about the possible destabilizing consequences of the United States projecting influence in the region.

But perhaps the most dramatic example of competitive "goods substitution" was the "base-bidding" war of 2009 between the United States and Russia over the status of Manas.[11] For some time, Moscow had been pressing the Bakiyev government to terminate the US lease, while Bakiyev himself was unhappy with the 2006 deal reached with Washington that committed the United States to provide $150 million in annual aid, but which included humanitarian assistance and United States Agency for International Development (USAID) programs in that figure without sufficient direct quid pro quo. At a joint press conference in Moscow in February 2009, then Russian Federation president Dmitry Medvedev and Bakiyev announced that the US base would be closed and that Kyrgyzstan would receive a $2 billion aid and stabilization economic package from the Russian Federation. Although Medvedev denied that the economic package was a bribe to convince Bakiyev to close the base, the move was widely perceived as Moscow's attempt to use a large monetary payment to force the United States out.

---

[10] http://eng.sectsco.org/load/197543/.
[11] This paragraph draws on Cooley (2012: chapter 7).

The announcement led to a frenzy among US negotiators from the incoming Obama Administration and culminated in a new deal signed between the United States and Kyrgyzstan that renamed the base a "Transit Center" and increased the direct rental payment from $17 million to $63 million per year. Tellingly, if the Russian aid package had been a bribe, Bakiyev blatantly double-crossed Moscow as the regime collected an initial $300 million wire payment from Moscow before concluding the new agreement with the United States. Following the deal, US and Russian officials – as part of the US–Russia "Reset"– expressed confidence that they had reached an understanding over the importance of Manas. However, over the course of the following year Russian media became increasingly hostile towards Bakiyev and, following his ouster in April 2010, the new interim government led by Roza Otunbayeva tacked sharply towards Moscow. US troops finally vacated Manas in Kyrgyzstan at the end of the Bakiyev lease extension in July 2014, after failing to secure a requested additional one-year extension.[12]

Since the US exit, both Russia and China have taken steps to consolidate their strategic presence in the region. In 2012, Russia consolidated all of its facilities in Kyrgyzstan into a joint military base governed by single agreement and in 2019 the two sides announced that they had reached an agreement to significantly expand the size of Kant.[13] Kyrgyz elites in the post-Bakiyev era have been eager to seek out Russian partnership, making their own status more akin to a client state of Moscow rather than the "multivector" diplomacy aggressively pursued in the 2000s under Bakiyev (Lewis 2015). Similarly, in 2012 Russia and Tajikistan signed a new agreement prolonging Russian basing rights for an additional thirty years, until 2042.[14]

But China has also increased it security footprint since the US departure. Investigative reports in US newspapers in 2019 confirmed that China established a security outpost in Tajikistan, near the Afghan Wakhan

---

[12] "U.S. Vacates Base in Central Asia As Russia's Clout Rises," *Reuters* June 3, 2014. www.reuters.com/article/us-kyrgyzstan-usa-manas/u-s-vacates-base-in-central-asia-as-russias-clout-rises-idUSKBN0EE1LH20140603S.

[13] "Bishkek, Moscow Agree to Expand Russian base in Kyrgyzstan," *RFE/RL* March 28, 2019. www.rferl.org/a/russian-military-base-in-kyrgyzstan-under-focus-at-putin-jeenbekov-talks/29847265.html.

[14] "Russia Signs Deal to prolong Troop Presence at Tajik Military Base," *RFE/RL* October 5, 2012. www.rferl.org/a/russia-signs-deal-troop-presence-tajikistan-military-base/24730251.html. The deal was ratified by the Tajik parliament the following year.

corridor, and was even patrolling swathes of the Tajik–Afghan border in Chinese military vehicles.[15] In 2016, China led the establishment of the Quadrilateral Cooperation and Coordination Mechanism (QCCM) – along with Tajikistan, Afghanistan and Pakistan– a new regional security agreement dedicated to fighting terrorism and sharing capabilities and intelligence.[16] China's confirmed presence in Tajikistan followed the confirmation that it was establishing a naval base in the Pakistan port city of Gwadar and news stories about a basing deal with Afghanistan. Five years after the United States departed from its last formal military base in Central Asia in Kyrgyzstan, Russia and China remain the two main external powers with an enduring military presence in the region.

Economics: From Post-Soviet Transition to the Silk Road

An equally dramatic shift has occurred in the economic sphere, as the dominant role that the West and Western-backed international financial institutions (IFIs) played in the 1990s of managing the economic transition has given way to the emergence of non-Western aid and investment providers, especially China, as the region's leading patrons.

Managing the Collapse and Transition and Collapse

The onset of independence constituted an economic shock to the region. The collapse of a centrally planned and coordinated system meant the national markets and institutions had to be constructed from scratch. During Soviet times, Central Asia had been held up by the Kremlin as a model of Communist-led Third World development, social modernization and large-scale infrastructure investment (Kalinovsky 2018). But Central Asian governments also had to cope with the loss of critical fiscal transfers that had helped to support their republican budgets during the late–Soviet era, meaning that new national governments simply could not afford to pay for Soviet-era social and welfare obligations. Transfers from

---

[15] Gerry Shih, "In Central Asia's Forbidding Highlands, a Quiet Newcomer: Chinese Troops," *Washington Post* February 19, 2019; and Greg Nelson and Thomas Grove, "Russia, China Vie for Influence in Central Asia As U.S. Plans Afghan Exit," *Wall Street Journal* June 18, 2019.

[16] "Afghanistan, China, Pakistan, Tajikistan Issue Joint Statement on Anti-Terrorism," *China Military Online* August 4, 2016. http://english.chinamil.com.cn/news-channels/2016-08/04/content_7191537.htm.

the Soviet Union budget as a percentage of republican government revenues in the late–Soviet era constituted 21.7 percent for Turkmenistan, 23.1 percent for Kazakhstan, 35.5 percent for Kyrgyzstan, 42.9 percent for Uzbekistan and 46.6 percent for Tajikistan (World Bank 1992: 14–15). One of the most compelling explanations for why post-Soviet Tajikistan descended almost immediately into a civil war that required the intervention of Russian and neighboring Uzbek forces is that the halt in Soviet subsidies effectively starved the republican-level patronage machine that had kept regional governors loyal to the center (Rubin 1993).

As post-Soviet states, all of the Central Asian states were considered and classified as post-Communist "transition economies." This meant that they fell within the purview of IFIs such as the IMF and EBRD, working on marketing restructuring, and were benchmarked against liberal ideals about a successful transition (Cooley 2015). But in Central Asia economic restructuring was especially difficult given that central authorities had promoted pockets of industrial production that were vertically, not regionally, linked (Dmitrieva 1996). These industries were neither autonomous nor economically viable in a market context, meaning that most industrial production collapsed throughout the region and the resulting output losses were staggering: In 1999, as a percentage of 1990 output, industrial production in Kazakhstan was just 47 percent, 35 percent in Kyrgyzstan and 22 percent in Tajikistan, with only autarkic Uzbekistan near its late Soviet level at about 83 percent.[17]

The bulk of external financing for the transition was undertaken by Western donors and multilateral organizations. The IMF, World Bank, Asian Development Bank (ADB) and EU were the region's main contributors, while the United States and Japan were the region's largest bilateral donors. After some donor fatigue in the late 1990s, US and Japanese aid peaked in 2002, just after security access arrangements were concluded in the wake of 9/11.[18]

Enter the Dragon

But if the 1990s involved seeking aid and investment from the West, the 2000s saw the region's economic reorientation towards Russia and

---

[17] Data from Cooley (2005: 116, table 5.2).
[18] On Japan as the leading regional Development Assistance Committee (DAC) donor in the 1990s, see Dadabaev (2016: 35–68).

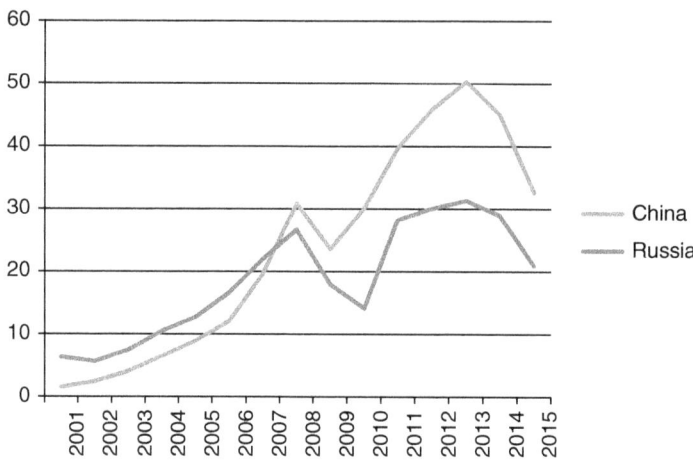

Figure 5.1 Central Asian trade with Russia and China, annual, 2001–15 (Source: IMF Direction of Trade Statistics, https://data.imf.org/?sk=9d6028 d4-f14a-464c-a2f2-59b2cd424b85)

China. First, as Figure 5.1 shows, the volume of Russian and Chinese regional trade exploded in the region, the latter increasing from just $1 billion in 2000 to over $50 billion a decade later. Russian trade also expanded significantly, with Moscow pushing a number of new regional economic organizations and architectures designed to boost economic activity in the post-Soviet region as an alternative to Western-led globalization and World Trade Organization (WTO) accession (Darden 2009).

Second, as trade and investment escalated in the 2000s, Chinese companies also heavily invested in large-scale infrastructure projects. The most important of these were in the field of energy and included the construction of two prominent regional pipelines. The first, the Kazakhstan–China oil pipeline, began in the Caspian city of Aktau and traversed Kazakhstan to the eastern city of Khorgos, while being fed by a number of small and intermediate oil fields across the energy-rich Central Asian state. The second, the China–Central Asia gas pipeline, was inaugurated in 2009. Originating in Turkmenistan, the pipeline traverses Uzbekistan and parts of Kazakhstan, before joining the internal China gas pipeline operated by the China National Petroleum Corporation (CNPC). After three initial lines were built (A+B+C), a proposed line D would extend to Tajikistan via Kyrgyzstan, thereby

From Post-Soviet Transition to the Silk Road 115

ensuring that the new pipeline network crosses all of the Central Asian states.

Beyond its geopolitical significance of reorienting Central Asian gas production from the old Russian-led Soviet pipeline network to the east, China's pipeline projects also cemented Beijing's role as a leading provider of regional club and public goods. During the financial crisis of 2008, China came to play the role of "lender of last resort" to Turkmenistan, providing $8 billion in emergency loans to be repaid by natural gas exports through the new pipeline. This effectively made Ashgabat dependent on Beijing as opposed to Western IFIs or commercial lenders. Similarly, China offered Kazakhstan $10 billion in emergency loans in 2009, and an additional $3 billion was offered in 2013 after CNPC was given a share of the flagship Kashagan Consortium that had been developed by Western energy majors in the 1990s.

The Belt and Road Initiative

In September 2013 at the prestigious Nazarbayev University in Astana, Kazakhstan, Chinese Premier Xi Jinping confirmed Beijing's plans to launch a "Silk Road Economic Belt" across the region designed to promote improvements in regional infrastructure and promote closer ties with China. Coupled with the Silk Road Maritime Belt, "One Belt, One Road" (soon after known as the Belt and Road Initiative or BRI) would take form as one of the most ambitious foreign policy initiatives of the post–Cold War era. Some media estimate the overall value of proposed BRI initiatives at about $1 trillion, including about 900 projects in over 60 partner countries, with the *South China Morning Post* describing the BRI as "the most significant and far-reaching project the nation has ever put forward."[19]

In the Central Asian context, the BRI takes on additional significance for two reasons. First, Central Asia not only represents an area of continued strategic interest that shares borders with China's Xinjiang province, but it is also the hub and transit route for many cross-regional (Europe–Asia, South Asia–Asia) projects designed to connect China's east with other global regions. Second, the announcement of the BRI in

---

[19] "Our Bulldozers, Our Rules," *The Economist* July 2, 2016; and "'One Belt, One Road' Will Define China's Role as a World Leader," *South China Morning Post* April 2, 2015, www.scmp.com/comment/insight-opinion/article/1753773/one-belt-one-road-initiative-will-define-chinas-role-world.

Central Asia came just after a period during which the United States had gone to great lengths to promote its own vision of "New Silk Road" that would enhance trade and investment along Afghanistan's neighbors and improve regional "connectivity." China's Central Asian BRI projects have not only substantially more financial resources backing them, but the involvement of new Chinese-led regional economic organizations such as the Asian Infrastructure Investment Bank (AIIB) and BRICS New Development Bank, as well as China's Exim bank, underscores Central Asia's deepening integration into the new governance architectures of the Chinese-led regional and international order.

By the end of the 2010s, the BRI and China's interest in its Central Asian neighbors had cemented its status as the region's leading project and development lender, while these countries' reliance on Western-led development finance had declined steeply from its peak in 2005–6 (see Figure 5.2). By 2017, China's share of Kyrgyzstan's total external debt (bilateral and multilateral combined) had reached 40 percent. Conversely, Kyrgyzstan's share of multilateral debt (Western-led IFIs) as a percentage of overall external debt, which had peaked at 49 percent in 2005, declined to just 18 percent in 2017.[20] Similarly, in Tajikistan multilateral debt as an overall percentage of external debt had dipped to 20 percent in 2017, while debt to China had reached 50 percent. Indeed, a report by the Center for Global Development identified Kyrgyzstan and Tajikistan as two of eight countries (out of a total of twenty-three examined) whose recent BRI-related debt to China raised the potential for debt sustainability problems (Hurley et al. 2018).[21]

Governance and Political Norms

Finally, the prevailing regional political norms and governing practices have also moved away from models associated with US hegemony and the international liberal order. During the 1990s, the Central Asian states, as with the economic reforms, were usually banded together with the other post-Communist states as countries in political or democratic transition. But with the exception of Kyrgyzstan – which publicly presented itself in the 1990s as a leading regional reformer – the Central

---

[20] World Bank, International Debt Statistics. https://databank.worldbank.org/.
[21] The eight countries were: Djibouti, the Kyrgyz Republic (Kyrgyzstan), Lao People's Democratic Republic (Laos), the Maldives, Mongolia, Montenegro, Pakistan and Tajikistan.

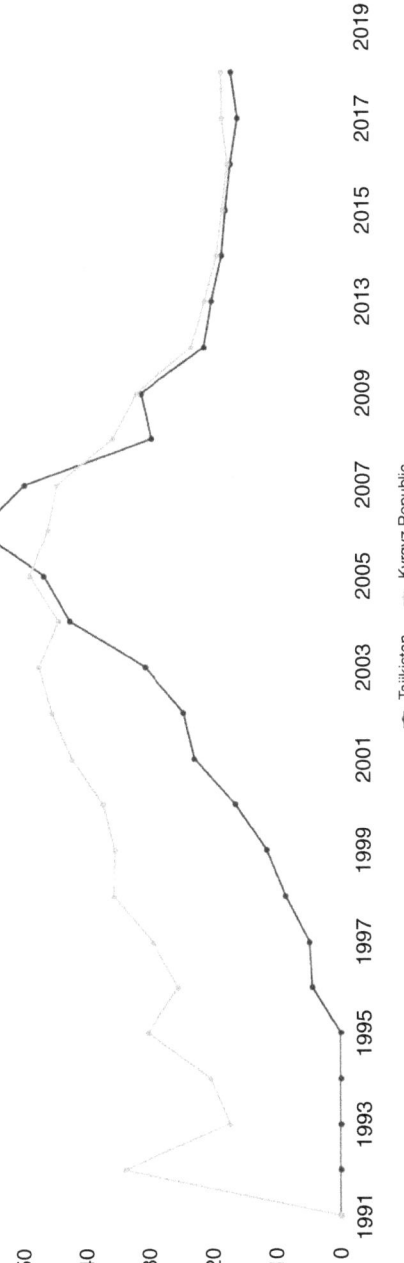

Figure 5.2 Post–Soviet era debt to multilateral organizations as a share of overall external debt, Kyrgyzstan and Tajikistan (Source: World Bank, International Debt Statistics, https://databank.worldbank.org/)

Asian regimes consolidated power and aggressively cracked down on opposition parties and movements.

The post-9/11 era also provided the pretext for the Central Asian regimes to expand – in the name of countering terrorism and extremism – the surveillance of domestic opponents and the capabilities of their internal security services.[22] Unlike the East European states that were now busy implementing the necessary conditions and reforms to join the EU and NATO, Central Asian security cooperation with the West, rather than acting as a moderating influence, appeared to embolden regimes and encourage authoritarian excesses. Not coincidentally, most democracy indicators for the region show an across the board decline since 2005, as civil liberties and freedom of expression were significantly curtailed, mirroring the crackdown in Russia.[23] In as much as the United States and its NATO partners (including France and Germany) continued to need basing and access rights in the region of Afghanistan operations, Central Asian governments leveraged the relationship to push back on criticism about human rights abuses and demanded more foreign aid and other forms of quid pro quo.

Moreover, on the values front, the intensifying insurgency in Iraq and the images of Abu Ghraib significantly damaged US credibility as a pro-liberalization reformer, fueling the criticism that the United States selectively championed political liberalism and human rights. In a series of focus groups exploring the dynamics of anti-Americanism in the Central Asian countries, Edward Schatz and Renan Levine found that local respondents did value the principles of democracy and human rights, but much more so when the sources of such endorsing statements were attributed to Central Asian advocates. However, when attributed to the US ambassador, or the President, respondents became far more skeptical about the sincerity of the US commitment to promoting liberal values (Schatz and Levine 2010). Russian-language propaganda and disinformation further fueled growing resentment of the US presence as well as suspicions about US and Western motives and influence.

---

[22] See, especially, Lewis (2008).
[23] Indeed, during the 2000s all Central Asian states saw significant declines in their political liberty scores as measured by the Democracy watchdog Freedom House. https://freedomhouse.org/regions/eurasia.

The Color Revolutions and the Rise of Illiberal Counternorms and Challenges

Other redefining political events of the 2000s were the Color Revolutions. Beginning with Georgia in 2003, then Ukraine in 2004 and Kyrgyzstan in 2005, a series of regime collapses followed street protests in response to crooked elections. These "revolutions" swept out long-standing regimes in favor of more pro-Western opposition figures such as Georgia's outspoken Mikheil Saakashvili, sending political shockwaves throughout the region and beyond. Moreover, as scholars have explored, the elections also had a "modular" quality to them, as they diffused across the region, with opposition activists and governments emulating previously effective tactics and counterstrategies (Beissinger 2007). Transnational networks that included US think tanks and activists justified these events as geopolitically advantageous for the United States, which was in competition with Russia for influence in the post-Soviet "Near Abroad" (Toal 2017). The role of foreign-funded NGOs, activists and election monitors was scrutinized, as the activities of NGOs and foreign-funded organizations were now recast from being a political nuisance to constituting a mortal security threat to existing regimes.

As a result, the region's regimes, supported by Russia and China, actively pushed new counternorms to undermine political liberalism and justify the backlash against Western influence. Three of these counternorms were particularly potent.[24] First, democracy protests and NGOs were recast as subversive foreign-funded opposition groups and transnational security threats, akin to transnational militant movements. After 2005, all of the Central Asian states passed new restrictive legislation on media and civil society activities. Anti-NGO laws sought to curtail funding or even ban NGO activities altogether in the name of safeguarding national security. In Uzbekistan, in the wake of Andijon, government authorities evicted a number of Western media outlets and foreign-sponsored NGOs and rights organizations.

The early and mid-2000s also saw a rise in intensive cooperation among Central Asian and Russian security services to coordinate their extraterritorial reach and target political opponents living across the region (Soldatov and Borogan 2010). Forced kidnappings and

---

[24] Some of this discussion of counternorms draws upon Cooley (2015: 49–63).

renditions became routine, in violation of international humanitarian norms and even national political asylum procedures, while many of these extraterritorial practices were codified in regional security agreements such as the SCO's 2009 anti-terror treaty or the CIS's Minsk Treaty, which have been cited as justifications for the transfer of political exiles and fugitives from one member country to the next (Cooley and Schaaf 2017). Indeed, since 2006, the SCO's Regional Anti-Terror Structure (RATS) has maintained a common regional list of suspected terrorists, extremists and separatists – both individuals and organizations – that has increased substantially; this appears to be a way for each member regime to list its most wanted political opponents and classify them as regional security threats. Political elites that had been in power or shared in regime coalitions and had been forced into exile were targeted overseas by being classified as terrorists or extremists on INTERPOL's list or even targeted for assassination by the extraterritorial actions of Central Asian state security services and their agents.[25]

A second prevalent counternorm in the region – backed strongly by China – has been the meme of civilizational diversity and noninterference. Like the norm of security, appeals to "civilizational diversity" also invoke the importance of state sovereignty and undermine the universality of liberalism, especially on questions of political and human rights, making the very act of rendering judgment on the domestic affairs of other states inappropriate interference. Civilizational diversity also comports with the normative mission of the SCO and its "Shanghai Spirit" that officially stresses cultural diversity, mutual development and trust, but which some scholars have interpreted as the basis for promoting authoritarian practices and undermining the regional status and importance of democratic norms (Ambrosio 2008). Similar language about civilizational diversity and respect has also informed the BRI agreements and other bilateral strategic partnerships that Beijing has concluded with individual Central Asian states. Although Western policymakers and scholars were initially skeptical of the influence of these counternorms, the SCO's "civilizational diversity and non-interference" agenda has been preferred by Central Asian governments to the democratic principles embedded in the region's supposedly preeminent security organization, the OSCE, as David Lewis

---

[25] On the growing political abuse of INTERPOL, see Lemon (2019: 15–29). On the targeting of political exiles overseas, see Cooley and Heathershaw (2017).

(2012) has shown. In fact, the OSCE has stagnated on the "human dimension" portfolio as no new major democratic initiatives have been announced since the 2000s. Illustrating the regime dynamics of "asset substitution," one report on OSCE police reform projects in Central Asia found that the OSCE had allowed recipient host governments to refuse to implement the political and human rights conditions originally associated with the projects, while still accepting funds to upgrade the capabilities of their forces (Lewis 2011).

A third counternorm has come in the form of the Russian-led "traditional values" agenda, associated with the promotion of traditional families, social conservatism, religion and the attempt to stymie the Western agenda of pressing for gender equality and LGBT rights. Moscow has been particularly keen to push the traditional values agenda as a counter to what it considers the extreme and morally bankrupt promotion of universal liberalism by the West. Its support of populism, right-wing European political parties and movements, and appeal to the moral values of "Eurasianism" has even made the Kremlin and its allies position themselves as the guardian and savior of Christian values internationally. In terms of global governance, Russia even took the lead, as part of the United Nations Human Rights Council, in passing two resolutions – one on promoting traditional values of mankind and the other on affirming the family. Anti-NGO campaigns in both Kyrgyzstan and Kazakhstan have openly drawn upon anti-LGBT agendas to justify cracking down on the activities and agendas of foreign-funded organizations (Fershtey and Sharifzoda 2019). Central Asian and Eurasian officials have also participated in the annual meetings of the World Congress of Families, an international network that seeks to disseminate the traditional values agenda across Eurasia and the West (Stoeckl 2018).

On their own, none of these three counternorms should be viewed as a challenger to global political liberalism with the same universal reach. But, taken together, the Central Asian governments, along with China and Russia, have pragmatically deployed these counternorms for the deliberate purpose of delegitimizing Western institutions, liberal democracy and civil society and constructing alternative bases for an emerging regional political community. Although democracy and political liberalism never really entrenched themselves in the region during the 1990s, three decades later the national and regional political landscape is characterized by normative and legal contestation in a manner that would have seen unthinkable in the early 2000s.

Example: The Rise of Alternative Election Observers

A striking illustration of the rise of alternative governance providers is how international election observation became a contested and geopolitically competitive field in Central Asia and the greater post-Soviet space. During the 1990s, as the international observation of elections became an international norm (Hyde 2011), the practice of election observation in post-Soviet Central Asia was dominated by the OSCE's Office for Democratic Institutions and Human Rights (ODIHR), based in Warsaw, that sent trained short-term and long-term observation teams to each national election to monitor the political and media environment. After a national election, the mission would release both a summary judgment and a detailed report assessing the quality of the elections. But the ODIHR's assessments, long considered the gold standard, proved especially bothersome to the Central Asian governments, as the organization sharply criticized all Central Asian elections held in the 1990s and the 2000s. The Color Revolutions not only recast the role of NGOs and civil societies with transnational links, but also pointed to the critical role of external assessments of election integrity in mobilizing protestors. After all, in Georgia, Ukraine and Kyrgyzstan, it was the ODIHR's proclamation that these post-Soviet elections were "not free and fair" that sparked street demonstrations and calls for new elections.

As a response, the Central Asian states – along with Russia, Armenia and Belarus – launched an effort to try and dilute the power of the ODIHR's observation mission by advocating the "reform of the group." A proposed package by Russia would have included placing observation missions under the auspices of the Parliamentary Assembly in Vienna (as opposed to the independent Warsaw-based office), allowing the assembly to appoint the head of mission, and mandating that the observation team issue a joint statement of findings in consultation with host governments. Effectively, this proposed reform package would have killed independent election observations as it was initially practiced.

However, a related countermeasure, grounded firmly in the logic of asset substitution, was introduced by Russia. In 2003, the CIS announced that it would also begin to send election observers to all the post-Soviet elections and, during its first observation mission in Ukraine in 2004, provided a positive assessment of the initial election in which Kremlin-backed Viktor Yanukovych was declared the winner (Fawn 2006). The CIS Election Monitoring Organization (CIS-EMO) also provides election monitors to national elections in disrupted or de facto states, such as the Georgian breakaway territories of Abkhazia and South Ossetia, and Transnistria, and has coordinated and subcontracted its activities with far-right groups in the West (Shekhovtsov 2015). In 2005, similarly, the SCO also began to send its own election observers to member state national elections and, like the CIS monitors, issued positive assessments of all the same Central Asian elections that were criticized by the ODIHR.[26]

As Judith Kelley has shown, the presence of multiple election observers also created a "multiple principals problem" (Kelley 2009), where the critical observations of any one mission were quickly discounted and drowned out by the positive local media coverage afforded to other monitors with more favorable observations. By the end of the 2000s, the Central Asian and other post-Soviet states had perfected the art of "election observation substitution" by inviting missions from other regional organizations and even previously unknown groups with seemingly respectable titles to further testify to the quality of elections – what I have elsewhere termed "zombie election monitors."[27] From occupying a status as the dominant and most credible election observation team in the 1990s, the ODIHR has become an organization espousing a minority view and often even the sole dissenting mission at many of these Eurasian polls. A stark illustration of this was visible in June 2019 when, in what were the first national presidential elections of the post-Nazarbayev era that saw over 500 protestors detained and widespread evidence of substantial electoral fraud, President-elect Tokayev commented on the ODIHR's acutely negative criticism by saying it was "just one of the international organizations" monitoring the vote and "we should not focus on the assessment of this organization."[28]

[26] For a table of contrasting summary assessments, see Cooley (2012: 185–194, appendix 2).
[27] See Walker and Cooley (2013). On the global rise and strategies of politically motivated election monitors, see Debre and Morgenbesser (2017).
[28] Tamara Vaal and Mariya Gordeyeva, "Nazarbayev's Hand-Picked Successor Tokayev Elected Kazakh President," *Reuters* June 10, 2019.

Conclusion

In the areas of security, economy and development, and political governance, Central Asia represents dramatic illustrations of how the rise of alternative patrons and asset substitution have served to rapidly hollow out US hegemony and erode the norms and institutions of the US-led liberal international order. Central Asia is now a true "multipolar region," where the military power, economic partnerships and normative rule-sets of different external powers compete, coexist with and even mimic one another, and where regimes use these competing and overlapping infrastructures of external powers to consolidate their own domestic political standing.

For sure, even in the 1990s, Central Asia was never an area characterized by strong Western influence; however, its experience holds two important comparative lessons. First, although Central Asia hosted a number of Russian and Chinese-led counterorder institutions such as the SCO and the CSTO in the early 2000s, the normative and economic contestation of the liberal order would spread in the next decade to the post-Communist space more broadly, including East Central Eurasian members of the EU and NATO – such as Hungary and Poland – that were once assumed to be firmly in the heat of the transatlantic core institutions of the US hegemonic order (see Cooley 2019). Central Asia has been a harbinger of the broader regional and now global backlash against the liberal international order.

Second, the rapid speed at which this contestation took place is also striking. US and Western influence peaked in about 2004 – the year in which many Eastern European post-Communist states were admitted into the EU and NATO and the time when the United States maintained multiple military facilities in Central Asia. Over the next fifteen years, however, the relative standing of the United States, the EU and Western-backed IFIs rapidly declined, while the role of Russia and China dramatically intensified in the areas of security, economy and norm projection. Accordingly, it should come as little surprise if sustained periods of asset substitution precipitate similar geopolitical shifts in other regions once thought of as firmly in the sphere of *Pax Americana*.

6 Goods Substitution in the USA's Back Yard: Colombia's Diversification Strategies under Conditions of Hierarchy

MORTEN SKUMSRUD ANDERSEN

From 2000–13, Chinese trade with Latin America grew from $12 billion to over $260 billion – that is, 2,400 per cent. Prior to 2008, China's loans to the region never exceeded $1 billion. In 2010, Chinese loans to the region accounted for $37 billion and, since 2005, China has transferred over $140 billion to Latin America in policy loans (Piccone 2016). Chinese presidents have made various high-profile visits to the region, accompanied by White Papers promising 'win-win' relations, support for new regional groupings, and finances with no strings attached. One such visit, accompanied by a release of a White Paper, took place a few days after Donald Trump's election and US withdrawal from the Trans-Pacific Partnership (TPP) (Piccone 2016: 5).[1] The presence of President Xi Jinping at the November 2016 Asia-Pacific Economic Cooperation (APEC) meeting in Peru triggered a former Ecuadorian foreign minister to declare that China has become 'the defender of free trade'. This is happening in a region that for two centuries has been considered the US' 'back yard' – a region characterized by US hegemony and exclusive ties to Washington. These developments prompted the understatement from the Heritage Foundation's Stephen Johnson that 'in a globalized world, the Monroe Doctrine has declining relevance' (Nolte 2013: 596).

The effects of goods substitution dynamics are certainly present in Latin America, but they manifest in different ways, depending on the nature of ties with alternative patrons. In this chapter, I distinguish between strategies of shifting ties and diversifying ties, and explore the conditions under which these may be present. Diversification, I argue, may centrally affect hierarchical ties, and concerns the question of

[1] Ministry of Foreign Affairs of the People's Republic of China, 'China's Policy Paper on Latin America and the Caribbean', 24 November 2016, www.fmprc.gov.cn/mfa_eng/wjdt_665385/2649_665393/t1418254.shtml.

whether and how goods substitution can happen under conditions of hierarchy.

Some Latin American states have heavily engaged with alternative patrons. Ecuador and Venezuela's direct challenge to US hegemony is well known, and so is the financial assistance they have received from Chinese banks in lieu of loans from traditional international creditors like the World Bank or the Inter-American Development Bank. Less known is how this initial Chinese incursion has triggered different types of goods and asset substitution effects beyond these countries, with potential unintended consequences for the fabric of international order and US hegemony. Other Latin American countries are not engaging with alternative patrons in the same way. What happens as China is aiming in on centrist governments and countries that appreciate free trade and traditional market values in a region traditionally under US dominance? How do countries in such a region engage with China? Can we observe goods and asset substitution effects even in a country like Colombia, often described as a US client state? After addressing the Latin American context overall, I take a closer look at the case of Colombia – one of the USA's closest allies in the region and as such a country that would be a least-likely case not only for theories of goods and asset substitution, but also for theories of soft balancing and hegemonic transition.

Colombia is the provider of a specific security asset for the USA (Lake 1996; 2001), given its role as a major production country for illegal drugs, and its internal conflict. The intimate relationship between the two countries has a long history, and Colombia's present relationship with the USA has less the characteristics of a rationally bargained 'contract' based on cost–benefit calculations (Lake 1996; 2009) than an ingrained hierarchical relationship based on informal authority and socialization, including a history of interrelations and informal practices among elites (Ikenberry and Kupchan 1990; Andersen 2016). In this context, can we see goods substitution mechanisms operating in Colombia, and how would that affect its relationship with the USA? I will argue that Colombia does not seek to *shift* ties by exiting the relationship or directly challenging US hegemony. Rather, Colombia is seeking to *diversify* its ties while staying within the context of a hierarchical relationship. In practice, this means exploring new avenues for increasing leverage to expand its autonomy, as well as hedging its bets in the face of uncertainty.

The case of Colombia shows how the country's leverage in its relationship with the USA may increase as a result of mounting Chinese goods substitution in the region at large; even if there is little evidence for actual goods substitution in Colombia, hedging strategies are indeed present, and are also used to *threaten* goods substitution in the context of China's central role in a global goods ecology. Added to this, goods substitution also plays a part in Colombian domestic politics. That is, the diversification of ties interacts with domestic and international politics, with one area having possible unintended effects on the other. This case further corroborates the viability of theories of goods and asset substitution as an aspect of contemporary power politics.

Tie Shifting, Diversification, and Hierarchy

Some countries in Latin America have engaged closely with China. Initially, Chinese incursions into the region took the form of loans to regimes that had swung left in the 2000s and became members of the Bolivarian Alliance (ALBA), like Venezuela and Ecuador, advancing a direct challenge to US hegemony and the international liberal order. Even so, the consensus view seemed to be that China's increasing presence in Latin America represented no geopolitical or strategic threat to the USA. The position of Washington has been that there is no 'evidence of Chinese interests in establishing a continuous military presence in the region' and that China is no 'direct conventional threat to the United States or its friends and allies' (Nolte 2013: 592). China, it is said, recognizes Latin America as a US sphere of influence, and is careful not to raise suspicions about its motives and intentions.

This debate concerns whether China's policies and potential 'soft balancing' in the region may promote counter-hegemonic capabilities or activities, or become a revisionist tool. However, as noted in Chapter 2 in this volume, it is crucial to distinguish between the logics of reformist, positionalist, and revisionist aims and effects when assessing goods and asset substitution mechanisms (see Figure 2.1, Chapter 2). One can be against both the current order and the current distribution of capabilities, or against only one of these. Further, the case of Ecuador discussed in that same chapter shows how, regardless of Beijing's intentions, demand-side factors effectively led Chinese loan practices to have counter-order effects. In other words, there is no need to assume or prove revisionist or reformist motivations on the part of the supplier for an undermining of hegemony to take place. Demand-side factors may in fact matter more than the intentions of the provider of alternative goods or assets when it comes to the *effects* of substitution, which is the main concern here.

I consider a good to be a material possession that *contains* value, like oil or loans, while an asset is a possession that *produces* value, like geography or status. Assets are therefore oriented more towards the future expectation of gains, while goods are more immediately valuable, as they can be sold and bought in a market. However, a good can be an asset if it generates future revenue. Thus, all goods can be assets, but not all assets can be goods (cf. Merton 1973; Veblen 1908). Assets are often more directly relevant for security, state goals and strategies, as their value is more intangible, complex, and dependent on circumstances. Goods are more directly relevant to present value for companies and people, although they are of more indirect value to state strategies. Note, again, that the distinction is not absolute, and that goods can easily be (constructed as) assets too.

There are two generic options for goods/asset substitution: one can *shift* ties to a new provider, or one can *diversify* ties. Further, one can acquire the same category of goods from a new provider, or one can substitute one type of good for another type of good that, however, serves the same goal. That is, the logic of goods substitution does not need the substituted goods to be the same, or equivalent, if the goal or effect of acquiring it remains the same – oil can substitute for coal, but so can a loan if the goal is to keep the state afloat. This also speaks to the presence of a global goods ecology, and interconnected hierarchies that might alter the 'exchange rate' for goods (see Nexon and Neumann 2018).

Diversifying ties would normally be the best strategy, but this is a difficult balancing act, which in most cases would increase transaction costs; political, cultural, and perhaps economic capital must be used both to reassure the current provider of your intentions and effects, and establish ties with a new provider without any previous history of interaction and procedures in place. The assumption is therefore that shifting ties reduces transaction costs – as that is normally the goal of shifting provider in the first place – while diversification increases transaction costs. Diversification, then, would imply investing the increased transaction costs in expected future gains from that diversification. Such gains could be purely economic, but could also take the form of hedging for future disagreements with providers or legitimacy challenges. In short, keeping your options open comes at a cost.

Demand-side mechanisms for goods/asset substitution are therefore:

- *shifting* ties to acquire the same category of goods, or a different category of goods serving the same goal, from a different provider at lower transaction costs
- *diversifying* ties to optimize the current realization of assets, or to expand future opportunities for shifting, incurring higher transaction costs.

Diversification of Ties and Hierarchy

How can one assess the effects of such demand-side mechanisms of goods substitution? Importantly, any one case of goods substitution may also be part of a broader *goods ecology*, which is one dimension of international order (see Chapter 1). That is, an international goods ecology, shaped by the nature of the providers and the goods provided, creates opportunities and constraints for action in international politics. Importantly, this ecology may also have effects on cases where no actual goods substitution is (yet) present.

When assessing single cases within a global goods ecology, we should therefore distinguish between the effects of actual goods substitution, and the effects of goods substitution becoming an option. Regarding the latter, when exit options become available, they may have crucial effects on international and domestic political dynamics even in the absence of *shifting* ties. A *diversification* of ties could expand such exit options, with similar effects.

Diversification, then, does not have to involve actual goods substitution (in the form of exiting or shifting links), but rather:

- *hedging*, and
- using threats of exit for political leverage, both
  - *internationally*, in seeking to improve existing arrangements with the goods provider, and
  - *domestically*, where goods substitution is used as a signalling device.

Such diversification strategies also contribute to a theoretical puzzle concerning whether and how goods substitution can operate in *hierarchical* relations. One assumption could be that goods substitution logics are hampered within hierarchies, as both the autonomy and cross-cutting ties of subordinate goods consumers are often limited (see Nexon and Wright 2007; Mattern and Zarakol 2016). Therefore, opposing a hierarchical arrangement will often be prohibitively costly, particularly when the transaction costs involved in changing to a new goods provider where there is no history of interaction and thus no common knowledge, are added. On the other hand, since goods and asset substitution need not be a direct challenge to either the hegemon or its position in a hierarchical order, it is to be expected that goods substitution can operate also within the confines of hierarchical relations.

Hierarchies are not simply about disparities in capacity or unequal relations – they also involve authority relations. As such, the claim is that goods substitution through diversification may challenge the exclusivity of hierarchical ties, without directly challenging the authority relationship or the hierarchical arrangement itself. *Hedging* is of relevance to goods substitution in the context of hierarchical authority relations, as declining to adopt or removing hedging strategies are shown to be an indication of relationships of trust in international politics (Keating and Ruzicka 2014). Similarly, new options for subordinate actors to use *threats of exit to increase political leverage* would indicate changes in political opportunity structures. As I show below, this is increasingly the case in Colombia – the USA's closest partner in the region.

Shifting mechanisms were prevalent in the early years of China–Latin America relations, particularly given the economic boost in oil-producing countries with counter-hegemonic regimes like Venezuela and Ecuador. The early excursion of China into Latin America was accomplished by countries with leftist regimes, such as Venezuela, Ecuador, and Bolivia, shifting their ties away from the USA and the institutions of the liberal order, to acquire similar goods elsewhere – namely loans. Following a Latin American boom in commodity prices caused by Chinese demand, decreasing oil prices triggered economic crises in Ecuador, Venezuela, and Brazil, which together make up the destination for 92 per cent of Chinese loans to the region. With prices crashing, these countries become further locked into China as a source of international financing. Facing crises in its most important partners in the region, China is partially reorienting its strategy towards investments in more centrist, market-oriented and open regimes like Peru, Chile, Argentina, and Colombia.

This may trigger more subtle goods and asset substitution strategies that have so far flown under the radar, as the focus has been on the first type of goods substitution – shifting mechanisms – and the potential strategic threat to the hegemon. The insecurities, policies, and controversial statements regarding the region from the Trump administration has played a part in this. That is, more countries may be willing to incur higher transaction costs in diversifying their asset portfolios when facing the uncertainties about US motives and future developments that the Trump administration leaves in its wake.

Below, I first address mechanisms of *shifting* ties in the region for context, before considering the *diversification* of ties with special reference to the case of USA–Colombia relations, arguing that goods substitution challenges the *exclusivity* of hierarchical ties although the hierarchical arrangement remains.

Mechanisms of Substitution in Latin America: Shifting Ties

In Latin America, most of the focus has been on tie shifting – that is, *exiting* a relationship and shifting to another provider. This applies to the group of countries in the region that have maintained close, direct ties with China, and is the most evident form of goods substitution. Policy loans in exchange for energy, such as in the cases of Ecuador and Venezuela, is a strategy of shifting ties to a new provider of the same category of goods.

In the 1990s, Latin American countries questioned and opposed the International Monetary Fund's (IMF) and World Bank's policy of loan conditionality, which was seen to interfere in sovereign decision making and impose debt repayment schemes that were too harsh.[2] This was, therefore, already fertile ground for China which, from about 2010, started giving loans to countries in the region that now had problems borrowing money from what had traditionally been the default option in times of trouble, namely, Washington-backed institutions like the World Bank, the Inter-American Development Bank, and the Andean Development Corporation. Currently, China's two

---

[2] Robert Soutar, 'China's Investment Splurge in Latin America Continues', *China Dialogue*, 24 February 2017, www.chinadialogue.net/blog/9632-China-s-investment-splurge-in-Latin-America-continues/en.

development banks provide more development finance to Latin America than these institutions combined, every year.

China's relationship with Venezuela is an example of the country's initial approach to Latin America, involving loans to commodity-exporting countries in exchange for guaranteed supplies of raw materials such as soy, copper, iron ore, and oil, all central to China's development. China may hold as much as $65 billion of Venezuelan debt. With regard to Ecuador, in 2014, 61 per cent of the country's borrowing needs were met by China, in exchange for 90 per cent of its total oil production.[3]

Despite China's partners suffering economic and political crises, this dynamic undermines the USA's agenda as it implies that economic development, or even regime survival, can in principle be achieved without the conditionalities and proscriptions of Washington or existing institutions of the liberal order. The Chinese option allows countries in the region to 'sidestep the negative consequences of actions deemed hostile to the interest of the United States and US companies – for example, defaulting on loans or nationalizing industries' (Nolte 2013: 595).

That is, loans-for-oil policies in Latin America have counter-order effects as: (a) these countries can escape the negative consequences of exiting the institutions of the global liberal order; and (b) such loans prolong the survival of anti-hegemonic regimes thus preventing any regional consensus on the rules and norms of the international order.[4] However, goods substitution in and of itself does not necessarily challenge the international order. China may in fact be substituting in a way that helps *uphold* the international order, but which simultaneously undermines US hegemony.

Immediately after the election of Donald Trump and US withdrawal from the TPP in 2017, APEC countries and observers met in Lima, Peru, to discuss and safeguard the future of the TPP and pacific trade, with or without the USA.[5] Whilst the TPP notably excludes China, the

---

[3] Daniel Capurro, 'Donald Trump's Trade Policy Is Driving Latin America into China's Arms', *The Telegraph* 17 January 2017, www.telegraph.co.uk/news/20 17/01/17/donald-trumps-trade-policy-driving-latin-america-chinas-arms/.

[4] Paul Coyer, 'Undermining America While Washington Sleeps: China in Latin America', *Forbes* 31 January 2016, www.forbes.com/sites/paulcoyer/2016/01/3 1/undermining-america-while-washington-sleeps-china-in-latin-america /#ced8d2b6c23f.

[5] Antonio Hsiang, 'Trump Makes China Great in Latin America', *The Diplomat* 21 April 2017, https://thediplomat.com/2017/04/trump-makes-china-great-in-latin-america/.

Chinese President Xi Jinping was notably present at the APEC meeting. Jinping used the occasion to promote the Regional Comprehensive Economic Partnership (RCEP) to Latin American Pacific nations – an alternative to the TPP led by China, and excluding the USA.[6] While the TPP covered 28 per cent of the world's exports, the RCEP would cover 38 per cent. This is part of a trend in which China, following Trump's election, has tried to position itself as the champion of free trade.[7]

What this shifting mechanism implies is Chinese *positionalist* goods substitution – the order is not challenged (rather, it is defended), but the distribution of capabilities within it is. The effect of giving loans to ALBA countries is counter-order goods substitution. However, as the Chinese engagement with Latin American countries is shifting towards another group of countries with more centrist governments, which are facing slumps in oil prices and challenges at home as well as questions about the viability of the present leftist regimes, the substitution mechanisms move away from order revisionism towards positionalist effects.

Also, Latin American countries without Venezuela's or Ecuador's close ties to China may increasingly look to China to uphold and promote liberal free trade, which would be order-enhancing goods substitution, and would face US retrenchment on the issue. In other words, paradoxically, it is the hegemon itself that is counter-order, while the main geopolitical rival has taken on the role of protecting at least one core part of the rules and values of the liberal world order, although the institutionalization and practices would be different.

The election of Trump made this shifting mechanism even more relevant. Trump promised to stand up to China, and to bring jobs back to the USA. However, the second goal undermines the first. The TPP may be in shatters, the North American Free Trade Agreement (NAFTA) is renegotiated, and free trade regimes are under attack, while the context is that bilateral trade between China and Latin America grew 2,400 per cent between 2000 and 2013, and further expansion is pending[8]

However, this is not exclusively positionalist, but may also include reformist effects. For some, Chinese trade plans may increasingly be

---

[6] Capurro, 'Donald Trump's Trade Policy'.
[7] See Reuters, 'China Says Chile Pacific Trade Meeting Not about TPP', 13 March 2017, www.reuters.com/article/us-trade-tpp-china-chile-idUSKBN16K15B.
[8] Capurro, 'Donald Trump's Trade Policy'.

considered an alternative strategy for achieving economic prosperity outside of existing liberal institutions. Furthermore, China and Latin American countries are seen to have a general common interest in the protection of national sovereignty and self-determination. Some see regional organizations as prioritizing this aspect over the consolidation of liberal norms and human rights, thus challenging the international order by preventing a status quo consensus on the South American continent.[9]

Diversifying Ties in Colombia: Asset Substitution under Conditions of Hierarchy

While tie shifting has been the most evident form of goods substitution in Latin America, this option would be costly for liberal, market-oriented economies, which are traditionally under the sway of US policy on the South American continent. A relevant theoretical and empirical question is therefore whether goods substitution can operate in hierarchical relations?

A hierarchy involves authority relationships between dominant and subdominant actors. Such authority is, most of the time, informal. That is, as opposed to hierarchies within states, regulated in formal procedures and law, international hierarchies are shaped by subtle socialization and informal practices – legitimacy in hierarchies is largely dependent upon a shared understanding fostered through socialization, culture, and tradition (Ikenberry and Kupchan 1990).

The key element to bear in mind is that even if this authoritative power position of the hegemon in a hierarchy is not challenged, the exclusivity of its ties can be – its exclusive access to, for example, infrastructure and elites. Goods and asset substitution may challenge the exclusivity of hierarchical ties, without directly challenging the authority relationship or the hierarchical arrangement itself. Such diversification – like hedging or threatening to exit – may however undermine the relationship over time. This has historical precedents. In the most hierarchical of international relationships – imperial ones – a key concern is avoiding subordinate entities becoming too

---

[9] Christopher Sabatini, 'Meaningless Multilateralism', *Foreign Affairs* 8 August 2014, www.foreignaffairs.com/articles/south-america/2014-08-08/meaningless-multilateralism.

independent or coordinating action against the imperial core. A problem faced by many empires was that even if the imperial core was not challenged directly, it could be slowly undermined by subordinate actors establishing their own ties with other actors outside of the hierarchy, or being allowed too much independence (Nexon and Wright 2007). That is, challenging the exclusivity of ties is not directly about power and resistance within a hierarchy; it is rather about the hegemon slowly losing its monopoly on unit interactions.

An instance of this is USA–Colombian ties, which have traditionally been strong and intimate, variably described as imperial, hegemonic, or clientelistic; the degree to which they remain so should not be underestimated. In terms of aid, trade, military assistance, and institutionalized cooperation mechanisms in general, the USA is still by far the most important actor for Colombia (Randall 1992; Tickner 2003a, 2003b). Therefore, in the context of this volume's theoretical framework, Colombia would be a least-likely case of goods substitution dynamics, being one of the USA's closest allies. Colombia would also be a least-likely case for alternative theories, like classical balancing, power transition theory, or liberal theories of world order. Such theories would find it difficult to explain any Chinese goods substitution resulting in weakened US influence in Colombia, other than as a result of the USA allowing for a gradual 'socialization' of China into the liberal world order. Significantly, Colombia is an even better test of goods substitution mechanisms than the ALBA countries, as they engage very differently with China. Colombia and other centrist countries have for many years had access to international creditors, and have not needed China in the same way as Venezuela and Ecuador (Myers and Wise 2016). Thus, if goods substitution is having effects in Colombia, this strengthens the theory of goods substitution and it is likely that similar mechanisms may be usefully employed to study other cases including US allies or client states.

Can we observe goods substitution effects in Colombia? Remember that we are focusing on the effects of goods substitution within an ecology. This means that international goods substitution can have effects in a country even in the absence of concrete goods substitution in that country. Put differently, within a global goods ecology, we should in particular (country) cases distinguish between the effects of *actual* goods substitution, such as link shifts, and the effects of goods substitution becoming an option even in the absence of actually shifting ties. Diversification would not necessarily involve actual goods substitution but it might involve *hedging*, and using the possibility of link shifting or exit for *leverage* – both domestically and internationally.

While there is little evidence of concrete goods substitution in Colombia, I have found that Colombia's quest for increased autonomy and weakening the influence of the USA has also taken the form of exploring agreements to provide public goods equivalent to those offered by the USA (Nexon 2009); that this is also being used domestically in party politics, and that factors within the USA itself may have a decisive influence on how closely Colombia aligns with partners in the region, or potentially with China, in the future.

In Colombia, goods substitution dynamics amount to challenges to the exclusivity of ties within a hierarchical relationship, and these dynamics draw on a traditional Colombian repertoire of foreign policy-making.

Colombian Foreign Policy: Between Dependence and Autonomy

Colombia's foreign policy has historically been marked by its dependence on individuals, its fragmented nature, and an intimate relationship with the USA.

Having presidentialist traits, Colombia is, to a remarkable extent, reliant on the sitting president to stake out foreign policy directions. The Foreign Ministry – whose functioning one informant described as 'the President's PR-agency'[10] – does not coordinate foreign policy and, above all, serves an administrative function rather than formulating long-term strategies or having negotiating capacities. There are, in addition, parallel diplomacies, often involving security actors such as the National Police or the Ministry of Defence. Consequently, the sites of foreign policy-making are often bilateral meetings – above all, with the USA – that predominantly address the topics of illicit drugs and Colombia's armed conflict. There is little public participation and debate about foreign policy; most discussions about Colombian

---

[10] This chapter has benefited from conversations with Colombian and US diplomats, scholars, and policy-makers during a research stay in Bogota in autumn 2016.

foreign affairs take place outside the country, such as in the US Congress (Drekonja-Kornat 1983; Pardo and Tokatlian 1989; Ardila et al. 2002: 17–18; Tickner 2003b). The result is a pragmatic and ad-hoc foreign policy decision-making procedure, where priorities and directions shift with the president, often in coordination with the USA.

Despite this, two broad foreign policy doctrines have historically existed in Colombia – so ingrained that they have received Latin names: *respice polum* and *respice similia*. The first implies a close alignment with, even 'active subordination' (Ardila et al. 2002: 29; Tickner 2003b) to, the USA; the latter asserts independence and autonomy through allying with similar countries in the region and globally (Ardila 1991). These are not merely analytical terms, but are operational among decision-makers.

Hegemonic socialization of secondary states tends to occur after crises or the use of coercive power, in periods marked by both international turmoil and domestic legitimacy crises (Ikenberry and Kupchan 1990). In 1903, Panama was separated from Colombia with the active participation of the USA, which supported a Panamanian separatist movement to secure prospects for building a canal. After this experience, Colombian President Marco Fidel Suarez (1918–21) accepted that resistance was futile, and argued that the only rational way to secure Colombia's national interests, was to align closely with the USA. This was captured precisely in his doctrine of *respice polum* – 'look to the North'. The doctrine promotes a policy of 'active' or even 'aggressive subordination' (Tickner 2002: 390), recognizing the region as a US sphere of influence and internalizing the hegemon's normative stance. The communist fear added to this during the Cold War, while naming drugs a national security threat to the USA in the 1980s strengthened ties further (Crandall 2002; Tickner 2002: 355). In exchange for its loyalty and subordination, Colombia has received economic and military aid from the USA (Tickner 2003b: 170). The 'Plan Colombia' devised in the 1990s, in addition to being an aid package, also instilled an image of Colombia as a problem country – both abroad and domestically. Again, the Colombian government accepted the US diagnosis of its situation and the associated cures, acknowledging the country's status as inferior and incapable (Tickner 2003b: 379) – a self-image based on US terms.

From the late 1960s, however, Colombia started diversifying its foreign relations to its regional neighbours and other countries, under a new doctrine named *respice similia* – 'look to your peers/equals' – coined by President Alfonso Lopez Michelsen (1974–8). The self-image was now based on Colombia's own terms: a Latin American, 'third world' country. The aim was to increase Colombia's room for manoeuvre vis-à-vis the USA. Policies associated with this doctrine occasionally opposed international, liberal institutions and Colombia resumed economic activity with socialist countries. The regional Andean Pact (now The Andean Community) was a priority during the administration of Carlos Lleras Restrepo (1966–70), and the Michelsen administration sought close association with the Group of 77 (G-77) – a coalition of developing countries in the United Nations – joined the Non-Aligned Movement, and supported the New International Economic Order proposals, which sought to replace the Bretton Woods system.

The pervasiveness of these doctrines means that in Colombian politics the relationship with the USA has become a marker of foreign policy orientation in general, and a domestic signalling device. The curious element of Colombian foreign policy, though, is how these doctrines cohabit. Given the fragmented nature of foreign policy, the precise combination of these two doctrines has varied considerably – even within the same administration (Ardila et al. 2002; Tickner 2002: 358). The mix between these strategies depends on the sitting president and domestic politics as well as on external conditions, which includes a global goods ecology increasingly involving China as a goods supplier.

Hedging, Threats, and Leverage in Colombia: International and Domestic Dynamics

In the dynamic between subordination and autonomy, the necessity to diversify and universalize relations as a strategy for gaining greater autonomy is and has been a key topic (Ardila et al. 2002: 23). Colombia seeks close relations with the USA, while at the same time consistently seeking to reduce the general influence of the USA in Colombia.

During interviews with Colombian civil servants and academics, it emerged that the relationship may not be universally considered so close and dependent as generally assumed, at least as viewed from the Colombian side. This is particularly so given the notable absence of strategic thinking on foreign policy, as most decisions rely on the president and the context of concrete bilateral negotiations. If this is correct, *hedging strategies* may be more prominent than assumed. Hedging is expanding future opportunities for shifting, incurring higher transaction costs. The basis for hedging may be domestic legitimacy concerns, or projected future disagreements with the current provider. There are indications of this mechanism in Colombia.

For instance, President Andres Pastrana (1998–2002) sought to open a wider policy agenda when negotiating the Plan Colombia. The USA agreed to financial initiatives concerning the economy, human rights, and peace, but only in return for a more comprehensive anti-drug strategy. Pastrana accepted this. Despite this compromise, however, the focus stayed almost exclusively on drugs, even militarizing the issue (Tickner 2002: 363–4) making Colombia the world's third largest recipient of military aid at the time.

Then, in 2001, Pastrana's chief of staff, Eduardo Pizano, travelled to China to seek funding for Plan Colombia. When the trip was casually revealed during a conference on US aid to Colombia, US policy-makers present were taken aback. One US State Department official noted that 'it's not as though they're talking with the Netherlands'. US Congress member Dana Rohrabacher stated that the USA should consider this a threat to the Western Hemisphere. After the conference, Pizano commented on Colombia's role as the leading world supplier of cocaine, and that international support is needed in the 'war on drugs'. Pizano invoked the American drug czar General Barry McCaffrey, who had said that the USA was sharing anti-drug intelligence with China. In other words, if the USA and China have a relationship, then why not Colombia and China? When asked why he had not consulted Washington, he answered, 'we are an independent, autonomous country' (Oxley 2012: 7).

However, senior officials in Washington pointed out that the greatest threat was not contacts with China, but potential divisions within the government of Colombia concerning its relationship with the USA – in short, the tension between the two foreign policy doctrines. As seen below, this dynamic is still visible in Colombian politics.

Nothing came of Pizano's approach to China. A year later, an attempt to acquire combat planes from Brazil failed due to US opposition. On hearing the news of the Colombian government's proposed acquisition, General James T. Hill of the US Southern Command sent a strongly worded letter to the Colombian government, stating that the US Congress would not view this favourably, and that it could impact further US financing. He argued that the money should be spent, rather, on modernizing the existing fleet of Lockheed-built Hercules C-130s. The Colombian government complied and reversed the decision only days later.[11] These examples demonstrate the high transaction costs involved in diversification within hierarchical relations.

Colombia has sought to diversify its ties, but has lacked the leverage to do so as Colombia is a very specific security asset for the USA. As noted in Chapter 1, in seeking this highly specific asset the USA has incentives to establish hierarchical control over Colombia as a provider. Colombia has therefore been met with US conditionalities and threats of decertifying it as a partner country in the fight against drugs – which would place the country in the 'rouge' category together with, for example, present-day Venezuela. At the same time, Colombia has worked hard to further relations with the USA and to remain relevant. After the 9/11 attacks, for instance, Colombia increasingly framed its internal conflict as part of the global war against terrorism (Tickner 2002: 368).

However, there are indications that with increasing Chinese goods substitution in the region at large, Colombia's *leverage* may increase as a result. In addition to expanding future opportunities for shifting, hedging strategies may also be the basis for *threats* of goods substitution, even when no actual goods substitution takes place (as seen also in Chapter 7 on the Arctic). China's expanding role in a global goods ecology may be used for leverage in US–Colombian relations. Additionally, as discussed below, goods substitution may function as a domestic signalling device in party politics – diversification dynamics in goods substitution interact with both domestic and international politics, with one area having possible unintended effects on the other.

An instance of this was a proposed Chinese 'dry canal' in Colombia as a competitor to the US-dominated Panama Canal. The context of the proposal was relative US disinterest in Latin America and Colombia, and a diversification of Colombian foreign policy rooted in the *respice similia* doctrine under President Juan Manuel Santos (2010–18). Like many of his predecessors, Santos actively sought to diversify

---

[11] *El Tiempo*, 'E.U. Bloquea Compra de Aviones', 11 November 2002, www.eltiempo.com/archivo/documento/MAM-1309556.

Colombia's foreign relations, at the same time as he was negotiating better terms in the relationship with the USA. When lobbying for a free trade agreement, Colombia was yet again met with conditionalities. This time, Santos pulled the China card.

Colombia had long been frustrated with the US Congress's repeated failure to ratify a free trade agreement (FTA), negotiated by former Colombian president Álvaro Uribe (2002–10) and the George W. Bush administration. This trade deal would not only lead to an increase in trade by an estimated $1 billion per year, but the deal would also liberate space for Colombia to actually bring about bilateral politics, and not be mired in continuous trade negotiations, including with US trade unions, over individual deals and minutiae concerning each commodity.[12] The US Congress stalled the ratification as it linked approval of the FTA to compliance with labour rights and human rights in Colombia – precisely the type of liberal conditionalities on aid or economic benefits that have been the basis of goods substitution elsewhere (e.g., Tan-Mullins et al. 2010).

Enter China. In February 2011, in an announcement reported globally, Santos declared that Colombia was now negotiating with China to build an alternative to the Panama Canal – a 'dry canal' linking the Atlantic and Pacific coasts by rail. Santos claimed that this 'was a real proposal ... and it is quite advanced'.[13] A WikiLeaks report[14] further detailed that a delegation from China's state rail construction company – the China Railway Group – met with president Santos in Colombia in late 2010 to discuss the 250 km railway, which would be administered by the company and funded by the China Development Bank. The estimated cost was $7.6 billion. The company was also interested in three other railway projects in Colombia. The Chinese Embassy stated that 'there is a project for a railway that connects the Atlantic coast of Colombia with the Pacific coast, but the fact is that they are still discussing it'.[15]

---

[12] Interview with Colombian diplomat, formerly posted to Washington, DC, August 2016.
[13] BBC, 'China and Colombia Announce "Alternative Panama Canal"', 14 February 2011, www.bbc.co.uk/news/business-12448580.
[14] Wikileaks.org, 15148_Proposed Chinese Railway Project in Colombia.docx.
[15] Vivian Sequera, 'Is Colombian "Dry Canal" for real?', *Washington Post* 10 March 2011, www.washingtonpost.com/wp-dyn/content/article/2011/03/10/AR2011031002777_2.html.

This move can be, and was, interpreted as leverage for the FTA, directed at a stalling US Congress and threatening with a goods-substitution strategy that would have the Chinese building competing infrastructure and increasing trade.[16] As Strauss and Armony summarize, the Santos administration used the ' "China threat" sentiment in Washington to bolster support in Congress' for the ratification of the FTA, and the proposal was 'intended to highlight Colombia's potential as a regional hub for trade with China, a component of a foreign policy agenda centered on geographic diversification and oriented to open up new business opportunities for Colombia' (Strauss and Armony 2012: 184).

For the present purpose, it is not necessary for this 'China threat' to be credible – the point is that this was invoked as an option, which indicated a major change in the region's space of possibilities. What is more, even non-credible and unsuccessful threats of shifting ties may lead to diversification. In the context of multilateral organizations, Morse and Keohane (2014: 391) argue that

> since dissatisfied actors have incentives to claim that they have outside options even when they do not, their incentives to misrepresent can generate problems of credibility. If the dissatisfied coalition is unable to make credible threats and promises about either its willingness or ability to leverage outside options to force change, it may take actions that result in contested multilateralism.

That is, even if there is no actual goods substitution, and even if a threat of goods substitution is not credible, it may still have the effect of moving an unsatisfied actor towards other providers.

The failure to ratify the FTA also prompted Santos to forge stronger ties with Venezuela's Hugo Chavez, who in turn used the opportunity of the failed FTA ratification to demonstrate how Washington would betray its friends.[17] Concurrently with the Chinese dry canal proposal, and in an unprecedented move, Venezuelan drug kingpin Walid Makled, arrested on a US warrant, was set to be extradited from Colombia to Venezuela instead of to the USA. The reason, according to Colombian President Santos, was that 'we have an extradition treaty

---

[16] Semana, 'Colombia's New China Story', 28 April 2011, www.semana.com/international/articulo/colombias-new-china-story/239042-3.

[17] *The Wall Street Journal*, 'The Chávez Democrats', 10 March 2008, www.wsj.com/articles/SB120510610822923099.

with Venezuela, we do not have an extradition treaty with the United States'.[18] A treaty was signed in 1979, but the ratification was nullified in Colombia in 1986. This had not, however, impeded hundreds of extraditions to the USA in the past.

Observing the deterioration of the relationship with the USA, and the resetting of relations with Venezuela, analysts and politicians in the USA and Colombia increasingly put their faith in a group of republican senators to maintain close ties with Colombia. And some indeed tried, but in a rather traditional way that no longer worked as it used to. On 8 April 2011 two republican members of a Colombia delegation, Schock and McCaul, sent a letter to President Santos calling the extradition of Makled to Venezuela a significant 'mistake'. Furthermore, they warned that the intense media coverage of the case may 'complicate' the ratification of the free trade agreement, and 'strongly suggest-[ed] reconsideration' of the extradition decision.[19] Santos did not comply.

Diversification and broadening the options, while maintaining the 'special relationship' with the USA, seemed to be the key goal of Santos's foreign policy. In addition to the dry-canal proposal, under Santos Colombia also started negotiating a FTA with China; acquired $1 million in Chinese aid to be used to buy back military non-lethal military hardware; announced a 'strategic partnership' with China; and signed a defence cooperation agreement, including places for Colombian generals in Chinese military academies (Ellis 2012, 2014). In these initiatives, the optics are more important than the dollars involved.[20] In addition, Santos advocated the legalization of drugs, and was conducting peace negotiation in Cuba before the normalization of relations with the USA. All of this angered Washington. In May 2017, Trump unsuccessfully lobbied Santos to resume spraying coca plants (to kill them) when the two met at the White House. During

---

[18] Jasmina Kelemen, 'Walid Makled's Extradition Case Highlights Warming Venezuela–Colombia Ties', *Christian Science Monitor* 8 April 2011, www.csmonitor.com/World/Americas/2011/0408/Walid-Makled-s-extradition-case-highlights-warming-Venezuela-Colombia-ties.

[19] Tom Heyden, 'Santos Meets with US Delegation to Smooth FTA Passage Process', *Colombia Reports* 19 April.2011, https://colombiareports.com/santos-meets-with-us-delegation-to-smooth-fta-threat-over-makled-extradition/.

[20] Sebastian Castaneda, 'Colombia's Santos Moves to Diversify Foreign Policy', *World Politics Review* 1 April 2011, www.worldpoliticsreview.com/articles/8383/colombias-santos-moves-to-diversify-foreign-policy.

an interview, one Colombian Foreign Ministry official argued that Santos effectively balanced the two doctrines of *respice similia* and *respice polum*; in this case, Chinese goods substitution was a new resource for the former.

The FTA with the USA was eventually approved, but whether the Venezuela and China threats worked, and whether they were at all credible, is debatable. Regardless, the case is indicative of a new dynamic of goods substitution concerning the core of the exclusivity of US ties with Colombia. Such hedging can be present even in countries that are neither counter-hegemonic nor counter-order; Colombia may seek to increase relative capability and leverage in its relationship with the USA in anticipation of changes in the world order and the distribution of capabilities therein (Tessman and Wolfe 2011: 220). A former Colombian foreign minister suggested the fact that 'China has won more space in the international community' might have helped this turn in the USA's stance on the FTA adding, 'all prognostics project that the US will lose its status as superpower'.[21] Compared with strong and successful US pressure regarding Colombia's proposal to buy fighter jets from Brazil in 2002, for instance, this is a different dynamic.

Domestic Politics and Current Prospects for Goods Substitution and Hedging in Colombia

Importantly, Santos's diversification strategy was also a way of distancing himself from his predecessor Álvaro Uribe in terms of the relationship with Washington. Uribe was intimately connected to Washington and George W. Bush. Santos, Uribe's former Minister of Defence, was seen to have turned against Uribe in promoting peace negotiations with the Revolutionary Armed Forces of Colombia (FARC) guerrillas, and by opposing aspects of US drug and anti-terror policy. Santos explicitly criticized Uribe for promoting Makled's extradition to the USA. This can be read as the differences between the *respice polum* and the *respice similia* doctrines playing out, now in the context of a global goods substitution ecology.

---

[21] Natalia Bonnett and José Antonio Sánchez, 'Las razones que influyeron para destrabar el TLC en Washington', *El Tiempo* 3 April 2011, www.eltiempo.com/archivo/documento/CMS-9138862.

With President Iván Duque (2018–present), Uribe's protégé, the emphasis seems to have returned to the *respice polum* doctrine, highlighting convergent views with Washington concerning drugs, counter-terrorism, and the crisis in Venezuela. 'When he is sworn in', a senior US official stated, 'Duque will overnight become the most pro-American head of state in Latin America'.[22]

At the same time, US rhetoric concerning China in Latin America has changed from being rather indifferent to confrontational. The US ambassador to Colombia called the Russian and Chinese presence in the region 'very detrimental', and maintained that China only invests in countries in the region to extract resources and leave with the surplus, comparing it to China in Africa. He added that president Duque is very aware of this.[23] Admiral Craig Faller, commander of US Southern Command, also warned of the presence of China, and that Chinese involvement in information technology infrastructure in allied countries in South America meant that the USA should stop trusting these allies with intelligence data.[24] Then Secretary of State Rex Tillerson said that China is 'getting a foothold in Latin America. It is using economic statecraft to pull the region into its orbit; the question is at what price'.[25] The Chinese ambassador to Colombia responded that these were baseless attacks.[26]

This culminated in September 2017: receiving reports of a surge in drug production in Colombia, Trump, like presidents before him, threatened to decertify Colombia as a partner against drugs, and

---

[22] Anne Gearan, 'Trump Administration Sees New Colombian President as an Ally in Drug War', *Washington Post* 6 August 2018, www.washingtonpost.com/politics/trump-administration-sees-new-colombian-president-as-an-ally-and-fellow-law-and-order-leader/2018/08/05/b7ad47d0-95cb-11e8-810c-5fa705927d54_story.html?utm_term=.ca1e5a8085dd.

[23] *Caracol Radio*, 'Embajador de EE.UU. cuestiona ayuda de Rusia y China a Venezuela', https://caracol.com.co/programa/2019/02/11/6am_hoy_por_hoy/1549890047_754727.html.

[24] Voa Noticias, 'Faller: "EE.UU. está enfocado en apoyar una solución política y diplomática" en Venezuela', 8 February 2019, www.voanoticias.com/a/entrevista-almirante-craig-faller-comando-sur-eeuu-venezuela-/4778220.html.

[25] Reuters, 'Latin America Should Not Rely on China: U.S. Secretary of State Tillerson', 1 February 2018, www.reuters.com/article/us-usa-diplomacy-latam-china/latin-america-should-not-rely-on-china-u-s-secretary-of-state-tillerson-idUSKBN1FL6D5.

[26] Kienyke Noticias, 'China fortalecerá inversiones en Colombia', 25 November 2018, www.kienyke.com/noticias/china-fortalecera-inversiones-en-colombia.

cancelled a planned visit to the country. This time, however, the coercive strategy was considered a 'huge mistake taking the bilateral relationship to its worst place in two decades'. The threat was the object of bipartisan critique in the US Congress.[27] Colombia retorted that there was no need to issue threats to make Colombia take the drug problem seriously.[28]

Faced with Colombia's increasing leverage in the relationship, it might be Washington that further weakens the informal hierarchical arrangements, facilitating diversification and hedging. Symptomatically, UN Ambassador Nikki Haley, a Trump confidante, led the US delegation at President Duque's inauguration ceremony, although Duque hosted Chinese Transport Minister Li Xiaopeng as an honoured guest at the event.[29] And despite the apparent reorientation towards Washington, in a statement that can be read precisely as hedging in the face of uncertainty in the North, Duque's Foreign Minister Trujillo pronounced that 'Colombia firmly adheres to the one-China policy and supports multilateralism', adding that the country is ready to work with China on strengthening multilateralism, safeguarding global free trade, and protecting the interests of developing countries.[30] Such hedging would amount to order-enhancing goods substitution. This is one example in a series of official pronouncements over recent years on Colombia–China relations that indicates the multivocality of Colombia's foreign policy signalling.

Combined with increasing preoccupation in Washington concerning China in Latin America, the mere presence of a China alternative is promoting political dynamics that weaken US influence in the region. In Colombia, the diversification strategies of hedging, threats of goods substitution for increased leverage, and substitution as a domestic

[27] Joshua Goodman, 'Trump Delivers Shock Rebuke to Colombia over Cocaine Surge', *AP News*, 14 September 2017, www.apnews.com/32f78da86d8443b2948a4c0e49a58f81.

[28] 'Comunicado del Gobierno Nacional', 14 September 2017. http://es.presidencia.gov.co/sitios/busqueda/noticia/170914-Comunicado-del-Gobierno-Nacional/Noticia.

[29] Agencia EFE, 'Enviado especial de Xi Jinping asistirá a la investidura de Iván Duque', 2 August 2018, www.efe.com/efe/america/mundo/enviado-especial-de-xi-jinping-asistira-a-la-investidura-ivan-duque/20000012-3709030.

[30] Xinhuanet.com, 'China, Colombia Hold New Round of Political Consultation between Foreign Departments', 13 December 2018, www.xinhuanet.com/english/2018-12/13/c_137671944.htm.

signalling device, all seem to play out. Still, there is, as yet, little evidence of concrete goods substitution in Colombia. As Colombia's leverage increases, it seems that the factor holding back more extensive goods substitution is informal hierarchy; a history of interactions, elite socialization, and the fact that relations with Washington is the default option.

However, the room for substitution and diversification of ties has expanded. The fact that other options are available, in the context of a USA decreasing the prioritization of Latin American relationships, can affect political dynamics even within a hierarchical relation – which the US–Colombia relationship remains. Colombian foreign policy-making is pragmatic – it is reactive in waiting for something to show up, and proactive in going for it when an opportunity arises. That should be very troubling for the USA in the context of a traditionally hierarchical relationship. A fragmented policy-making context, combined with the dynamics of a global goods ecology, can lead to changes in political opportunity structures, which in turn trigger innovations in how Colombia's two foreign policy doctrines are deployed. The *respice polum* heritage may be fragile, as the other traditional foreign policy doctrine of *respice simila* is now deployed in a context with China as a new regional actor, and may link up with hedging strategies. The possibilities for actual goods substitution, or closer alignments with China, is therefore not only a theoretical possibility – even for the closest allies in the USA's own back yard.

Conclusion: Goods Substitution and Client States

In sum, *shifting* ties in a hierarchical relationship – effectively challenging that relationship itself – is often prohibitively costly, but diversifying ties can be done *within* an existing hierarchical relationship. This corresponds to the point that goods substitution does not necessarily challenge the hegemon, but it may slowly undermine the order that it relies on and upholds. A parallel is semi-autonomous subordinate actors in empires cultivating cross-segment ties, thus undermining an imperial order relying on exclusive ties. The implication is that Colombia may unintentionally be transforming the international order, even if it qualifies as a positionalist or status quo power – you do not need to be a Venezuela or an Ecuador to challenge the international order.

These dynamics can also be observed in other cases involving US 'client states' engaged in diversification and hedging strategies. For instance, in the Middle East, recent developments in Israel and Saudi Arabia follow a similar pattern. Both countries are closely aligned to the USA, but are simultaneously diversifying their ties to other actors in the region and globally. Israel increasingly seeks to diversify its diplomatic and economic ties away from Europe and the USA (Efron et al. 2019), and can draw on a history of interactions with China in this process (Goldstein 2004) without necessarily compromising its relationship with the USA. Beginning in the 1980s, Israel and China secretly worked on defence technology transfers between the two countries (Kumaraswamy 2005; Ayyadi and Kamal 2016). However, the USA intervened: in 2000, Israel yielded to US pressure and cancelled the transfer of radar systems technology to China. In 2005, as Israel was planning to support Chinese upgrades of HARPY UAVs, the USA halted cooperation with Israel on the F-35 Joint Strike Fighter programme, demanded the firing of senior Israeli Ministry of Defense officials, and enforced an 'agreement' that all defence related exports to China should be subject to US approval (Efron et al. 2019).

In recent years, in part triggered by US withdrawal from the Middle East, Israel has again been seeking out alternative patrons, and Israeli–Chinese ties are reopening (Chen 2012). The two countries have now, however, shifted from technological to economic cooperation. This has led to a surge in bilateral ties and Chinese investments, and the countries are poised to sign a FTA.[31]

In addition, in recent years Israel has vastly expanded its cooperation with untraditional partners such as India, Russia, Bahrain, Oman – and Saudi Arabia.[32] Saudi Arabia has itself been emerging as a patron in the Middle East. It is one of the USA's closest allies in the region, and has traditionally been aligned against Russia. However, Mohammed Bin Salman's unprecedented visit to Moscow in 2017 expanded Saudi Arabia's options and possible leverage in the region without exiting

---

[31] Daniel J. Samet, 'Can China Replace the United States in Israel?', *Foreign Policy* 3 February 2020, https://foreignpolicy.com/2020/02/03/can-china-replace-the-united-states-in-israel/.

[32] Jake Novak, 'Israel Will Soon Have to Choose between China and the US', *CNBC* 29 August 2019, www.cnbc.com/2019/08/29/israel-will-soon-have-to-choose-between-china-and-the-us.html.

the close relationship with the USA (Dannreuther 2012).[33] Saudi Arabia and Russia have subsequently signed a number of economic, technical, and military cooperation agreements.

Few would question the special relationship between the USA and these two countries. Yet, just as in the case of Colombia, simply being present as alternative goods providers means that Russia and China challenge the exclusivity of US ties in the region.

As we have seen, deviating from standards set by Washington has traditionally been met with severing ties or threatening a 'rouge state' label. In Colombia's case, the threat has been to decertify the country as a partner in the war against drugs, cutting aid and barring trade. Previously, such threats have allowed patrons to impose strict conditionalities. With the increasing availability of exit options, such threats have weaker effects on the recipients, and may be counterproductive if it increases the chances of recipients actually exiting. In addition, the options for diversifying ties in new areas – above all economic – are expanding as a global goods substitution ecology becomes more widespread.

Even if the hegemonic authority or the hierarchical ties are not directly challenged, goods substitution challenges the hegemon's exclusivity of ties with the recipient. This means that the mere prospect of goods substitution may weaken hegemonic influence in a region. It has not, however, been the purpose of this chapter to prove any large-scale shift in the international order, but to illustrate the broad application of a theory of international goods and asset substitution, even in prima facie least-likely cases. In short, by focusing on how order and hegemony may be slowly undermined by 'a thousand paper cuts', we can see dynamics and mechanisms of order transformation, or order resilience, that remain hidden when using other lenses, such as asking whether China is a direct 'strategic threat' to the USA in Latin America, or assessing future great-power war scenarios where China might possibly use its influence in Latin America or in other regions for military purposes. The broader story is rather about how patrons in general

---

[33] Jared Malsin, 'Putin Welcomes Saudi Arabia into His Middle East Sphere of Influence', *TIME*, 5 October 2017, https://time.com/4970217/saudi-arabia-king-salman-moscow-vladimir-putin/; Adam Taylor, 'Why Washington Will Be Watching the Saudi King's Visit to Moscow', *The Washington Post* 4 October 2017, www.washingtonpost.com/news/worldviews/wp/2017/10/04/why-washington-will-be-watching-a-saudi-kings-visit-to-moscow/.

and Latin American states in particular approach alternative goods provision, how they exit, diversify, or threaten to do either, and the effects of this regardless of status quo or revisionist intent from either goods providers or the individual regimes on the demand side.

Even if US–Colombian ties remain solid, the hierarchical arrangement could eventually come to rest on tradition and personal relations alone, rather than on any form of institutionalized power. The implications can be generalized to other (client) states and allies such as Israel and Saudi Arabia. If the stakes are raised, the benefits of goods substitution could trump such concerns. This means that even in the presence of a hierarchical relationship, goods substitution dynamics may still prevail, eventually undermining the structural relationship itself. Taking on the USA or its ties with allies directly, as has been the goods substitution strategy of the ALBA countries, is not the only option – undermining the exclusivity of ties may indirectly affect the architecture of international order, since diversifying ties or threats of exit will influence policies. Hierarchies are not only about power and dominance; so when goods substitution takes additive form – hedging your bets, relating with new actors, or changing dominant narratives – this does not imply an exit from existing hierarchical ties, but it challenges their exclusivity.

7 | Goods Substitution at High Latitude: Undermining Hegemony from below in the North Atlantic

REBECCA ADLER-NISSEN, BENJAMIN DE CARVALHO AND HALVARD LEIRA

In 2016, years after having withdrawn from the Keflavik airbase in Iceland, the United States announced that it would resume a presence on the base (Barents Observer 2016). In a similar vein, the US Department of Defense issued a statement in late 2018 confirming American interest in financing Greenlandic airport infrastructure (Over the Circle 2018). This statement came after years of downscaling of the US presence on the island. More spectacularly, in August 2019 President Trump suggested that the United States should buy Greenland from Denmark. The suggestion caused diplomatic friction, and although that plan was soon scrapped, the United States moved ahead with plans to open a consulate in Greenland (Reuters 2019). What can explain these changes in policy, and to what extent can they be made sense of within a framework of goods substitution?

The polities of the North Atlantic – Iceland, Greenland and the Faroe Islands – have been central to Western strategic thought for more than a century. During both world wars, German submarines entered the Atlantic by going north of the United Kingdom and, during the Cold War, the strategically important area in the northern Atlantic between Greenland, Iceland and the United Kingdom – the GIUK-gap – was central to NATO strategic planning for the relief of Europe in case of attack. The US Air Force had a base at Keflavik in Iceland, and the Thule radar station in Greenland was a central node in the US early warning system in case of intercontinental ballistic missile (ICBM) attack (Powers 2017). Iceland was an independent founder member of NATO, while Greenland and the Faroe Islands were included by virtue of Danish membership. On the face of it, it would seem preposterous to think of US hegemony being undermined in this area, which is of significant strategic interest to the United States and has been close to the core of the Western alliance – and so close to 'home'.

Even so, in this chapter we suggest that there were indisputable signs of decline of US hegemony in the North Atlantic before 2019, and of at least potential goods substitution by Russia and China. Our analysis builds on a growing research literature, but also on thirty-four interviews with politicians, bureaucrats, diplomats, journalists, private sector actors and academics in Reykjavik, Torshavn, Nuuk, Copenhagen and Washington, DC, between 2011 and 2017.

When the financial crisis hit Iceland in 2008, and stopgap loans proved hard to come by, Russia and Iceland, in secret negotiations, agreed in principle on a deal which would have Russia lend all the required money to Iceland. As Greenland has been inching towards independence over the last decade, in the process seeking to diversify the economy, Chinese-associated mining companies have been at the forefront. When the West imposed sanctions on Russia following the Ukraine crisis in 2014 and Russia retaliated against countries that sanctioned it with a food-import embargo, the fishing dependent Faroes, which are not European Union (EU) members but had themselves suffered fisheries sanctions from the EU the year before, were handed a virtual monopoly in Russia for their biggest export: fresh salmon.

However, this potential goods substitution has not primarily been initiated from above, with Russia and China offering what the United States or the West have ceased to offer. Rather – and this is the main claim of this chapter – alternative goods provision has been sought out from below, by polities with complex post-colonial and potential hegemonic relationships with a variety of states. In short, these polities are experimenting with new ways of playing the United States, Russia and China against each other, with the EU and Denmark also playing important roles, and Norway a more distant one. Greenland, Iceland and the Faroes exploit their strategic positions in a variety of ways to push great powers to compete in offering a variety of public and private goods. These Northern polities have effectively found cracks in the liberal order where they can thrive – economically, strategically and culturally. While the United States and Europe would prefer to keep them in the fold, for obvious reasons, in the context of liberal international norms, post-colonial sensitivities and independence dreams, there are limits to how far the hegemons will go in order to discipline these polities. Furthermore, regardless of whether these attempts at playing the United States, China and Russia off one another are successful, the fact that these states do so is important, and indicates that there is potential political gain from openly challenging the consensus on upholding elements of the liberal order. Absent external shocks of a certain magnitude, such as dramatic shifts in the arctic policies of the great powers, we argue here, the cracks in the liberal order in the High North have the potential to grow in the coming years.

The chapter proceeds in four steps. First, we spell out the theoretical rationale for looking at goods substitution from the bottom up. Then, we briefly present the background for our cases, and the post-colonial and layered dimensions of goods substitution and the maintenance of hegemony. In the longer, third, section, we present our analysis of the three cases, followed by the conclusion.

Undermining Hegemony, Bottom Up

As spelled out in Chapter 1 of this volume, the politics of goods substitution hinges on both supply-side and demand-side drivers. On the supply side, goods substitution is easier if the good sought has high substitutability (like a loan or an investment), and if the number of actors in a position (and willing) to provide it is higher than one. On the demand side, intrinsic as well as extrinsic costs of goods, as well as renegotiations of existing deals about goods, are likely to influence whether and how goods substitution takes place. To reiterate, by *goods substitution* we thus mean competitive dynamics surrounding efforts by states to seek – or provide – alternative sources for economic, military or social assets. When actors view the existing supply of such assets as politically or substantively problematic, they face incentives to seek substitutes. They may *provide the relevant good for themselves, contract with another actor* for supply of the good or *pool their resources* to jointly produce the good.

The politics of goods provision by hegemonic powers is central in upholding international order, but is only now receiving sustained scholarly attention. Even less attention has been paid to the interplay of goods provision and 'goods-shopping' and how this influences the agency of receiving states. While aspiring hegemons can attempt to attract clients through offering goods, client states can seek to diversify their goods portfolio by bringing in more providers, they can exchange one provider for another, or they can use the possibility of changing providers as a form of leverage vis-à-vis the original provider. For economic and military assets, the possibility of additivity or exchange is fairly straightforward; a new provider can be added to, or exchanged for, a former provider. For social assets, the equation is less straightforward, highlighting how symbolic goods are jointly produced; switching providers of social assets thus undermines hegemony in two ways: first, by undercutting the manifest hegemony, and second, by questioning the notion of that hegemony as such. When making sense of the agency of client states, one also needs to take into account the historic specificity of the relationship between hegemon and client. Of high relevance to this chapter, we would, for instance, expect post-colonial relationships to come with more possibilities of extrinsic costs of goods than relationships without a colonial back story.

From our perspective, thus, models of goods substitution should allow specified room for agency from below. We would like to highlight four points. First, closely tied to the notion of substitutability, is the possibility of clients using the threat of substitution as strategic leverage. As the model specifies, attempts at renegotiation from the hegemon might drive the clients to seek alternative providers of goods. However, the logic also works in reverse, namely, clients seeking out alternative providers of goods might drive the hegemons to renegotiate. Closely related to this is the second point, namely, that client leverage will be highest where the client can easily switch goods provider, but where the hegemon cannot easily find an alternative client. Third, cultural specificity matters and local logics might create unexpected demand-side drivers. In particular, in post-colonial settings we hypothesize that seeking out alternative goods suppliers might have a value in and of itself, as is implicit in the model's focus on the extrinsic costs of goods provision. Post-colonial identity might make the desire for goods substitution higher than strategic or economic factors alone would suggest (Adler-Nissen 2014a; Adler-Nissen and Gad 2013). The imperial history of the 'liberal order' itself might make it particularly attractive to seek out goods providers from outside of that order. Fourth, in following through on post-colonial identity, status might be a double-edged good. While post-colonial clients will tend to want their status to be recognized by the hegemon, in the end the status provided in relationships where there is no historical hierarchy might prove more satisfactory. And, as we have argued elsewhere, for smaller polities the status game is probably even more important than it is to great powers (Wohlforth et al. 2018).

Layers of Hegemony in the North Atlantic

The hegemonic relations of the North Atlantic polities have their roots in Viking expansion more than 1,000 years ago. Iceland and the Faroes were largely populated by Norwegian Vikings (and their slaves), as were enclaves on Greenland. By the middle of the thirteenth century, these islands, in addition to the Orkneys, Shetland, the Hebrides and the Isle of Man were part of the Norwegian polity. When Norway became subordinated to the Copenhagen-centred Danish polity in 1380, the islands of the North Atlantic were part of the package.[1] When Norway was ceded from Denmark to Sweden in 1814, the islands remained with Denmark. Even though formal political ties to Norway have thus not been in place for more than 600 years, Norway retains at least some nimbus as an ancestral home in Iceland and the Faroes. There are also perceived cultural ties to Norway, an interest in Norway as an example of a small state managing outside of the EU and recognition of Norway's active Arctic policy. This is not to say that Norway has a hegemonic role in the North Atlantic, but still, at times, these polities look to Norway (Dodds and Ingimundarson 2012: 32–33).[2]

Much more important, and complicated, is the relationship between the islands and Denmark. As was the case with many colonies and possessions, control and direct intervention from the metropole intensified during the nineteenth and twentieth centuries, in turn leading to the emergence of independence movements. Iceland eventually became independent in 1944. The Faroes voted for independence in 1946, a vote that was rejected by the Danes, but home rule was granted in 1948 and deepened in 2005. Greenland was granted Home Rule in 1979, and this was deepened in 2008. Current relationships with Denmark are ambivalent, and to fully appreciate the relations between these polities and the wider liberal order, it is important to recall that seen from below, that very order has been imperial (see also Adler-

---

[1] De facto control over Greenland lapsed between the late middle ages and 1721.
[2] Likewise, some in Greenland, and more in the Faroes, refer to Iceland as a state that they look to for inspiration and guidance.

Nissen and Zarakol in press). Iceland is now an independent state with a distinct national identity, which takes few cues from the former colonial power, although the former colonial relationship still has political meaning and can be used to mobilize Icelandic national identity (Loftsdottir 2015). In the Faroes and Greenland, Denmark is still the provider of economic security, and the self-perception among many respondents in these polities is that Denmark is the hegemon.[3] In the Faroes, cultural affinities imply that even if independence is a constant in the political imagination, ever increasing local competencies might be satisfactory to a majority of the Faroese population. In Greenland, political tensions are overlaid by cultural tensions, and a stark colonial relationship (perceived as such by both parties) between Greenlanders and Danes. Of the three cases, Greenland has the most obvious postcolonial self-identity, expressed in essentialist terms (Gad 2009)

Beyond Denmark, the EU figures in a hegemonic role to all three polities, even though none of them are members. The Faroes rejected membership when Denmark joined in 1973, while Greenland opted out in 1985. Iceland did apply for membership in 2009, after the financial crash of 2008, but the application was withdrawn in 2015. Even so, all the polities have close relations with the EU. Iceland is a member of the European Free Trade Association (EFTA), the European Economic Area (EEA) and the Schengen Area, and through Danish EU membership both the Faroes and Greenland are affected regularly by EU decisions.[4] In a sense, the EU is a hegemon which all three polities have rejected, but which they still cannot escape.[5]

To outsiders, the USA might seem to be the clear-cut hegemon of the North Atlantic. To the polities in question, this is not so clear. In Iceland, NATO membership and the Keflavik base have implied that US military hegemony has been readily acknowledged. At the same time, a strong national identity has ensured that even an openness towards US popular culture has not led to acceptance of US cultural

---

[3] One should be careful not to conflate such self-perception and identity with the analytical concept of hegemony; but, at the very least, such self-perceptions suggest that hegemony could productively be seen as layered (or nested).

[4] And, as a not unimportant curiosity, inhabitants of the Faroes and Greenland, even though their polities are not members of the EU, are EU citizens through their Danish citizenship.

[5] In the Faroes, some floated the idea that the United Kingdom might be a sort of hegemon of last resort if push came to shove. Others rejected this as a flight of fancy,

hegemony. In Greenland, the US presence at Thule is ambiguous, and there is little acknowledgement of any form of US hegemonic influence. In the Faroes, the openness towards the US is more obvious, but still with little explicit acknowledgement of any hegemony.

In sum, hegemony in the North Atlantic is ambiguous. For analytical purposes, there is no doubt that there is a 'Western' hegemony in the region, but as self-perceptions remind us, this comes in different varieties and with multiple layers, with local hegemonic relations nested within more overarching ones. This is of obvious importance to the ensuing analyses. What might look to the casual observer like counter-hegemonic behaviour – seeking to undermine American hegemony – might better be interpreted as assertion of leverage towards Denmark or the EU. Likewise, what might look like US indifference must be understood in light of the obvious client role of Denmark vis-à-vis the USA. As long as Denmark is able to function as a local hegemon for Greenland and the Faroes, there is no need for the USA to act openly as the hegemon of last resort. The recent uptick in US interest towards Greenland could be interpreted as a sign that the USA is no longer certain that Denmark can fulfil this role.

Conversely, while policy-makers in these polities themselves might not acknowledge US hegemony, there is no doubt that both Russia and China recognize the importance of these islands to US strategic planning, and that they also see the opportunities and limitations inherent in the current political set-up of the region. While these powers might desire more influence, and are happy to see the USA retreating, we would expect the supply-side powers to be hesitant to challenge the hegemon too obviously.

Finally, it is important not to overestimate the strategic interaction capacity of the North Atlantic polities. Iceland tilts towards the small end of the small-state category, and the two other polities, if independent, would be classified as micro-states. Iceland, with a population of some 330,000 people, is smaller than Anaheim, California or Belfast in the United Kingdom. Greenland and the Faroes, both with populations around 50,000, are comparable to the Morningside Heights neighbourhood of New York City. Smallness necessarily implies less capacity to attend to a wide palette of policy choices. If we simplify, and argue with Hobbes that polities seek security, gain or glory, these polities are decidedly tilted towards the latter two. While the wider world has paid increasing attention to security issues in the North

Atlantic, a clear majority of local respondents are largely indifferent to such issues. On the other hand, economic welfare is paramount, and a number of status-signifiers are in play. To foreshadow the analyses: while the North Atlantic polities have been actively seeking goods substitution, they have not deliberately been undermining hegemony. The notion that their actions might help establish a new regional or world order has surely not crossed the minds of relevant policy-makers.

The Spectre of Goods Substitution in the North Atlantic

In the eyes of both external observers and internal stakeholders, the North Atlantic has become a site of renewed great-power interest over the last decade. While the USA has changed its hegemonic presence, other powers, in particular China and Russia, have been perceived to actively pursue Arctic strategies, perhaps seeking to undermine the Western hegemony in the area. We should stress at the outset that even though they are both positioned to provide goods substitution, these two powers play different roles in the region. Russia is a major Arctic power in its own right and was, throughout the Cold War, the 'Other' of Western Alliance thinking in the North Atlantic. This creates some obvious path dependencies for how Russia perceives itself in the region, and how other states perceive Russia (interestingly, in all three cases, these perceptions are not the same in the North Atlantic microstates as in Copenhagen or Washington, DC). China, on the other hand, is a relative newcomer in the region, associated primarily with economic interests and activities.

Institutionally, Russia is actively engaged in the Arctic Council, and China has become an observer in the council. While the Arctic Council – a high-level intergovernmental forum counting the eight states[6] that have sovereignty over lands within the Arctic Circle – works primarily on sustainable development, environmental and social issues and economics, a number of policy commentators have claimed that great-power interest in the region is about more than cooperation over natural resources and climate change. It has been suggested that we are witnessing a 'scramble for the Arctic', which may herald renewed geopolitical engagement in the region. It can thus be argued

---

[6] Canada, Denmark, Finland, Iceland, Norway, Russia, Sweden and the USA, in addition to thirteen non-Arctic states with observer status.

that Russia and China are seeking to achieve economic, strategic and status-associated goals in the Arctic. Below, we set out to explore below the concrete ways in which this plays out. On one hand, we analyze whether we are seeing classical balancing, acquiescence to the existing hegemony or hegemony being undermined. On the other hand, we investigate whether initiatives come from the great powers or the local polities. For each of the polities, we start by presenting the local background and the case for great-power involvement, before detailing whether and how Russia and China have been involved.

Iceland

Iceland was a founder member of NATO, and hosted a substantial US military presence at Keflavik from 1951to 2006 (Ingimundarson 2011). There has also been considerable influence from American popular culture, although Iceland has been fiercely protective of its cultural heritage. Icelanders have constructed themselves as different, but also as distinctively Nordic, and, over recent decades, as part of the Arctic (Dodds and Ingimundarson 2012; Ingimundarson 2015; Jones and Clark 2016). While there has been no doubting a Western hegemony with a strong American flavour, Iceland has also traditionally had a good relationship with the USSR/Russia. Two major events from the previous decade could be perceived as challenging to the hegemonic relations between the rest of the West and Iceland: the closure of the Keflavik airbase in 2006, and the financial crisis and bank collapse of 2008. Both are ripe for analysis in light of goods substitution.

Until 2006, Iceland's defence was directly guaranteed through a direct US presence at Keflavik; since then the guarantee has been associated with moveable forces (Winger and Petursson 2016). If material power was the sole dimension of hegemony, one might expect there to be a greater interest in Iceland on the part of Russia and China after the closure of the base. In addition to the material loss of defence capabilities, the closure left a political rift. While it had long been announced, the way in which negotiations between Iceland and the USA took place left many Icelanders unhappy with the hegemon, particularly those who had supported the US military presence for decades. Interviewees in Reykjavik, both journalists and politicians, noted that many key supporters of the US alignment had felt a sense of betrayal. Two years later, the economic crisis of 2008 brought new challenges. Icelanders felt a sense of 'shock' at how Iceland was portrayed by Western media at the time, and by the fact that it took so long before any financial help was pledged from Iceland's allies. The United Kingdom's enforcement of anti-terrorist legislation against Icelandic banks was perceived as particularly provoking. In sum, a cross section of respondents agreed that there is now a sense of a reduced attachment to the West in Iceland.

The Russian interest in Iceland connects both of these challenges to hegemony, but is largely associated with the handling of the economic crisis. As the Icelandic economy was cratering, and Iceland struggled to find loans which would secure the economy, attempts were made to negotiate such a loan with Russia, covering all of Iceland's needs. During the crisis, Icelandic officials made no secret of the fact that Iceland needed to look for help anywhere they could get it, with the Icelandic Prime Minister Geir Haarde explicitly chastising 'old friends' for not helping, and arguing that Iceland needed to seek out 'new friends'.

Although the negotiations with Russia had started in the summer of 2008, before the final collapse, they had received no public attention. As Iceland was denied help from both the USA, the International Monetary Fund (IMF) and other Western states, the head of the Icelandic central bank went public about the negotiations, without informing the Russians. Many actors with intimate knowledge of Icelandic politics agreed that the negotiations had reached an advanced stage, yet it is virtually impossible to get information about the process and the conditionalities, if any, attached to the proposed loan itself. While the conditions of the loan package Iceland eventually accepted from the IMF and Western states have been the object of academic scrutiny, the Russian deal has been left almost in the dark (however, see Ingimundarson 2015: 87–88). It is likely that only four to five people on the Icelandic side were fully informed about the process. Conversely, on the Russian side, the negotiations apparently bypassed the normal bureaucratic channels and were handled directly via the Russian Embassy in Reykjavik and the Kremlin. The Russian Ministry of Finance, allegedly, was kept outside of the process. This would suggest that, on the Russian side, the deal could have been eyed as an opportunity to advance a more security-oriented agenda in the Arctic.

Russia later denied that there had been any conditionalities attached to the proposed loan. The content of a meeting between Icelandic President

Ólafur Ragnar Grímsson and the Reykjavik diplomatic corps, which was partially leaked to the Norwegian newspaper *Klassekampen*, nevertheless paints a more nuanced picture. It was reported that the Russian ambassador had denied any Russian interest in the Keflavik airbase. Those we interviewed in Reykjavik, nevertheless, suggested that what had been said during the meeting was not that there was no Russian interest in Keflavik at all, but that there was none '*at the present moment*'. Again, this would suggest that although there are few examples of goods substitution by the Russians, this is certainly a possibility that remains open from the Russian side. While full Russian use of a former US airbase is still beyond the pale for Iceland, the possibility of allowing the Russians refuelling rights and the partial use of Keflavik was not inconceivable.

Although the loan negotiations were quite advanced, the Russia loan never materialized. Other loans were made available to Iceland, by Western states and institutions, at the last minute. This case is thus particularly interesting from a bottom-up goods perspective, as it could be argued that Iceland actively sought substitutions from Russia, given the initial refusal from Western states and institutions, only later to turn around and use Russia as leverage. Our interviewees, including commentators, journalists and politicians, were quite open about how this would have fitted the pattern of Iceland's relations with the West, and particularly the USA, during the Cold War, when Iceland kept trading channels with the USSR open (Thorhallsson and Gunnarsson 2017: 3) and did not hesitate to pressure the West for better deals. As Icelanders put it, the country had experience in playing the 'Russia card'.

The secrecy surrounding the loan negotiations has led to different interpretations. Some of the people we interviewed saw the negotiations that had been going on as the outcome of a real belief in the need to find 'new friends' on the part of Icelandic officials; others pointed to over-zealous Russian diplomats with connections directly to the Kremlin who had oversold the possibility of reaching an agreement with Reykjavik; while, finally, others saw it as an overture on the Icelandic side which needed leverage against its Western allies reticent to help them. These interpretations are obviously not mutually exclusive, and only the last one can be partially confirmed; the proposed loan was indeed used as leverage to get Iceland a better deal with the West.

While Russian interests in Iceland have been relatively limited, and fairly obviously connected to material gains, Chinese involvement has been more diverse and less exclusively material. Local discussion about Chinese interest in Iceland revolves around four main issues: two manifest and two more speculative. Perhaps tellingly, respondents were much more interested in the latter ones. The two manifest issues are scientific and cultural cooperation on the one hand, in particular the Aurora observatory, and economic cooperation on the other, especially the free trade agreement. The two more speculative issues are an attempted Chinese land buy in northeast Iceland in 2011 and the general Chinese presence in Iceland.

The Aurora Observatory, which involved substantial Chinese–Icelandic scientific cooperation (Lanteigne 2017), was frequently acknowledged, as was the 2012 visit by the icebreaking research vessel *Snow Dragon*, but the information we were able to gather was vague and the people we interviewed did not seem to know the exact scope of this collaboration. The same goes for cultural cooperation in the form of mutual cultural exchanges; they were noted, perhaps as a form of public diplomacy, but little more. Scientific collaboration and cultural exchange are fairly straightforward ways of interacting, and the typical tools of states wanting to increase their visibility in international relations.

The remaining three issues do seem more puzzling, and while estimates about Chinese involvement varied a great deal between respondents, few were able to make sense of it. The free trade agreement, although substantial enough, provides a first example. Signed in 2013, it figures prominently in discussions about China's involvement in the Arctic (Lanteigne 2016). In practice, the agreement did little to better trade relations, as Iceland is too small a market to attract direct Chinese imports. Thus, goods travel through third countries (EU, USA) in spite of the agreement. The negotiation process, though, was perceived by Icelanders to have been fair and unproblematic, and in line with Iceland's general belief in free trade. If anything, Icelanders were believed to have been more in the lead than the Chinese, and were able to change a number of points to their liking. As to the drivers behind the agreement on the part of China, there is little consensus. Some saw the agreement and the increase in mutual official visits as beneficial to China, as they were seen to boost China's internal legitimacy by showcasing support in the West for Chinese internal policies, thereby discouraging dissidents at home. Icelandic officials too, our interviewees stressed repeatedly, cherished the opportunity of being photographed alongside important foreign state officials. On the whole, the image that emerged was one in which China is seeking to gain friends and increase its presence in the Arctic, but also as having signed the agreement with Iceland as a 'test case' for further agreements with European states.

Locally, much more attention was paid to the attempts by Chinese tycoon/philanthropist Huang Nubo to buy a large stretch of land at Grímsstaðir in the northeast of the island in 2011, an attempt that was seen as a key indicator of Chinese interest. This was often mentioned in conjunction with the possible opening of Arctic trade routes, and the possibility of building a trade hub in Iceland in the future. The attempted purchase covered a large tract of land, amounting to about 0.3 per cent of Iceland's total land area, the goal allegedly being to build a holiday resort including golf courses and hotels. The purchase had gained the backing of local and national political interests, and it was prevented only at the last minute by the Minister of the Interior – against strong pressure (New York Times 2011, 2013). Few Icelanders, however, have found Nubo's plan to be viable, and there has thus been widespread belief that there must have been ulterior motives. Some have, for instance, mentioned the possibility of building an airstrip or a harbour along the northern sea route.

On the whole, China has more of a presence in Icelandic discourse than Russia, but this presence is ambiguous. Public diplomacy efforts aside, there is a fair amount of distrust of China, and its policies raise some suspicion. A case in point is the new Chinese Embassy building in downtown Reykjavik. Based on our interviews, the estimate of the number of people working there varied enormously, between 15 and 500 people. In general, representations of a threat from China seem to go hand in hand with a more nationalistic stance on Iceland's foreign policy; one respondent even suggested what seems a highly unlikely argument, that the Chinese were 'infiltrating' Icelandic society (cf. Einarsson et al. 2014).

In sum, it is important not to overestimate great-power interest in Iceland, or the role of the great powers in Icelandic discourse. The current sanctions regime implies that Russia is on the Icelandic agenda (Reykjavik Economics 2016; Thorhallsson and Gunnarsson 2017), but this is related to the export of fish, not to questions of political order. Other than that, Russia is largely absent from debates. China has been higher on the agenda, to the extent that many interviewees seemed genuinely preoccupied with the modest Chinese presence in Iceland. The Chinese overtures have been met with scepticism and outright distrust. If they have been intended as public diplomacy initiatives, with ulterior motives of undermining Western hegemony, they have been extremely poorly executed.

However, reflections on the strategic course of Iceland today are few and far between, at least beyond academic circles and specific policy debates (Bailes and Ólafsson 2014). Defence in Iceland, respondents argued repeatedly, was about safety, or at most societal security, and the population feared natural disasters more than they did military threats (see also Petursson 2014). Indeed, to Icelanders, as they themselves stress, all politics is local. Whereas Iceland is an outward-looking country, with a strong interest in the world, the political discourse is decidedly local, in the sense that the world is made to matter for Icelandic politics. As is evident in the cases of the proposed Russian loan, the Chinese attempted land acquisition and the Chinese Embassy, the important factor is how these things play out (or not) in local discourse. 'Russia' and 'China' can be used for political leverage and to mobilize support domestically. The focus is nevertheless almost exclusively local – what the implications will be for Iceland – rather than geopolitical or economic. As noted by Thorhallsson (2013: 16): 'Iceland's foreign policy still bears the hallmark of the past. Accordingly, the political discourse has been structured by a quest for self-determination, protection of identity and the concept of preserving the country's sovereignty and independence.'

'Russia' and 'China' can also be used for international leverage. While we cannot conclude that either China or Russia have attempted to gain influence at the expense of the USA in Iceland through goods substitution, the case of the proposed Russian loan to Iceland nevertheless highlights an important feature of goods substitution. The mechanism of goods substitution is not only one though which great powers may compete for influence over smaller 'client' states, but also one which these 'client' states can take advantage of by enticing competition for the provision of goods with a view to forcing the hand of an unwilling hegemon. And, interestingly, there are some signs that the USA might once again have an increasing interest in Iceland (Winger and Petursson 2016). Thus, rather than concluding that there is, and has been, a clear great-power competition over influence in Iceland, we suggest that much of the great-power presence and interest in Iceland is the result of Iceland's willingness to play great powers off against one another.

Greenland

Until 1953, Greenland was run as a Danish colony, and had had an American military presence since 1941. With geopolitical tensions, growing American interests and increasing international sentiments in favour of decolonization, Greenlanders were then given equal rights, and Greenland was incorporated as a Danish province (Beukel et al. 2010). Growing nationalism led to home rule being established in 1979, which deepened in 2009 through the Self Government Act. Desires for full independence are explicit in Greenlandic politics, but tempered by economic dependence on Denmark and the EU (Gad 2014). This can be seen in the block grant from the Danish state, which covers just over 50 per cent of the government budget (and around 30 per cent of GDP), but also in the way Greenlandic economics are still heavily focused on Denmark. For Greenland to become independent, alternative revenue streams have to be established (Mortensen 2013; Taagholt and Brooks 2016). Greenland is, furthermore, dependent on Denmark beyond its financial situation. Most of the central Greenlandic administration is staffed by Danes, and Greenland is dependent on Copenhagen for skilled labour to staff other key functions such as the health sector. Danish is still the working language of the Greenlandic administration. Even though the EU provides economic support to Greenland through various mechanisms, the EU does not assume the role as hegemon or proxy hegemon in domestic Greenlandic politics. As such, dependence on the EU does not structure the domestic policy space. Therefore, we do not discuss Greenlandic–EU relations in great detail (Adler-Nissen and Gad 2013).

A background of colonialism has led to a level of distrust of Denmark in Greenland, and potential Greenlandic independence was mentioned by many commentators in the aftermath of increased home rule. Nationalist arguments reached a peak in 2011–13 (Taagholt and Brooks 2016). However, Greenlandic identity is oriented more towards post-colonial politics than around Greenland's current and future role in the world. Greenlandic external relations are largely formulated and put into action by a limited group of individuals in politics and the government administration. Several of these have had an explicitly nationalist agenda. Politicians in Nuuk make no secret of their medium-term ambitions to achieve independence from Denmark. This, quite often, is based on a vision of large future foreign investments in Greenland. Thus, alternative sources for revenue are high on the agenda, and the possibility of goods substitution in the form of revenue from new sources would seem to be both likely and desirable by many people in Greenland.

This local interest in external investments has been mirrored by a significant uptick in global interest in Greenland, described as a virtual 'gold rush' (or 'cold rush') (Boersma and Foley 2014; Wilson 2017). One of the most talked about features of this new interest has been the alleged Chinese desire to become engaged in Greenlandic mining. In October 2013, Greenland lifted its ban on uranium mining (Vestergaard 2015), and it was widely assumed that Chinese companies (and workers) would be prominently present in the mining of Greenland's uranium and other rare earth elements, as well as iron ore and other (as of yet) unexplored minerals. Yet, despite the 'hype' about Chinese interest in Greenland, little of this has materialized.

In the diplomatic realm, Greenland has had its own Brussels office since 1992 (Ackrén 2014). The opening of a Greenlandic Representation in Washington, DC in 2014 was seen as a first step towards establishing a presence in Beijing. Although Nuuk's strategic vision was to forge closer ties with China with a view to facilitating a larger Chinese financial investment in Greenland, there was an understanding that, for tactical reasons, representation in the USA had to come first. Representation in Beijing has nevertheless not yet materialized. These elements of a separate foreign policy, alongside Denmark yet distinguished from it, have come to a halt, largely due to lack of development of the mining sector. Conversely, the practical consequences of Greenland's current attachment to Denmark for the Danes are unresolved. When, for instance, Denmark claimed the North Pole in 2014, it was stressed in Greenland that the initiative was strictly Greenlandic, and based on a long-term view of the interests of an independent Greenland. Greenland had dictated the terms of the Danish Arctic policy.

Outside the circle of pro-independence politicians, the prospects of Greenlandic independence seemed to most interlocutors rather unlikely, both at the present time and in the near future. Greenland is still strongly dependent on revenues from Denmark, and few developments suggest that this is likely to change. Denmark is still committed to Greenland, although the reason for being so pertains less to financial issues than to the status consequences of being the Kingdom of Denmark and Greenland (Jacobsen 2016; Kjærgaard Rasmussen and Merkelsen 2017). Greenland connects Denmark to a greater and more glorious past, and gives Denmark a seat at tables where it would not otherwise be present (Henriksen and Rahbek-Clemmensen 2017). Greenland gives Denmark an Arctic presence, the possibility of being alongside the USA, China and Russia in the Arctic Council and, on the whole, making Denmark something bigger than 'just another of the Benelux kingdoms' as one respondent put it. It is nevertheless hard for Copenhagen to admit to this. Structurally, then, Denmark, more so than the USA, must be understood as the local hegemon.

This does not mean that the USA has shown no interest in Greenland. The USA still has a significant military presence on the island through the Thule airbase (Berry 2016; Petersen 2011). Although downsized when compared to the Cold War, the Thule base plays an important part in current US global military engagement as a communications hub and for missile early warning and defence. Greenland is also of key importance to the USA and NATO through its geopolitical situation in the Arctic, although this is largely managed by Denmark rather than any direct US involvement. While Greenland is important strategically, until recently this does not seem to have given the island itself any leverage towards the USA; rather, it has made Denmark a more attractive defence partner of the USA and in NATO. From the American side, before 2019, there seems to have been little concern about Greenland's current situation and set-up, with formal independence within the Kingdom of Denmark. The USA, on the whole, seemed to be happy with the current arrangements. From the other side, some concern has been voiced in Nuuk that the USA has not been sensitive enough in its interactions with the local population. A case in point was the award of a large civilian contract on the Thule airbase to an American rather than a Greenlandic bidder. However, no major concerns were generally voiced about the US military presence at Thule in our interviews.

The current situation suggests the *potential* of goods substitution in Greenland; *demand-side drivers* are certainly in place. Should other states such as Russia or China wish to compete with Denmark for influence in Greenland, there might well be a desire for such a deal in Nuuk. But while Greenland today has the ability to declare its independence should it wish to do so, and while Denmark in principle has opened the door to this, it is unlikely that such a process would take place without US involvement.

Given the enthusiasm for independence in Nuuk, the question which must be answered is why there is so little great-power interest in Greenland, and why the anticipated mining rush has not taken place. Despite much being written and the 'hype' around Greenland, even dubbed by some the 'scramble for Greenland', one obvious fact is that there is virtually no Russian interest in the island. And Chinese interests in Greenland are mainly in the mining sector and mainly indirect, subject to a number of limitations. Neither Russia nor China can thus be said to be engaged in direct goods substitution in Greenland.

Rhetoric aside, both South Korea and Japan have been more active towards Greenland than China, with the former sending delegations and engaging in cultural diplomacy. The former South Korean president has visited Greenland, and there have been numerous visits to Greenland by various ambassadors. There is also one consul general (from Iceland) and around ten honorary consuls (although only from 'the West', with the Philippines and Thailand being further candidates) in Nuuk.

Considered from the Chinese side, this situation may seem puzzling at first sight. Although China is present indirectly through partial ownership of Australian mining companies, there is little Chinese presence in Greenland, notwithstanding China's global drive for natural resources. In 2014, it was argued that 'Chinese companies have demonstrated little interest to date in projects in Greenland, despite substantial efforts to attract Chinese investment' (Boersma and Foley 2014: vii) and, in 2017, a survey of Chinese mining interests concluded that 'Greenland is not a high-priority area for Chinese companies because it continues to be seen as an extreme and remote environment (Têtu and Lasserre 2017: 9). The investments foreshadowed only a few years ago have never materialized.

Respondents in Nuuk mentioned that investing in Greenland would represent tremendous outlays, as distances are vast and infrastructure is almost non-existent. Furthermore, China seemed unwilling to incur the political trouble represented by investing in Greenland. Indeed, as the island is solidly within the USA's sphere of influence, large-scale investments there may have been perceived as more of a direct challenge to US influence than China actually intended in the Arctic. As talk increased of the possibilities of China investing in Greenland, it was also argued that the Copenhagen media came to overplay Chinese investment, turning it into an imminent takeover of Greenland when the interest, in practical terms, was only a few Chinese-backed companies looking for investment possibilities (Zeuthen 2017). Against the backdrop of the current lack of great-power interest in Greenland, the scramble for Greenland which was heralded in 2012–13 seems to have been blown out of proportion. Only when Greenlandic authorities had opened up for foreign labour was it announced that this would pave the way for a US$2 billion investment from China in mining, and that several thousand Chinese workers would come to work in Greenland.

The prospects of any large-scale Chinese mining project reduced as the Danish reaction played out. China, wary of international attention to Tibet, did not want to be caught meddling in internal Danish affairs. Consequently, the Chinese Ministry of Foreign Affairs does not have any relations or contact with Greenlandic authorities. Such contacts are handled by issue-specific ministries (mining, fisheries) to underline that China has no political interest in Greenland. These ministries, which are not so concerned with issues of sovereignty, were much easier for Greenland to deal with.

The image of an imminent Chinese takeover, which still is not uncommon tin commentaries, emerged out of the confluence of several factors: first, a general interest in the Arctic over the last decade or so; second, general Chinese interest in the Arctic, as witnessed by its observer status in the Arctic Council; and third, Chinese interest in large mining projects requiring the import of foreign labour due to the lack of skilled local labour. All these factors combined with the Greenlandic interest in foreign investments and the pro-independence Greenlandic agenda, which meant actively seeking alternatives to Danish money.

These developments were picked up by the Danish media and government, which exaggerated China's tentative interest, creating a scare that Greenland might be slipping away (Kjærgaard Rasmussen and Merkelsen 2017) and becoming merely 'a Chinese appendix' (Zeuthen 2017: 2). This 'China hype', made Copenhagen less willing to go along with Greenlandic wishes. Seen from Greenland's perspective, this hype was rather surprising, as it did not reflect the realities of Chinese interest in mining in Greenland, nor the degree of cooperation between the large island and the Asian power. The hype did, in all likelihood, deter some Chinese investments, and probably led to the Chinese backing off somewhat, as they felt unwanted. Yet the major fear on the Greenlandic side was that the USA would be caught up in the China hype. Today, both Greenland and China would seemingly prefer there to be less talk about Chinese interests in Greenland, thus enabling what is perceived as more constructive cooperation. However, there is clearly more Greenlandic interest in China than Chinese interest in Greenland. There is also little Chinese interest in an independent Greenland, as this would undoubtedly imply heightened US presence. Furthermore, the most explicit pro-independence rhetoric stands in contrast to the outside impression that Greenland might be a risky place to do business. This, in combination with the slump in mineral prices, and the many bureaucratic challenges associated with mining in Greenland, has meant that most mining projects in Greenland have been put on hold. Greenland was thus left without the needed investments it had hoped for, and unable to use Chinese investments to leverage political gain

While public goods substitution may be a favoured way for great powers to gain influence at the expense of the hegemon, the case of Greenland suggests that such substitution is more likely to be effective if it is not being constructed as an outright political challenge. This constraint is amplified by Greenland's political status. During interviews in Nuuk, it was time and again stressed how China cares dearly about its reputation, does not take public shaming lightly and is sensitive to challenges about meddling in the internal affairs of other states.

Overall, while the case would at first hand seem to be one in which China would actively engage in public goods substitution, and where Greenlandic pro-independence promoters could turn economic and political dependence on Copenhagen into independence due to Chinese investments, this has not really happened. Probing the case for public goods substitution, it becomes obvious that the extent of Chinese interest in Greenland might not have been as great as Danish and international media reported, and that the hype may in fact have been intended to deter further Chinese involvement.

While there is certainly a desire among some in Greenland for alternative sources of revenue, direct Chinese involvement runs into a number of economic, political and logistical challenges. For China, in short, investing in Greenland may have come to cost more, economically and politically, than the Chinese were willing to risk. Close observers argue that the narrative of heavy Chinese interest and involvement in Greenland probably says less about China and Chinese interests, than about the dynamics of the relationship between Greenland and Denmark. Even with Greenlandic independence a possibility in the intermediate future, there seems to be no obvious hegemon to take the place of those already existing. On the contrary, it seems reasonable to interpret the recent strong uptick in US interest in Greenland as an unintended consequence of the Greenlandic push for diversification and Chinese investments, and the strong Danish response. While this might over time lead to a shift from Denmark to the USA as the general hegemon, such a shift would obviously not undermine the Western hegemony in Greenland more generally.

The Faroe Islands

The Faroes have not been subject to the same geopolitical interest as their more northerly neighbours. Their Cold War role was less pronounced, and both the strategic potential and the resource potential are less obvious than for Iceland and Greenland. Nevertheless, as a semi-sovereign polity in the North Atlantic, with a long-standing desire for independence, its place in the Western orbit must be explored. The islands have their own trade policy, and increasing control over foreign affairs, with representation in London (for historical reasons, the first to be opened), Brussels, Moscow, Copenhagen and Reykjavik, and Washington and Beijing being discussed. Historical ties to the United Kingdom have been strong and some Faroese expect that, in a crisis situation, the United Kingdom would be more likely to come to the rescue than Denmark. This, combined with no US base and the continued connection to Denmark, has implied that the islands are less Americanized than Iceland. The mindset is decidedly Western but, according to local respondents, there is no fear of Russia. In economic terms, Russia is actually much more important than the USA. All told, American hegemony is decidedly indirect, with most locals referring to Denmark as the hegemon, and some outsiders jokingly suggesting that the true hegemon, in these fairly religious islands, is God. The Faroes nevertheless became part of great-power calculations with the sanctions regime established by the West after the Russian annexation of the Crimea in 2014.

Gradually established, and tightened in the spring and summer of 2014, the Western sanctions against Russia were met in August of the same year by a Russian import ban on foodstuffs from most Western states. The food import ban posed a problem both for Western food companies and Russian consumers, for whom the Russian government vowed to find alternatives. The Faroe Islands, as non-members of the EU and in charge of their own trade policy, offered such an alternative for Russia. The Faroese government simply declared that the food import ban imposed by Russia did not cover the Faroe Islands, making it possible to continue the export of fish to the Russians. This was confirmed at subsequent meetings in Copenhagen and Moscow. At the time of the Faroese–Russian meeting in Moscow, the Faroese had just ended a longer dispute with the EU concerning the quotas on fishery of Atlanto–Scandian herring, and they were thus not on good terms with the EU anyway.

The decision by the Faroese authorities to deepen economic relations with Russia in a time of crisis led to widespread criticism both in Denmark and locally. Sjúrdur Skaale, a Faroese member of the Danish parliament, said that the Faroese 'stabbed the West and NATO in the back' by helping Russia with the embargo (Gardel 2014a). Mr. Skaale has also called the Faroese Prime Minister 'Putin's useful idiot' (Gardel 2014b). Later, however, he recanted somewhat, arguing that Faroese trade with Russia promotes peace-keeping (Skaale 2015). The self-perception of the Faroes as actually doing the West a favour by keeping open lines of communication with Moscow seems fairly widespread in the islands. The Faroese Prime Minister (*Løgmand*) further argued, in August 2015, that the Faroese did not exploit the situation but merely conducted business as usual. He also stated that the Faroes had no other option than to trade with the Russians because export of fish is the main source of income on the Faroe Islands (Højgaard Sørensen et al. 2015). This attitude was mirrored by a number of local respondents – they are not really proud of make money from the sanctions, but pragmatically they will take the opportunity when it is offered.

The Faroese authorities have also anticipated cooperation with Russia on other areas as well as fish exports. In March 2015, the Faroe Islands opened a representation in Moscow, and the leader of the representation has repeatedly visited the Russian Arctic to prepare for further collaboration on fishing and aquaculture. In the islands, the increased contacts with Russia are read into a narrative of long-standing contact, particularly regarding fisheries, with Russian trawlers frequenting Faroese waters since the 1980s. However, apart from the current mutual interest in fish being sold, there is little perceived interest in the Faroes by Russia. On the other hand, while the Faroese are sceptical about Putin, a number of respondents perceived the possibility of closer ties with Russia, even after the sanctions are at some point lifted.

Thus, while the Faroese are eager to exploit the possibilities offered by closer connections with Russia, there is limited reciprocal interest. And China does not really appear in the conversation. As one interviewee noted, the islands are too far south to be considered Arctic, and thus they do not really register in China. The local desire to position the islands as 'Arctic' must necessarily be understood as part of a wider push to be recognized. One state which appears to offer increased recognition is the USA. Unlike Russia and China, the alleged indirect hegemon appears to have a new-found interest in the Faroes. Over recent years there has been an increase in official visits, and from more high-ranking officials than ever before. And, as one local respondent noted, when their American guests were asked why they were suddenly so interested in the Faroes, the reply was simple: 'look at the map'. From the Faroese perspective, the USA is suddenly seeing a need to establish better relations in the area, even bypassing mainland Denmark in the process.

In sum, the current situation allows the Faroes to play on a fluid international setting, and to pragmatically benefit from an intermediate position. Even respondents who are in principle eager to see full independence mentioned that there are benefits to having an ambiguous status. As of now, fish can be sold, without much consideration of global politics. Relatedly, when a formal representation was opened in Moscow in 2015, the Faroese authorities focused on trade rather than broader strategic repercussions. From the Faroese perspective, trade with the USA was unproblematic; thus there was no need for a local representation. The USA, on the other hand, was not happy, as pointedly relayed to Faroese diplomats.

Many Faroese have a self-perception as a Western society, and even though there is obvious resentment against what is perceived as Danish ignorance of Faroese affairs, the calls for outright independence are less prevalent than in Greenland. Furthermore, despite the current exploitation of the rift in the sanctions regime, there is no serious push in the islands for goods substitution. There is a forthright desire to diversify the economic portfolio, and explore whether Russia might have something to offer, but there is also a distinct appreciation of a perceived increased American focus on the Faroes.

Conclusion

The islands of the North Atlantic are quite different from each other, and they have quite different relations with the great powers of the world. The three cases discussed in this chapter thus illustrate a number of points about potential and actual goods substitution: activism from below, the persistence of hegemony and the nestedness of hegemonic relations. To begin with the latter two points, while all three polities understand themselves to be part of 'the West' and are, from an analytical point of view, clearly part of the basis for American hegemony, Iceland is the only polity where an explicit US hegemony is acknowledged (and has been questioned). In Greenland, the USA, at least until President Trump's suggestion of buying the island, has been largely absent from political discourse, and much the same is the case in the Faroes, where more US interest would nevertheless be perceived as positive. To most locals, far more important than the American hegemon, is the (former) Danish imperial centre. Denmark has been the local upholder of Western hegemony, and while there are in general few critics of American hegemony in the Faroe Islands, many would like to see Danish influence reduced or even removed. There is a feeling, not without reason, that Denmark holds the place it does in world politics because of 'the colonial holdings', and that there is little Danish interest in the North Atlantic apart from this enhanced status.

To the extent that American hegemony in the North Atlantic has relied on Danish hegemony in the area being nested within US hegemony over Denmark, the weakening of the Danish link may come to undermine US hegemony. To this should be added the quite obvious Icelandic displeasure with both the USA and the West, following the withdrawal from Keflavik and the bank collapse. Even so, none of these polities would welcome an alternative hegemon, and they all strongly prefer an orderly world, much as they have grown accustomed to. They are, however, seeking to expand their room for agency. Following the typology discussed in Chapter 2, they could thus tentatively be classified as *positionalist*. This point should not be pressed too hard, though, as it assumes more strategic intentionality than we can substantiate. As stressed above, the external relations capacity in the North Atlantic is limited. There is, quite simply, limited exploration of the possible long-term repercussions of specific foreign policies. Symptomatically, we were told during our interviews in Tórshavn that Faroese parliamentarians had been a little surprised about why the then US Secretary of the Navy Ray Mabus chose to visit the Faroe Islands in 2016 (and that US diplomats had been equally astonished about what they saw as a lack of strategic outlook). What matters is largely economic gain and status; the notion that local policies might undermine the order that the polities rely on is not widely debated.

One further reason to downplay the general weakening of hegemony in the North Atlantic is the actions, or the lack thereof, of Russia and China. Russia may have put out feelers towards Iceland in 2008, but it is completely absent from Greenland, and seems to have little interest in the Faroes, beyond importing fish. China is absent from the Faroes, but has some presence in Iceland and Greenland. In Greenland, the interest seems largely economic, while in Iceland there has been more of a political component as well. However, Chinese relations with Denmark complicate approaches to Greenland, and in Iceland the Chinese are viewed with such suspicion that moves intended to undermine hegemony are likely to be met with a severe backlash. Complicating any attempts at establishing new hegemonic relations are strong pro-independence streaks in all three polities. While there is a desire to reduce the importance of Denmark, there is absolutely no desire to accept a new hegemon. All three polities feature a degree of suspicion of foreign powers, and they are hard cases for any aspiring hegemon to crack. The USA, on the other hand, is in a position of relatively unacknowledged hegemony, and could probably even increase its presence in the region without incurring negative blowback.

Thus, while one can observe a lot of local agency in trying to establish contacts and relations with Russia and/or China, and while we can analytically see these processes as undermining hegemony, we need to specify clearly exactly what this agency implies. Local politicians are undoubtedly both seeking to diversify their portfolio of goods providers and use the possibility of having alternative goods providers as leverage towards the West. This finding ties in well with what Sharman (2017: 572) found concerning the relative sovereignty of other microstates that practise 'hierarchy *à la carte*' and enjoy unprecedented latitudes of action. Local policies are nevertheless not explicitly directed towards the West. When hegemony is being undermined, it is a form of collateral damage in the process whereby the North Atlantic polities seek economic betterment, more political independence and increased status. If American hegemony is eventually undermined in the North Atlantic, it seems likely that it will be as a result of a combination of unintended consequences: local actors seeking to gain wealth or glory and reduce the Danish presence; external great powers also trying to make money; and Denmark and the USA failing to step up their game.

8 | *Reflections on the Volume*

OLE JACOB SENDING AND IVER B. NEUMANN

Among the many ways in which this volume has expanded our understanding of the dynamics by which political orders are maintained and may be undermined, two stand out. They are the adding of a bottom layer of goods ecology to extant conceptions, and the suggestion of a new two-by-two matrix which is not based on intentions but rather on the effects of goods substitution. The matrix has two axes: whether or not a state is satisfied with a given order, and whether or not a state is satisfied with the distribution of goods within that order at any one given time. A state that is satisfied with both is status quo-oriented, whereas a state that is satisfied with the order but not with the distribution, is positionalist (in the sense that it wants to change relative positions within the order). A state that is satisfied with the order but not with the distribution of goods is revisionist, while a state that is dissatisfied with both is revolutionary. A key purchase of this scheme is that it helps us specify how one and the same state – say, China – may generate effects that are both reformist and positionalist, and so the scheme may help us specify what it means to be a revisionist power. In this concluding chapter, we sum up the value added of talking about goods ecology, and suggest three ways in which the conceptualization may be further developed. These concern the question of identity, the search for recognition and coproduction, and the prospect of hegemonic self-harm.

Goods Ecology

This book gives us a new set of analytical tools with which to analyze the dynamic by which international political orders in general, and hegemony in particular, are produced and maintained, and how they may unravel. Rather than focusing on hegemonic clout, balancing, or on changes in material or ideational power structures, the editors provide us with an original and analytically powerful framework organized around *goods substitution*. Hegemonic orders are sustained, they argue, by the provision of public, private, and pool goods in exchange for political support. This is in keeping with a social contract view, much like David Lake's view of hierarchy in which hierarchy is based on an exchange, as are international orders more generally (Lake 2009). A hegemon provides a subordinate state, like Norway or Colombia, with a good – security – in exchange for political loyalty.

In Chapter 1 of this book, Nexon, Cooley, and Andersen elaborate on this approach by adding a new bottom layer to the picture. They suggest that it is not sufficient to look at such contracts or exchanges in terms of norms and rules that guide specific exchanges, or even in terms of the institutional setting within which this happens, for underneath these two strata we find a layer that constitutes the very terrain upon which states graft their strategies. This layer they name the *ecology* of goods provision. This ecology may include a whole range of actual and potential competing suppliers. It is also a terrain where one will find unintended consequences of state and nonstate action. From such a perspective, international relations emerge as a marketplace where suppliers of public goods are typically great powers, and consumers of such goods are all other states. Crucially, this means that hegemonic orders are products not so much of one state's ability to legitimate or coerce others into complying with its demands, but of the configuration of goods provision by a range of different actors. One empirical implication is that a US-led hegemonic order may be undermined not only through direct confrontation between the USA and China, but also by China succeeding in providing alternative goods that undermine the value of US-produced goods. The upshot of this is that hegemonic orders may depend as much on the agency, and choices, of subordinate actors choosing between rival producers of public goods.

The idea that American hegemony may be undermined by "a thousand papercuts" is a highly significant one, and flows directly from the enlarging of asset substitution through a bottom layer of ecological goods. As the editors note, "the most consequential undermining of hegemony is typically more routine and proceeds through a slow hollowing out – or alteration – of the existing order" (Chapter 1). This move opens a whole new empirical terrain, where hegemonic orders are made and remade, in the form of institutional frameworks through which foreign policy is made in subordinate states. Small shifts in the assessment by policymakers in client states of the goods provided by the

USA may lead to hedging and pooling of resources, with a view to making the client states less dependent on the USA as a provider of security.

For example, while commitment to club good-providing NATO is still strong among EU members, it is worth noting that the recent Permanent Structured Cooperation (PESCO) initiative among EU members gained momentum amid increased uncertainty about US commitments to European security. Similarly, many developing countries remain equally committed to the Organisation for Economic Co-Operation and Development – Development Assistance Committee (OECD-DAC) model of development assistance, where the USA and its allies coordinate modes of providing development assistance. However, the relative importance of official development assistance has decreased significantly, with private funding increasing significantly at the same time as China is increasingly offering loans on different terms to many developing countries. The result is not a shift in alliances and political loyalties as such, but a small change in the configuration of goods provided, where the political and economic costs of defecting from US demands or wishes are reduced, the results of which may be significant.

By introducing the language of a "goods ecology," the editors shift our focus from rules and norms that are typically said to define and structure the international system to a whole new dimension: the rules and norms of the system emerge here *as* goods. The rules and standards of the international financial system, for example, are goods provided principally by the USA. The recent spat over the Joint Comprehensive Plan of Action with Iran between the USA and Europe demonstrates this: The USA is using its considerable clout over international financial markets to police the behavior of others with regard to economic relations with Iran. This power comes from the fact that the USA is the key provider of this "good," in the form of Society of Worldwide Interbank Financial Telecommunications (SWIFT) and other mechanisms for transnational financial flows. European states – having opted to uphold the Iran deal – have developed an alternative system – a rival good – for financial interaction with Iran to bypass the US-controlled system (Farrell and Newman 2019).

The analytical intent and purchase of this approach lies in how the actors of the system are conceptualized. The power of the USA is analyzed in terms of the scope and contents of its goods provision relative to other states, such as China. This means at least three things:

- The stress is on relations between units. However, in contrast to much of the emerging literature on "relationalism," which tends to excel at abstract theorizing but fail on empirical operationalization, the focus on goods ecologies anchors these relations in the production and consumption of goods, whether in terms of security provision, financial systems, or global infrastructures for transport (e.g., freedom of navigation at sea). In effect, we move from relationalism as a nominal or thin concept to a thick one. For relations are now expressed within and through the logic of asset substitution, understood as an ecological system for the production and consumption of goods.
- The focus on the dynamics of goods production and consumption resolves the thorny issue of intentions. We need not discuss whether China intends to challenge US hegemony, since US hegemony may be undermined by asset substitution regardless of Chinese intentions. As both Bader and Cooley discuss (Chapter 4 and Chapter 5, respectively) with regard to the Asia Infrastructure Investment Bank (AIIB), this *does* undermine the USA's position by virtue of providing an alternative source of funding for infrastructure that is not funded or controlled by the USA. And as Adler-Nissen, de Carvalho, and Leira (Chapter 7) and Andersen (Chapter 6) discuss, the effects of Chinese asset substitution with regard to Greenland and to several Latin American countries may be both reformist and positionalist, depending not on Chinese intentions, but on the responses from subordinate actors.
- The focus on goods substitution makes the discussion of hegemony a much more social one. Here, we are moving towards the already noted second major contribution of this volume, which is to specify the phenomenon of revisionism (see, especially, Chapter 2). Extant agent-oriented approaches see states other than the hegemon either as status quo-oriented, or as revisionist. The corollary is that extant approaches tend to treat any nonmilitary and actually or potentially revisionary action as analytically uninteresting or, at the very best, as a case of what is called soft-balancing. If we want a proper social analysis, however, this will not do. By focusing on goods substitution, this volume offers a social and hence more fine-grained

approach to this issue, which captures the importance of intended as well as nonintended action, be that of a nonconflictual or conflictual nature. By the same token, instead of being seen simply as revisionist, action may be further specified as being undermining either of a certain hegemonic order, or of the hegemon as such. Agents and/ or actions that undermine order are called reformist, while agents and/or action that undermine the hegemon specifically, or the pecking order (distribution of power) more generally, are called positionalists. Only agents and/or actions that do both are revisionist.

The empirical chapters demonstrate how these distinctions matter. There are a number of empirical examples here of reformist action, be it intentional or unintentional. The framework also allows for analysis of how actions by the hegemon itself may undermine the hegemon's own position. The George W. Bush presidency threw up a number of examples of this, and the Trump presidency spawned even more. Cooley and Nexon (Chapter 2) and Bader (Chapter 4) both use the distinction between all-out revisionists like Russia on the one hand, and a reformist state like China on the other, to pinpoint why an institution such as the Shanghai Cooperation Organization (SCO) does not pose more of a challenge to American hegemony than it does. Where extant scholarship tends to see the SCO simply as a revisionist institution, an ecological goods substitution analysis highlights how the different kinds of counter-hegemonic policies we may observe from Russia and China clash and lead to an institutional gridlock. Here, we have a very clear example of the value of accessing the analysis relationally from an underlying ecological layer, for such an access point makes it possible to explain what happens on the institutional layer where state agents clash.

The Symbolic Dimension of Goods: Between the Social and the Material

If the first major contribution of the book is to add a new structural layer called a goods ecology to the asset substitution approach, the second contribution is to specify the category of "revisionism." A revisionist, Andersen, Cooley, and Nexon aver, may be out either to revise the international order as such, or it may have the more limited aim of changing the distribution of power within the system, usually by strengthening its own position and weakening the position of the hegemon (Chapter 1). In Chapter 2, Cooley and Nexon suggest a two-by-two matrix which yields four kinds of revisionists: those who want to change both the order and its distribution of power – the revisionists proper; those who want change the order but not the distribution – the reformists; those who want to change the distribution but not the order – the positionalists; and those two want to change neither – the status quo oriented.

The book delivers a thorough theoretical examination of the difference between the revisionist and reformist cells of this two-by-two, and is politically pertinent in drawing out how this distinction is analytically apposite for it illuminates the differences between Russian revisionist and Chinese reformist challenges to the present American-led international order. It spends little time on status quo powers beyond noting how an ecology perspective is useful in spelling out exactly how devastating it may be for a hegemon to reduce side payments in the face of increased competition from new rising powers (a point to which we will return in the section "Identity and Coproduction" below). That leaves the positionalist cell, which Andersen discusses in Chapter 6, demonstrating that China, for example, is both reformist and positionalist, depending on the reception in the specific region.

While this differentiation between types of revisionism is important, it also highlights a tension in conceiving of international orders as two dimensional, with rules and norms defining the *architecture* of that order, and the goods ecology capturing the *distribution of power* within it (Chapter 1). That is: If the architecture is distinct from the distribution, we have to assume that what constitutes a "good" is relatively independent from the rules and norms (architecture) of the system. In Chapter 1 and in Chapter 2, we see this distinction being used to good effect. However, Chapter 1 *also* stresses that rules and norms may alternatively be considered *as* goods, and that what "counts" as a good is shaped by the dominant meanings embedded in the rules and norms of the international architecture. This analytical tack is most clearly on display when the editors draw on Bourdieu to discuss how different forms of capital (aka goods) take on different significance and purchase depending on the configuration of international fields. This more social take on goods ecology is also on display in Chapter 7 by Adler-Nissen, de Carvalho, and Leira on the centrality of status, and in Chapter 3 by Rumelili and Towns on the performative effects of country performance indicators. Had the editors stayed with the fields and capital analytic, the interdependence of the architectural and distributive aspects of international orders would have looked different.

For example, the examples offered for the analytical value of both positional and reformist states would highlight that reformists rarely want to change only the rules, and not the distribution of power. Rather, they want to change the rules in order to increase the value of the type of capital, or goods, where they hold a comparative edge over others, so that they may improve their relative position within the distributive dimension. In Chapter 2, Cooley and Nexon argue that "reformist" states "may seek changes in areas of international order besides the distribution of capabilities," but then they go on to suggest that "international economic order may look unfavorable to politically ascendant economic sectors or interests; or a newly empowered coalition may dislike the international order for ideological reasons." Similarly, they suggest that a case of a positional strategy would be if "the United States continues down the path of trying to revise the international order along less liberal lines," prompting European powers to engage in goods substitution, while still insisting that this is counter-goods substitution, but not counter-order substitution.

The conception of goods may thus be a bit too muscular in its approach to ecology, for it occludes the lingering importance of hierarchies of what counts as goods, and competition over how they should be valued. In short, the social dimension is somewhat marginalized. This has knock-on effects beyond the categories of revisionism. As we discuss in the next section, "Identity and Coproduction," the social dimension of hegemony, and of international orders more generally, also comes up when we consider how subordinate states – consumers of goods provided by a hegemon – develop self-identities that ward off strategic bargaining and the logic of goods substitution over time.

Identity and Coproduction

The beauty of the model of goods substitution is that it has a clear logic, providing a new framework for capturing how states assess the cost and benefits of relying on a single producer of, say, security, and make choices about how to procure it accordingly. At its core is a social contract view, where subordinate actors assess the value of the goods in question and choose what it sees as the best provider of that good. What a social contract view leaves out follows from the analytical separation between goods considered as straightforwardly economic or military, and the social meaning and definition of what counts as a good. As noted above, the valuation and meaning attached to goods does not only vary over time; it can also, we suggest, become constitutive of the identity of the consumer.

In Chapter 6, on Colombia, Andersen highlights how a supply-side factor – to what degree a client state sees a certain purveyor of a good as a problem for political legitimacy – will affect that state's proclivity to seek goods substitution. This is one way in which symbolic meaning attached to the provider of the good, as opposed to the consumption of the good, matters. But there is more going on here: Subordinate states may develop a self-understanding and identity tied to the consumption of goods provided by a hegemon, even investing in producing that very good for the hegemon. States that see themselves as being dependent on the USA as a provider of economic or security goods may make virtue out of necessity, developing narratives about who they are that confirm and justify a subordinate position as not only necessary, but virtuous and good. For example, Norway has developed – much like a number of other Western European states – an identity as a loyal ally of the USA. The logic is that of using one's own resources to, in fact, help *coproduce* the goods in question as a means to be recognized by the USA as a trustworthy, important, and relevant ally (Paul et al. 2014; Wohlforth et al. 2018).

There may be a range of cases where there may be fierce competition between great powers to produce public goods, but where "consumer decisions" are heavily biased in favor of one provider. States may be conservative, opting to do business with a known provider rather than try a new one, or they may have developed a foreign policy identity that is organized around seeking recognition from the hegemon. In some cases, this identity may evolve into one where the good provided by the hegemon is not seen as a good, but as a political project in which one seeks to be part. In such cases, the goods provided by the hegemon will not only be consumed, but the subordinate state will also try to embed itself within the hegemonic order by seeking to become a coproducer. It becomes a part of that state's narrative of what it wants to be, where the self-understanding shifts from being solely a consumer to a coproducer of the hegemon's global political project (Neumann 2015), seeking recognition from the hegemon on terms set by the hegemon (Sending 2017).

In prolongation of Chapter 3, identity may be thought of as a normative good. An analytical shift of focus in the direction of questions of identity allows us to see how goods provision may shape identities in ways that complicate the pure logic of goods substitution. A strategy of coproduction is consistent with the logic of asset substitution in that it is a strategy of subordinate states to have a say in the design and delivery of public goods. However, an added focus on identity will also nuance the goods substitution perspective by considering the pull of ideological alignment: States assess both the contents of the good *as well as* (i) the character or identity of the producer, and (ii) the political and identity costs of shifting to a new producer. It is hardly conceivable that, say, Denmark, Norway, or the Netherlands would jeopardize their relationship with the USA, given the ideological apparatus and identity-alignment organized around the security good provided by the USA.

This issue goes to the heart of a question that is played down in Chapter 1 and Chapter 2, but that receives more attention in the subsequent chapters even if not theorized as such, namely, the difference between goods and assets (Andersen, Chapter 6). Goods disappear when they are consumed, whereas assets generate value. If we factor in the identity dimension, we may need to differentiate more clearly between goods and assets. Put differently, what is a good to a subordinate actor, may be an asset to the superordinate actor, because the consumption of security by the subordinate actor is an asset for the superordinate actor beyond the loyalty it may generate; the subordinate actor – seeking recognition – seeks to be a coproducer of the very good that is supposed to be provided by the superordinate actor. Elsewhere, we have analyzed Norwegian foreign policy in such terms, as having to do with "systems maintenance" of the US-led international order through investments in disaster relief, peace and reconciliation efforts, and other practices that may forestall crises, or alleviate them as they play out (Neumann 2015). Another example would be how Norway tries to use humanitarian assistance to secure a seat at the table next to the USA, as in the case of the significant funding to the Palestinian Authorities, which has provided Norway with the position as chair of the Ad Hoc Liaison Committee that coordinates aid to the Palestinian Authorities, in which the USA and the EU are both cosponsors (Sending 2015). Norwegian diplomats note explicitly that this is the key reason why Norwegian Foreign Ministers can call up the US Secretary of State directly (authors' interviews).[1]

The question boils down to whether the actors *themselves* actually treat the currency of foreign policy – alliances, trade deals, economic support, security guarantees, etc. as "goods" to be consumed. Given the inspiration from social contract theory, one may ask whether Lake´s discussion of hierarchy is worth exploring in more detail in this regard. For Lake (2009), there is a clear transaction at work in establishing and maintaining hierarchies, similar to what the editors discuss in this book. However, Lake introduces another element, which is efforts aimed at *legitimizing* the arrangements in place. The economic and political costs of defection increase for the subordinate actor, and the cost of securing loyalty and support from the subordinate actor decreases if the arrangement is legitimized. Depending on how naturalization and legitimization works within a particular case of hierarchy/hegemony, the asset in question may not be approached as a "good" to be consumed at all, but as reflecting an already legitimized hierarchical order, where subordinate actors think in terms of loyalty and trust in the provider. Put differently, loyalty to the "brand" of a good (this brand being linked to its provider) may be important in explaining subordinate state behavior as it ponders which supplier to choose. This may help explain why the most clear-cut examples of states shifting from one provider to another mentioned in this book are Turkey, Egypt, and the Philippines, whose ideological ties with the USA are less strong than most European states.

Relatedly, initial power differentials may not be well captured by the contractual dynamic that seems to underwrite good substitution. The case of the AIIB seems to be primarily about how a range of European states want to be part of *supplying* or coproducing rather than consuming the "asset" that China, through the AIIB, can be said to provide (Bader, Chapter 4). This suggests that the logic of goods substitution may operate as much on the supplier side as on the demand/consumption side for many states: would-be consumers want to be part of the

---

[1] Access to policymakers in the USA is a top priority of Norwegian governments (as is also the case for most other states of similar size and military strength which rely on US protection and support). Norway´s investments in peace and reconciliation efforts, for example, tracks US strategic interests (see Neumann 2015).

supply-side as a way to secure their position as trusted partner in the eyes of the hegemon.

Conclusion: Hegemonic Self-Harm?

The focus on goods substitution shifts the analytical terrain on which to discuss the dynamics, and possible unraveling, of hegemonic orders. This book gives a number of valuable examples of how different types of revisionist states, wittingly or unwittingly, are at the present time dismantling the American-led international order. Let us end by looking at how the USA is reacting to all this. Brock Tessman, and Wojtek Wolfe argue that: "second-tier states often benefit from public goods or direct subsidies that are provided by the system leader. If the leading state sees its relative power advantage erode as the system shifts toward multipolarity, it may choose to reduce or eliminate some or all of the public goods and subsidies it provides" (Tessman and Wolfe 2011, 219–20).

This hypothesis seems about to be verified. On June 1, 2017, US President Donald announced that the USA would not participate in the 2015 Paris Agreement on Climate Change. The USA has a history of reservation about participation in a range of international agreements, cases in point being the International Criminal Court (ICC) and the Kyoto Protocol on greenhouse gas emissions. Such decisions notwithstanding, the USA has been able to uphold a position as the major provider of goods for other states, both in terms of economic interaction and of security guarantees. The USA invests far more than other states in securing freedom of navigation – a key ingredient of maritime trade routes – and in backstopping the international financial system, both directly through the dollar as international currency, and indirectly, through its position as major shareholder in the International Monetary Fund (IMF). As has become clear during the last three years, however, Trump´s "transactional" approach to established allies has meant that broader institutional frameworks for the production of security goods – NATO in particular – have come under strain.

The signal to allies seems to be that the USA will no longer pay for their security. Trump's failure to reach consensus on a G7 communique, his criticism of the EU, and his outright support for Brexit, is similarly an indication that the USA under Trump was far less committed to providing goods for others in exchange for political support.

The uncertainty thereby produced in European capitals and beyond is a good illustration of the analytical purchase of goods substitution: The Atlantic bond depends less than we think on shared history and ideological convergence, and much more on the USA's commitment to producing goods that European allies consume. However, this illustration comes with a twist, for the dynamic by which hegemony is now being undermined before our very eyes is not caused by the emergence of a rival producer of goods, nor by the decision in Europe to pool resources of its own accord. Rather, it is caused by the USA making decisions that obviously undermine its own position, distancing itself from states that are ideologically aligned with it, and creating uncertainty for subordinate states about the continued value of engaging in coproduction. It is a case of hegemonic self-harm – of increasing uncertainty about the consistency and quality of the goods to be provided, which prompts allies to look elsewhere, as Cooley and Nexon (2020) discuss extensively.

This means that the logic of the analytical framework can be extended from goods "substitution" to also include the consistency and quality of the goods produced: Hegemony can be undermined not only by a thousand papercuts, but by decisions, such as the signature to withdraw from the Iran agreement, which reduce the quality of the goods in the eyes of subordinate actors. Indeed, such actions may further exacerbate the push by rival actors, such as China, to move in and fill the gap by insisting on its commitment to multilateralism and the provision of public goods. We should stress that this does not challenge the analytical framework applied here, but it does bring us back to the question of the decisions by the hegemon itself that affect both the perception of the goods or assets, and of the configuration of goods producers in the hegemon's environment. The analytical and political relevance of the theoretical and empirical job done in this book could hardly have been more timely.

Bibliography

Ackrén, Maria (2014). "Greenlandic Paradiplomatic Relations," pp. 42–61 in Lassi Heininen (ed.) *Security and Sovereignty in the North Atlantic*: Houndmills, UK: Palgrave.

Adamson, Fiona B. (2005). "Global Liberalism versus Political Islam: Competing Ideological Frameworks in International Politics." *International Studies Review* 7(4): 547–569.

Adler-Nissen, Rebecca (2008). "The Diplomacy of Opting Out: A Bourdieudian Approach to National Integration Strategies." *JCMS: Journal of Common Market Studies* 46(3): 663–684. https://doi.org/10.1111/j.1468-5965.2008.00799.x.

Adler-Nissen, Rebecca (2014a). "The Faroe Islands: Independence Dreams, Globalist Separatism and the Europeanization of Postcolonial Home Rule." *Cooperation and Conflict* 49(1): 55–79.

Adler-Nissen, Rebecca (2014b). "Stigma Management in International Relations: Transgressive Identities, Norms, and Order in International Society." *International Organization* 68(1): 143–176.

Adler-Nissen, Rebecca and Ulrik Pram Gad (2013). *European Integration and Postcolonial Sovereignty Games: The EU Overseas Countries and Territories*. London: Routledge.

Adler-Nissen, Rebecca and Vincent Pouliot (2014). "Power in Practice: Negotiating the International Intervention in Libya." *European Journal of International Relations* 20(4): 889–911. https://doi.org/10.1177/1354066113512702.

Adler-Nissen, Rebecca and Ayşe Zarakol (2020). "Struggles for Recognition: The Liberal International Order and the Merger of its Discontents." *International Organization*: 1-24. https://doi.org/10.1017/S0020818320000454.

AIIB (2020). "The Asian Infrastructure Investment Bank." www.aiib.org/en/about-aiib/index.html.

Allan, Bentley B., Srdjan Vucetic, and Ted Hopf. (2018). "The Distribution of Identity and the Future of International Order: China's Hegemonic Prospects." *International Organization* 72(4): 839–869. https://doi.org/10.1017/S0020818318000267.

Allison, Graham (2017). *Destined for War: Can America and China Escape Thucydides's Trap?* Boston, NY: Mariner Books.

Allison, Roy (2004). "Regionalism, Regional Structures and Security Management in Central Asia." *International Affairs* 80(3): 463–483.

Alter, Karen J. and Sophie Meunier. (2009). "The Politics of International Regime Complexity." *Perspectives on Politics* 7(1): 13–24. https://doi.org/10.1017/S1537592709090033.

Ambrosio, Thomas (2008). "Catching the 'Shanghai spirit': How the Shanghai Cooperation Organization Promotes Authoritarian Norms in Central Asia." *Europe–Asia Studies* 60(8): 1321–1344.

Anderlini, Jamil (2015). "UK Move to Join China-Led Bank a Surprise Even to Beijing." *Financial Times*, March 26. www.ft.com/intl/cms/s/0/d33fe d8a-d3a1-11e4-a9d3-00144feab7de.html#axzz4AyCorXTm.

Anderlini, Jamil and Kiran Stacey (2015). "George Osborne Rejected Diplomatic Advice to Join China-Led Bank." *Financial Times*, March 26.

Andersen, Morten Skumsrud (2016). "Semi-Cores in Imperial Relations: The Cases of Scotland and Norway." *Review of International Studies* 42 (1): 178–203.

Antonenko, Oksana (2007). "The EU Should Not Ignore the Shanghai Co-operation Organisation." Centre for European Reform, May 11.

Arase, David (2015). "What to Make of the Asian Infrastructure Investment Bank." *The Asan Forum*, June 26.

Ardila, Martha (1991). *Cambio al Norte?* Bogotá: Tercer Mundo.

Ardila, Martha, Diego Cardona, and Arlene B. Tickner (2002). "Introducción. El análisis de la política exterior colombiana: Lugares communes y grendes silencions," pp. 17–44 in Martha Ardila, Diego Cardona, and Arlene B. Tickner (eds.) *Prioridades y Desafíos de la Politica Exterior Colombiana*. Bogotá: Friedrich Ebert Stiftung/Hanss Seidel Stiftung.

Aris, Stephen (2009). "The Shanghai Cooperation Organisation: 'Tackling the Three Evils'. A Regional Response to Non-traditional Security Challenges or an Anti-Western Bloc?" *Europe–Asia Studies* 61(3): 457–482.

Armijo, Leslie Elliott and Cynthia Roberts. (2014). "The Emerging Powers and Global Governance: Why the BRICS Matter," pp. 503–520 in Robert Looney (ed.) *Handbook of Emerging Economies*. New York: Routledge.

Asian Development Bank (2009). *Infrastructure for a Seamless Asia*. Tokyo: Asian Development Bank Institute.

Ayyadi, Islam and Mohammed Kamal. (2016). "China-Israel Arms Trade and Co-operation: History and Policy Implications." *Asian Affairs* 47(2): 260–273.

Bader, Julia (2015). "China, Autocratic Patron? An Empirical Investigation of China as a Factor in Autocratic Survival." *International Studies Quarterly* 59(1): 23–33. https://doi.org/10.1111/isqu.12148.

Bader, Julia (2019). "To Sign or Not to Sign. Hegemony, Global Internet Governance, and the International Telecommunication Regulations." *Foreign Policy Analysis* 15(2): 244–262.

Bailes, Alyson J. K. (2007). "The Shanghai Cooperation Organization and Europe." *China and Eurasia Forum Quarterly* 5(3): 3–18.

Bailes, Alyson J. K. and Kristmundur Þór Ólafsson (2014). "Nordic and Arctic Affairs: + Iceland's National Security Policy: Latest Progress." Centre for Small State Studies, University of Iceland, Reykjavik.

Bailes, Alyson J. K. and Orvar Rafnsson (2012). "Iceland and the EU's Common Security and Defence Policy: Challenge or Opportunity?" *Stjornmal & Stjornsysla* 8(1): 109–131.

Barents Observer (2016). "U.S. Military Returns to Iceland," 10 February. https://thebarentsobserver.com/en/security/2016/02/us-military-returns-iceland.

Barkin, J. Samuel (2010). *Realist Constructivism: Rethinking International Theory*. Cambridge: Cambridge University Press.

Barma, Naazneen, Giacomo Chiozza, Ely Ratner, and Steven Weber (2009). "A World without the West? Empirical Patterns and Theoretical Implications." *The Chinese Journal of International Politics* 2(4): 525–544. https://doi.org/10.1093/cjip/pop013.

Barnhart, Joslyn (2016). "Status Competition and Territorial Aggression: Evidence from the Scramble for Africa." *Security Studies* 25(3): 385–419. https://doi.org/10.1080/09636412.2016.1195620.

BBC (2017). "Russian MPs Pass Bill to Soften Domestic Violence Law," January 27. www.bbc.com/news/world-38767873.

BBC News (2015). "UK Support for China-Backed Asia Bank Prompts US Concern," March 13. www.bbc.com/news/world-australia-31864877.

Beckley, Michael (2012). "China's Century? Why America's Edge Will Endure." *International Security* 36(3): 41–78.

Beissinger, Mark R. (2002). *Nationalist Mobilization and the Collapse of the Soviet State*. Cambridge Studies in Comparative Politics. Cambridge: Cambridge University Press.

Beissinger, Mark R. (2007). "Structure and Example in Modular Political Phenomena: The Diffusion of Bulldozer/Rose/Orange/Tulip Revolutions." *Perspectives on Politics* 5(2): 259–276.

Bermeo, Sarah B. (2016). "Aid Is Not Oil: Donor Utility, Heterogeneous Aid, and the Aid-Democratization Relationship". *International Organization* 70(1): 1–32.

Berry, Dawn Alexandrea (2016). "The Monroe Doctrine and the Governance of Greenland's Security," pp. 102–121 in D. A. Berry, Nigel Bowles, and Halbert Jones (eds.) *Governing the North American Arctic: Sovereignty, Security, and Institutions*. Houndmills, UK: Palgrave.

Beukel, Erik, Frede P. Jensen, and Jens Elo Rytter (2010). *Phasing out the Colonial Status of Greenland, 1945–54*. Copenhagen: Museum Tusculanum Press.

Bitar, Sebastian E. (2015). *US Military Bases, Quasi-bases, and Domestic Politics in Latin America*. London: Palgrave.

Boersma, Tim and Kevin Foley (2014). *The Greenland Gold Rush: Promise and Pitfalls of Greenland's Energy and Mineral Resources*. Washington, DC: Energy Security Initiative, John Thornton China Center, Brookings Institution.

Bourdieu, Pierre (2011). "The Forms of Capital" pp. 81–93 in Imre Szeman and Timothy Kaposy (eds.) *Cultural Theory: An Anthology*. Malden, MA: Wiley-Blackwell.

Bower, Adam (2017). *Norms without the Great Powers: International Law and Changing Social Standards in World Politics*. Oxford: Oxford University Press.

Bradley, Christopher G. (2015). "International Organizations and the Production of Indicators: The Case of the Freedom House," pp. 27–73 in Sally Engle Merry, Kevin E. Davis, and Benedict Kingsbury (eds.) The Quiet Power of Indicators: Measuring Governance, Corruption, and Rule of Law. Cambridge: Cambridge University Press.

Brautigam, Deborah (2009). *The Dragon's Gift: The Real Story of China in Africa*. New York: Oxford University Press.

Brooks, Stephen G. and William C. Wohlforth (2005a). "International Relations Theory and the Case against Unilateralism." *Perspectives on Politics* 3(3): 509–524.

Brooks, Stephen G. and William C. Wohlforth (2005b). "Hard Times for Soft Balancing." *International Security* 30(1): 72–108.

Brooks, Stephen G. and William C. Wohlforth (2008). *World Out of Balance: International Relations and the Challenge of American Primacy*. Princeton, NJ: Princeton University Press.

Broome, André (2010). *The Currency of Power: The IMF and Monetary Reform in Central Asia*. Basingstoke, UK: Palgrave Macmillan.

Brütsch, Christian and Mihaela Papa (2013). "Deconstructing the BRICS: Bargaining Coalition, Imagined Community, or Geopolitical Fad?" *Chinese Journal of International Politics* 6(3): 299–327.

Bueno de Mesquita, Bruce and Alastair Smith (2016). "Competition and Collaboration in Aid- for-Policy Deals." *International Studies Quarterly* 60(3): 413–426.

Bukovansky, Mlada (2015). "Corruption Rankings: Constructing and Contesting the Global Anti-Corruption Agenda," pp. 60–84 in Alexander Cooley and Jack Snyder, (eds.) *Ranking the World: Grading States as a Tool for Global Governance.* Cambridge: Cambridge University Press.

Bull, Hedley (1977). *The Anarchical Society: A Study of Order in World Politics.* London: Macmillan.

Bunce, Valerie (1985). "The Empire Strikes Back: The Evolution of the Eastern Bloc from a Soviet Asset to a Soviet Liability." *International Organization* 39(1): 1–46.

Busch, Marc L. (2007). "Overlapping Institutions, Forum Shopping, and Dispute Settlement in International Trade." *International Organization* 61(4): 735–761.

Buzan, Barry (2010). "China in International Society: Is 'Peaceful Rise' Possible?" *The Chinese Journal of International Politics* 3(1): 5–36. https://doi.org/10.1093/cjip/pop014.

Buzan, Barry and Richard Little (2000). *International Systems in World History.* Oxford: Oxford University Press.

Byman, Daniel (2019). "Israel's Four Fronts." *Survival* 61(2): 167–188. https://doi.org/10.1080/00396338.2019.1589094.

Callaghan, Mike and Paul Hubbard (2016). "The Asian Infrastructure Investment Bank: Multilateralism on the Silk Road." *China Economic Journal* 15(3): 116–139.

Campbell, Kurt M. and Rush Doshi (2020). "The Coronavirus Could Reshape Global Order." *Foreign Affairs*, March 18. www.foreignaffairs.com/articles/china/2020-03-18/coronavirus-could-reshape-global-order.

Carrère, Cèline (2006). "Revisiting the Effects of Regional Trade Agreements on Trade Flows with Proper Specification of the Gravity Model." *European Economic Review* 50(2): 223–247. https://doi.org/10.1016/j.euroecorev.2004.06.001.

Chan, Lai-Ha (2017). "Soft Balancing against the US 'Pivot to Asia': China's Geostrategic Rationale for Establishing the Asian Infrastructure Investment Bank." *Australian Journal of International Affairs* 71(6): 568–590.

Chan, Steve (2008). *China, the U.S., and the Power Transition Theory: A Critique.* New York: Routledge.

Chapman, Terrence L., Patrick J. McDonald, and Scott Moser (2015). "The Domestic Politics of Strategic Retrenchment, Power Shifts, and Preventive War." *International Studies Quarterly* 59(1): 133–144.

Charap, Samuel and Timothy J. Colton (2018). *Everyone Loses: The Ukraine Crisis and the Ruinous Contest for Post-Soviet Eurasia.* Abingdon, UK: Routledge.

Chen, Yiyi (2012). "China's Relationship with Israel, Opportunities and Challenges, Perspectives from China." *Israel Studies* 17(3): 1–21.

Chin, Gregory T. (2014). "The BRICS-Led Development Bank: Purpose and Politics Beyond the G20." *Global Policy* 5(3): 366–373.

Christensen, Thomas J. (2015). *The China Challenge. Shaping the Choices of a Rising Power*. New York: W. W. Norton & Company.

Clarke, Michael (2010). "Widening the Net: China's Anti-Terror Laws and Human Rights in the Xinjiang Uyghur Autonomous Region." *International Journal of Human Rights* 14(4): 542–558.

Clarke, Michael E. (2011). *Xinjiang and China's Rise in Central Asia, 1949–2009*. New York: Routledge.

Clark, Samuel (2016). *Distributing Status: The Evolution of State Honors in Western Europe*. Montreal: McGill-Queens University Press.

Cohen, Ariel (2006). "After the G-8 Summit: China and the Shanghai Cooperation Organization." *China and Eurasia Forum Quarterly* 4(3): 51–64.

Cohen, Benjamin J. (2012). "The Yuan Tomorrow? Evaluating China's Currency Internationalisation Strategy." *New Political Economy* 17(3): 361–371.

Colgan, Jeff D. and Nicholas J. Miller (2019). "Rival Hierarchies and the Origins of Nuclear Technology Sharing." *International Studies Quarterly* 63(2): 310–321.

Cooley, Alexander (2005). *Logics of Hierarchy: The Organization of Empires, States and Military Occupations*. Ithaca, NY: Cornell University Press.

Cooley, Alexander (2009). "Cooperation Gets Shanghaied: Russia, China and the SCO." *Foreign Affairs*, December 14. www.foreignaffairs.com/articles/china/2009-12-14/cooperation-gets-shanghaied/.

Cooley, Alexander (2012). *Great Games, Local Rules: The New Great Power Contest in Central Asia*. Oxford: Oxford University Press.

Cooley, Alexander (2013). "The League of Authoritarian Gentlemen." Foreign Policy, January 31.

Cooley, Alexander (2015). "The Emerging Politics of International Rankings and Ratings: A Framework for Analysis" pp. 1–38 in Alexander Cooley and Jack Snyder (eds.) *Ranking the World: Grading States as a Tool for Global Governance*. Cambridge: Cambridge University Press.

Cooley, Alexander (2019). "Ordering Eurasia: The Rise and Decline of Liberal Internationalism in the Post-Communist Space". *Security Studies* 28(3): 588–613. https://doi.org/10.1080/09636412.2019.1604988.

Cooley, Alexander and John Heathershaw (2017). *Dictators without Borders: Power and Money in Central Asia*. New Haven, CT: Yale University Press.

Cooley, Alexander and Daniel Nexon (2013). "'The Empire Will Compensate You': The Structural Dynamics of the U.S. Overseas Basing Network." *Perspectives on Politics* 11(4): 1034–1050.

Cooley, Alexander and Daniel Nexon (2020a). *Exit from Hegemony: The Unraveling of the American Global Order*. New York: Oxford University Press.

Cooley, Alexander and Daniel Nexon (2020b). "Why Populists Want a Multipolar World." *Foreign Policy*, April 25. https://foreignpolicy.com/2020/04/25/populists-multipolar-world-russia-china/.

Cooley, Alexander and Daniel Nexon (2020c). "Trump Says the U.S. Will Pull Out of the World Health Organization. China Will Happily Fill the Void." *Washington Post*, May 29. www.washingtonpost.com/politics/2020/04/14/trump-threatened-defund-who-that-could-leave-another-global-initiative-under-chinas-influence/.

Cooley, Alexander and James Ron (2002). "The NGO Scramble: Organizational Insecurity and the Political Economy of Transnational Action." *International Security* 27(1): 5–39.

Cooley, Alexander and Matthew Schaaf (2017). "Grounding the Backlash: Regional Security Treaties, Counternorms, and Human Rights in Eurasia," pp. 159–188 in Stephen Hopgood, Jack Snyder, and Leslie Vinjamuri (eds.) *Human Rights Futures*. Cambridge: Cambridge University Press.

Cooley, Alexander and Hendrik Spruyt (2009). *Contracting States: Sovereign Transfers in International Relations*. Princeton, NJ: Princeton University Press.

Cooley, Alexander, Daniel H. Nexon, and Steven Ward (2019). "Revising Order or Challenging the Balance of Military Power? An Alternative Typology of Revisionist and Status-Quo States." *Review of International Studies* 45(4): 699–708.

Cornes, Richard and Todd Sandler (1996). *The Theory of Externalities, Public Goods, and Club Goods*. 2nd ed. Cambridge: Cambridge University Press.

Crandall, Russel (2002). *Driven by Drugs. U.S. Policy Toward Colombia*. London: Lynne Rienner.

Crawford, Timothy W. (2011)."Preventing Enemy Coalitions: How Wedge Strategies Shape Power Politics." *International Security* 35(4): 155–189.

Curanovic, Alicja (2015). "The Guardians of Traditional Values. Russia and the Russian Orthodox Church in the Quest for Status," *2014–2015 Paper Series No. 1*. Transatlantic Academy.

Dadabaev, Timur (2016). *Japan in Central Asia: Strategies, Initiatives, and Neighboring Powers*. London: Palgrave Macmillan.

Dannreuther, Roland (2012). "Russia and the Middle East: A Cold War Paradigm?" *Europe–Asia Studies* 64(3): 543–560.

Darden, Keith A. (2009). *Economic Liberalism and Its Rivals: The Formation of International Institutions among the Post-Soviet States*. Cambridge: Cambridge University Press.

Darwin, John (2009). *The Empire Project: The Rise and Fall of the British World-System, 1830–1970*. Cambridge: Cambridge University Press.

Davidson, Jason W. (2006). *The Origins of Revisionist and Status-Quo States*. New York: Palgrave Macmillan.

Davis, Kevin E., Angela Fisher, Benedict Kingsbury, and Sally Engle Merry (eds.) (2012). *Governance by Indicators: Global Power through Classification and Rankings*. New York: Oxford University Press.

Debre, Maria J. and Lee Morgenbesser (2017). "Out of the Shadows: Autocratic Regimes, Election Observation and Legitimation." *Contemporary Politics* 23(3): 328–347.

Debusscher, Petra and An Ansoms (2013). "Gender Equality Policies in Rwanda: Public Relations or Real Transformation?" *Development and Change* 44(5): 1111–1134.

de Carvalho, Benjamin and Iver B. Neumann (eds.) (2014). *Small State Status Seeking: Norway's Quest for International Standing*. London: Routledge.

Denber, Rachel and Iain Levine (2005). "Bullets Were Falling Like Rain": The Andijan Massacre, May 13, 2005." *Human Rights Watch*, June 6.

DiCicco, Jonathan M. and Jack S. Levy (1999). "Power Shift and Problem Shifts: The Evolution of the Power Transition Research Program." *Journal of Conflict Resolution* 43(6): 675–704.

Dilanian, Ken (2016). "New Cold War? Russia, U.S. Relations at Lowest Point Since 1970s". *ABC News*, October 5. www.nbcnews.com/news/us-news/new-cold-war-russia-u-s-relations-lowest-1970s-n660126.

Dmitrieva, Oksana (1996). *Regional Development: The USSR and After*. London: UCL Press.

Dodds, Klaus and Valur Ingimundarson (2012). "Territorial Nationalism and Arctic Geopolitics: Iceland as an Arctic Coastal State." *The Polar Journal* 2(1): 21–37.

Dollar, David (2015). "China's Rise as a Regional and Global Power: The AIIB and the 'One Belt, One Road'." *Brookings*, July 15. www.brookings.edu/research/chinas-rise-as-a-regional-and-global-power-the-aiib-and-the-one-belt-one-road/.

Downs, Erica (2011). "Inside China, Inc: China's Development Bank's Cross-border Energy Deals." Brookings.

Drekonja-Kornat, Gerhard (1983). "Colombia: Learning the Foreign Policy Process." *Journal of Interamerican Studies and World Affairs* 25(2): 229–250.

Drezner, Daniel W. (2009). "The Power and Peril of International Regime Complexity." *Perspectives on Politics* 7(1): 65–70. https://doi.org/10.1017/S1537592709090100.

Drezner, Daniel (2010). "Will Currency Follow the Flag?" *International Relations of the Asia-Pacific* 10: 389–414.

Drezner, Daniel W. (2014). *The System Worked: How the World Stopped Another Great Depression*. New York: Oxford University Press.

Dunning, Thad (2004). "Conditioning the Effects of Aid: Cold War Politics, Donor Credibility, and Democracy in Africa." *International Organization* 58(2): 409–423.

Duque, Marina G. (2018). "Recognizing International Status: A Relational Approach." *International Studies Quarterly* 62(3): 577–592. https://doi.org/10.1093/isq/sqy001.

Ebert, Hannes and Tim Maurer. (2013). "Contested Cyberspace and Rising Powers." *Third World Quarterly* 34(6): 1054–1074.

Eckstein, Arthur M. (2006). *Mediterranean Anarchy, Interstate War, and the Rise of Rome*. Berkeley, CA: University of California Press.

Economy, Elizabeth C. (2010). "Game Changer: Coping with China's Foreign Policy Revolution." *Foreign Affairs* 89(6): 142–152.

Edelstein, David M. (2017). *Over the Horizon: Time, Uncertainty, and the Rise of Great Powers*. Ithaca, NY: Cornell University Press.

Edson, Gary. (2020). "Abandoning the World Health Organization Will Benefit China." *The National Interest*, June 7. https://nationalinterest.org/feature/abandoning-world-health-organization-will-benefit-china-160951.

Efron, Shira, Howard J. Shatz, and Arthur Chan et al. (2019). *The Evolving Israel-China Relationship*. Santa Monica, CA: RAND Corporation.

Einarsson, Sveinn K., Ingjaldur Hannibalsson, and Alysob Bailes (2014) *Chinese Investment and Icelandic National Security*. Reykjavík: Félagsvísindastofnun Háskóla Íslands.

Ellis, Evan (2012). "Las relaciones China–Colombia en el contexto de la relación estratégica entre Colombia y los Estados Unidos," pp. 297–326 in Benjamin Creutzfeldt (ed.) *China en América Latina. Relfexiones sobre las relaciones transpacíficas*. Bogotá: Universidad Externado.

Ellis, Evan (2014). *China on the Ground in Latin America: Challenges for the Chinese and Impacts on the Region*. New York: Palgrave Macmillan.

Erickson, Andrew S., Ladwig C. Walter III, and Justin D. Mikolay (2010). "Diego Garcia and the United States' Emerging Indian Ocean Strategy." *Asian Security* 6(3): 214–237.

Eyre, Dana P. and Mark C. Suchman (1996). "Status, Norms, and the Proliferation of Conventional Weapons: An Institutional Theory Approach," pp. 79–113 in Peter J. Katzenstein (ed.) *The Culture of*

National Security: Norms and Identity in World Politics. New York: Columbia University Press.

Farrell, Henry and Abraham Newman (2019). "Weaponized Interdependence: How Global Economic Networks Shape State Coercion." *International Security* 44(1): 42–79.

Fawn, Rick (2006). "Battle over the Box: International Election Observation Missions, Political Competition and Retrenchment in the Post-Soviet Space." *International Affairs* 82(6): 1133–1153.

Fawn, Rick (2013). *International Organizations and Internal Conditionality: Making Norms Matter.* Basingstoke, UK: Palgrave Macmillan.

Fershtey, Anastassiya and Khamza Sharifzoda (2019). "Life in the Closet: The LGBT Community in Central Asia." The Diplomat, January 29.

Finnemore, Martha (1996). *National Interests in International Society.* Ithaca, NY: Cornell University Press.

Flores-Macías, Gustavo A. and Sarah E. Kreps (2013). "The Foreign Policy Consequences of Trade: China's Commercial Relations with Africa and Latin America, 1992–2006." *The Journal of Politics* 75(2): 357–371.

Foot, Rosemary (2014). " 'Doing some Things' in the Xi Jinping Era: The United Nations As China's Venue of Choice." *International Affairs* 90(5): 1085–1100.

Fougner, Tore (2008). "Neoliberal Governance of States: Competitiveness Indexing and Country Benchmarking." *Millennium: Journal of International Studies* 37(2): 303–326.

Friedman, Max Paul and Tom Long (2015). "Soft Balancing in the Americas: Latin American Opposition to US Intervention, 1898–1936." *International Security* 40(1): 120–156.

Fuchs, A. and N. H. Klann (2013). "Paying a Visit: The Dalai Lama Effect on International Trade." *Journal of International Economics* 91: 164–177.

Fumagalli, Matteo (2007). "Alignments and Realignments in Central Asia: The Rationale and Implications of Uzbekistan's Rapprochement with Russia." *International Political Science Review* 28(3): 253–271.

Gad, Ulrik Pram (2009). "Post-Colonial Identity in Greenland: When the Empire Dichotomizes Back – Bring Politics Back in." *Journal of Language and Politics* 8(1): 136–158.

Gad, Ulrik Pram (2014). "Greenland: A Post-Danish Sovereign Nation State in the Making." *Cooperation and Conflict* 49(1): 98–118.

Gallagher, Kevin P., Amos Irwin, and Katherine Koleski (2012). "The New Banks in Town: China in Latin America." *Inter-American Dialogue*, February 15.

Gardel, U. (2014a). "Ingen har spurgt om vores mening". *Berlingske Business*, 12 September. www.business.dk/oekonomi/ingen-har-spurgt-om-vores-mening.

Gardel, U. (2014b). "Færøerne bad Danmark holde sig væk fra eksportmøde med Rusland". *Berlingske Business*, 12 October. www.business.dk/global/faeroeerne-bad-danmark-holde-sig-vaek-fra-eksportmoede-med-rusland.

Gates, Robert M. (2014). *Duty: Memoirs of a Secretary at War*. New York: Alfred Knopf.

Ghoble, Vrushal T. (2019). "Saudi Arabia–Iran Contention and the Role of Foreign Actors." *Strategic Analysis* 43(1): 42–53.

Gilady, Lilach (2018). *The Price of Prestige: Conspicuous Consumption in International Relations*. Chicago, IL: University of Chicago Press.

Gilpin, Robert. (1981). *War and Change in World Politics*. New York: Cambridge University Press.

Gilpin, Robert. (1988). "The Theory of Hegemonic War." *The Journal of Interdisciplinary History* 18(4): 591–613.

Go, Julian (2008). "Global Fields and Imperial Forms: Field Theory and the British and American Empires." *Sociological Theory* 26(3): 201–227.

Go, Julian and Monika Krause (2016). "Fielding Transnationalism: An Introduction." *The Sociological Review* 64(2 suppl.): 6–30.

Goddard, Stacie E. (2018a). "Embedded Revisionism: Networks, Institutions, and Challenges to World Order." *International Organization* 72(4): 763–797. https://doi.org/10.1017/S0020818318000206.

Goddard, Stacie E. (2018b). *When Right Makes Might: Rising Powers and World Order*. Ithaca, NY: Cornell University Press.

Goddard, Stacie E. and Daniel H. Nexon (2016). "The Dynamics of Global Power Politics: A Framework for Analysis." *Journal of Global Security Studies* 1(1): 4–18. https://doi.org/10.1093/jogss/ogv007.

Goddard, Stacie E. , Paul K. MacDonald, and Daniel H. Nexon (2019). "Repertoires of Statecraft: Instruments and Logics of Power Politics." *International Relations* 33(2): 304–321.

Goh, Evelyn (2006). "Understanding 'Hedging' in Asia-Pacific Security." *PacNet* 43(August 31): 1–2.

Goh, Evelyn (2013). *The Struggle for Order: Hegemony, Hierarchy, and Transition in Post- Cold War East Asia*. Oxford: Oxford University Press.

Goldstein, Jonathan (2004). "The Republic of China and Israel, 1911–2003." *Israel Affairs* 10(1–2): 223–253.

Grieco, Joseph (1993). "Anarchy and the Limits of Cooperation: A Realist Critique of the Newest Liberal Institutionalism," pp. 116–142 in David A. Baldwin (ed.) *Neorealism and Neoliberalism: The Contemporary Debate*. New York: Columbia University Press.

Grunberg, Isabelle (1990). "Exploring the 'Myth' of Hegemonic Stability." *International Organization* 44(4): 431–477.

Gunitsky, Seva (2017). *Aftershocks: Great Powers and Domestic Reforms in the Twentieth Century*. Princeton, NJ: Princeton University Press.

Haas, Mark L. (2003). "Ideology and Alliances: British and French External Balancing Decisions in the 1930s." *Security Studies* 12(4): 34–79.

Halper, Stefan (2010). The Beijing Consensus: How China's Authoritarian Model Will Dominate the Twenty-First Century. New York: Basic Books.

Hamanaka, Shitaro (2016). "Insights to Great Power's Desire to Establish Institutions: Comparison of ADB, AMF, AMRO and AIIB." *Global Policy* 7(2): 288–292.

Harris, Peter (2017). "China in British Politics: Western Unexceptionalism in the Shadow of China's Rise." *The Chinese Journal of International Politics* 10(3): 241–267.

Harris, Tobias (2015). "The U.S. Response to the Asian Infrastructure Investment," pp. 43–52 in *Asian Infrastructure Investment Bank: China As Responsible Stakeholder?* Washington: Sasakawa Peace Foundation USA.

He, Kai (2008). "Institutional Balancing and International Relations Theory: Economic Interdependence and Balance of Power Strategies in Southeast Asia." *European Journal of International Relations* 14(3): 489–518.

He, Kai, and Huiyun Feng (2008). "If Not Soft Balancing, Then What? Reconsidering Soft Balancing and US Policy Toward China." *Security Studies* 17(2): 363–395.

Heilmann, Sebastian, Moritz Rudolf, Mikko Huotari, and Johannes Buckow (2014). "China's Shadow Foreign Policy: Parallel Structures Challenge the Established International Order". China Monitor No. 18, Mercator Institute for China Studies, Berlin.

Henke, Marina E. (2017). "The Politics of Diplomacy: How the United States Builds Multilateral Military Coalitions." *International Studies Quarterly* 61(2): 410–424.

Henriksen, Anders and Jon Rahbek-Clemmensen (2017). "Grønlandskortet: Arktis' betydning for Danmarks Indflydelse i USA." Center for Military Studies, Copenhagen.

Hilpert, Hanns Günther and Gudrun Wacker (2015). *Geoeconomics Meets Geopolitics*. Berlin: German Institute for International and Security Affairs.

Hirai, Tadashi (2017). *Creation of the Human Development Approach*. Cham, Switzerland: Palgrave Macmillan.

Højgaard Sørensen, B. , M. Crone, and S. Kruse (2015). "Færøsk fiskeeventyr slår revner i rigsfællesskabet". *Berlinske Business*, 20 August. www

.business.dk/oekonomi/faeroesk-fiskeeventyr-slaar-revner-i-rigsfaellesskabet.

Hui, Victoria Tin-bor (2004). "Towards a Dynamic Theory of International Politics: Insights from Comparing Ancient China and Early Modern Europe." *International Organization* 58(1): 175–205.

Hui, Victoria (2005). *War and State Formation in Ancient China and Early Modern Europe*. Cambridge: Cambridge University Press.

Human Rights in China (HRIC) (2011). *Counterterrorism and Human Rights: The Impact of the Shanghai Cooperation organization*. New York: HRIC.

Hurd, Ian (2007). "Breaking and Making Norms: American Revisionism and Crises of Legitimacy". *International Politics*, 44(2–3): 194–213.

Hurley, John, Scott Morris, and Gailyn Portelance (2018). "Examining the Debt Implications of the Belt and Road Initiative from a Policy Perspective." Center for Global Development Policy Paper 121.

Hyde, Susan D. (2011). *The Pseudo-Democrat's Dilemma: Why Election Observation Became an International Norm*. Ithaca, NY: Cornell University Press.

Ikenberry, G. John (2001). *After Victory: Institutions, Strategic Restraint, and the Rebuilding of Order After Major War*. Princeton, NJ: Princeton University Press.

Ikenberry, G. John (2002). "Introduction," pp. 1–26 in G. John Ikenberry (ed.) *America Unrivaled: The Future of the Balance of Power*. Ithaca, NY: Cornell University Press.

Ikenberry, G. John (2009). "Liberal Internationalism 3.0: America and the Dilemmas of Liberal World Order." *Perspectives on Politics* 7(1): 71–87.

Ikenberry, G. John (2011). *Liberal Leviathan: The Origins, Crisis, and Transformation of the American World Order*. Princeton, NJ: Princeton University Press.

Ikenberry, G. John and Charles A. Kupchan (1990). "Socialization and Hegemonic Power." *International organization* 44(3): 283–315.

Ikenberry, G. John and Daniel H. Nexon (2019). "Hegemony Studies 3.0: Hegemonic-Order Theory." *Security Studies* 28(3): 395–421.

Ingimundarson, Valur (2011). *The Rebellious Ally: Iceland, the United States, and the Politics of Empire, 1945–2006*. Dordrecht: Republic of Letters.

Ingimundarson, Valur (2015). "Framing the National Interest: The Political Uses of the Arctic in Iceland's Foreign and Domestic Policies." *The Polar Journal* 5(1): 82–100.

Jacobsen, Marc (2016). "Den grønlandske forbindelse." *Udenrigs* 2016(1): 65–73.

Jacques, Martin (2009). *When China Rules the World: The End of the Western World and the Birth of a New Global Order.* New York: Penguin Books.

Johnson, Juliet (2016). *Priests of Prosperity: How Central Bankers Transformed the Postcommunist World.* Ithaca, NY: Cornell University Press.

Johnston, Alastair I. (2003). "Is China a Status-Quo Power?" *International Security* 27: 5–56.

Jones, Alun and Julian Clark (2016). "Contemporary Geopolitical Positionings of Iceland Towards 'Europe' and the Nordic States." *Tijdschrift voor Economishe en Sociale Geografie* 107(2): 147–161.

Kagan, Robert (2004). "America's Crisis of Legitimacy". *Foreign Affairs*, March/April.

Kalinovsky, Artemy M. (2018). *Laboratory of Socialist Development: Cold War Politics and Decolonization in Soviet Tajikistan.* Ithaca, NY: Cornell University Press.

Kassenova, Nargis (2009). "China as an Emerging Donor in Tajikistan and Kyrgyzstan." Institut français des relations internationales (IFRI), Paris.

Kastner, Scott L. (2014). "Buying Influence? Assessing the Political Effects of China's International Trade." *Journal of Conflict Resolution* 60(6): 980–1007.

Kastner, Scott L. and Phillip C. Saunders (2012). "Is China a Status Quo or Revisionist State? Leadership Travel as an Empirical Indicator of Foreign Policy Priorities." *International Studies Quarterly* 56(1): 163–177.

Katzenstein P. (ed.) (1996). *The Culture of National Security. Norms and Identity in World Politics.* New York: Columbia University Press.

Kauffman, Stuart, Richard Little, and William Wohlforth (2007). "Introduction: Balance and Hierarchy in International Systems," pp. 1–21 in Stuart Kauffman, Richard Little, and William Wohlforth (eds.) *The Balance of Power in World History.* New York: Palgrave.

Kawai, Masahiro (2015). "Asian Infrastructure Investment Bank in the Evolving International Financial Order," pp. 5–26 in *Asian Infrastructure Investment Bank: China as Responsible Stakeholder?* Washington: Sasakawa Peace Foundation USA.

Keating, Vincent. C. and Ruzicka, Jan (2014). "Trusting Relationships in International Politics: No Need to Hedge." *Review of International Studies* 40(4): 753–770.

Kelley, Judith (2005). "Strategic Non-Cooperation As Soft Balancing: Why Iraq Was Not Just about Iraq." *International Politics* 42(2): 15–173.

Kelley, Judith (2009). "The More the Merrier? The Effects of Having Multiple International Election Monitoring Organizations." *Perspectives on Politics* 7(1): 59–64.

Kelley, Judith G. and Beth Simmons (2015a). "The Power of Ranking: The Ease of Doing Business as Soft Power." Unpublished manuscript.

Kelley, Judith G. and Beth Simmons (2015b). "Politics by Number: Indicators As Social Pressure in International Relations." *American Journal of Political Science* 59(1): 55–70.

Kennedy, Paul (1987). *The Rise and Fall of the Great Power: Economic Change and Military Conflict from 1500 to 2000*. New York: Random House.

Keohane, Robert Owen (1980). "The Theory of Hegemonic Stability and Changes in International Economic Regimes, 1967–1977." Center for International and Strategic Affairs, University of California.

Kim, Tongfi (2016). *The Supply Side of Security: A Market Theory of Military Alliances*. Stanford, CA: Stanford University Press.

Kindleberger, Charles (1973). *The World in Depression 1929–1939*. Berkeley, CA: University of California Press.

Kissinger, Henry (2017). *A World Restored: Metternich, Castlereagh, and the Problems of Peace, 1812–22*. Auckland: Pickle Partners Publishing.

Kjærgaard Rasmussen, Rasmus and Henrik Merkelsen (2017). "Post-Colonial Governance through Securitization?" *Politiken* 20(3): 83–103.

Klotz, Audie (1993). "Norms Reconstituting Interests: Global Racial Equality and US Sanctions against South Africa." *International Organization* 49(3): 451–478.

Knoerich, Jan and Francisco Urdinez (2019). "Contesting Contested Multilateralism: Why the West Joined the Rest in Founding the Asian Infrastructure Investment Bank." *The Chinese Journal of International Politics* 12(3): 333–370.

Koga, Kei (2018). "The Concept of 'Hedging' Revisited: The Case of Japan's Foreign Policy Strategy in East Asia's Power Shift." *International Studies Review* 20(4): 633–660. https://doi.org/10.1093/isr/vix059.

Kopstein, Jeffrey S. and David A. Reilly (2000). "Geographic Diffusion and the Transformation of the Postcommunist World." *World Politics* 53(1): 1–37.

Korolev, Alexander (2016). "Systemic Balancing and Regional Hedging: China–Russia Relations." *The Chinese Journal of International Politics* 9(4): 375–397. https://doi.org/10.1093/cjip/pow013.

Krahmann, Elke (2005). "American Hegemony or Global Governance? Competing Visions of International Security." *International Studies Review* 7(4): 531–545.

Krahmann, Elke (2008). "Security: Collective Good or Commodity?" *European Journal of International Relations* 14(3): 379–404.

Krebs, Ronald R. (1999). "Perverse Institutionalism: NATO and the Greco–Turkish Conflict." *International Organization* 53(2): 343–377.
Kreiger, Miriam, Shannon L. C. Souma, and Daniel Nexon (2015). "US Military Diplomacy in Practice," pp. 220–255 in Ole Jacob Sending, Vincent Pouliot, and Iver B. Neumann (eds.) *Diplomacy and the Making of World Politics*. Cambridge: Cambridge University Press.
Kroenig, Matthew (2010). *Exporting the Bomb: Technology Transfer and the Spread of Nuclear Weapons*. Ithaca, NY: Cornell University Press.
Kucera, Joshua (2012). "US Military Aid to Central Asia: Who Benefits?" Occasional Paper No. 7, Open Society Foundations, New York.
Kugler, Jacek and A. F. K. Organski (1989). "The Power Transition: A Retrospective and Prospective Evaluation," pp. 171–194 in Manus I. Midlarksky (ed.) *Handbook of War Studies*. Boston, MA: Unwin Hyman.
Kumaraswamy, P. R. (2005). "Israel-China Relations and the Phalcon Controversy." *Middle East Policy* 12(2): 93–103.
Kupchan, Charles A. (2014). "The Normative Foundations of Hegemony and The Coming Challenge to Pax Americana." *Security Studies* 23(2): 219–257.
Kurlantzick, Joshua (2007). *Charm Offensive: How China's Soft Power Is Transforming the World*. New Haven, CT: Yale University Press.
Kurowska, Xymena (2014). "Multipolarity as Resistance to Liberal Norms: Russia's Position on Responsibility to Protect." *Conflict, Security & Development* 14(4): 489–508.
Laffey, Mark and Jutta Weldes (1997). "Beyond Belief. Ideas and Symbolic Technologies in the Study of International Relations." *European Journal of International Relations* 3(2): 193–237.
Lake, David A. (1993). "Leadership, Hegemony, and the International Economy: Naked Emperor or Tattered Monarch?" *International Studies Quarterly* 37(4): 459–489.
Lake, David A. (1996). "Anarchy, Hierarchy and the Variety of International Relations." *International Organization* 50(1): 1–33.
Lake, David A. (1999). *Entangling Relations: American Foreign Policy in Its Century*. Princeton, NJ: Princeton University Press.
Lake, David A. (2001). "Beyond Anarchy: The Importance of Security Institutions." *International Security* 26(1): 129–160.
Lake, David A. (2007). "Escape from the State of Nature: Authority and Hierarchy in World Politics." *International Security* 32(1): 47–79.
Lake, David A. (2009). *Hierarchy in International Relations*. Ithaca, NY: Cornell University Press.

Lanteigne, Marc (2016). " 'Smått er godt' Islands økonomiske diplomati med Kina." *Internasjonal Politikk* 74(3): 1–9.

Lanteigne, Marc (2017). "Walking the Walk: Science Diplomacy and Identity-Building in Asia–Arctic relations," *Jindal Global Law Review* 8 (1): 87–101.

Larson, Deborah Welch and Alexei Shevchenko (2010). "Status Seekers: Chinese and Russian Responses to U.S. Primacy." *International Security* 34(4): 63–95.

Larson, Deborah Welch and Alexei Shevchenko (2014). "Russia Says No: Power, Status, and Emotions in Foreign Policy." *Communist and Post-Communist Studies* 47(3–4): 269–279.

Larson, Deborah Welch, T. V. Paul, and William Wohlforth (2011). "Status and World Order," pp. 3–29 in T.V. Paul, Deborah Welch Larson, and William Wohlforth (eds.) *Status in World Politics*. Cambridge: Cambridge University Press.

Laruelle, Marlène and Sébastien Peyrouse (2012). *The Chinese Question in Central Asia: Domestic Order, Social Change, and the Chinese Factor.* New York: Columbia University Press.

Layne, Christopher (1993). "The Unipolar Illusion: Why New Great Powers Will Arise." *International Security* 17(4): 5–51.

Layne, Christopher (2006). "The Unipolar Revisited: The Coming End of the United States' Unipolar Moment." *International Security* 31(2): 7–41.

Lee, Ji-Young (2016a). *China's Hegemony: Four Hundred Years of East Asian Domination*. New York: Columbia University Press.

Lee, Ji-Young (2016b). "Hegemonic Authority and Domestic Legitimation: Japan and Korea under Chinese Hegemonic Order in Early Modern East Asia." *Security Studies* 25(2): 320–352.

Legro, Jeffrey W. (2007). "What China Will Want: The Future Intentions of a Rising Power." *Perspective on Politics* 5(3): 515–534.

Lemke, Douglas (2002). *Regions of War and Peace*. Cambridge: Cambridge University Press.

Lemon, Edward (2019). "Weaponizing Interpol." *Journal of Democracy* 30 (1): 15–29.

Lewis, David (2008). *The Temptations of Tyranny in Central Asia*. New York: Columbia University Press.

Lewis, David (2011). *Reassessing the Role of OSCE Police Assistance Programing in Central Asia*. New York: Open Society Foundations.

Lewis, David (2012). "Who's Socialising Whom? Regional Organisations and Contested Norms in Central Asia." *Europe–Asia Studies* 64(7): 1219–1237.

Lewis, David (2015). "Reasserting Hegemony in Central Asia: Russian Policy in Post-2010 Kyrgyzstan." *Comillas Journal of International Relations* 1(31): 58–80.

Liao, Steven and Daniel McDowell (2015). "Redback Rising: China's Bilateral Swap Agreements and RMB Internationalization." *International Studies Quarterly* 59: 401–422.

Lieber, Keir A. and Gerard Alexander (2005). "Waiting for Balancing: Why the World is Not Pushing Back." International Security 30(1): 109–139.

Lissner, Rebecca Friedman and Mira Rapp-Hooper (2018a). "The Day after Trump: American Strategy for a New International Order." *The Washington Quarterly* 41(1): 7–25. https://doi.org/10.1080/0163660X.2018.1445353.

Lissner, Rebecca Friedman and Mira Rapp-Hooper (2018b). "The Liberal Order Is More Than a Myth." *Foreign Affairs*, July 31. www.foreignaffairs.com/articles/world/2018-07-31/liberal-order-more-myth.

Loftsdottir, Kristin (2015). " 'The Danes Don't Get This': The Economic Crash and Icelandic Postcolonial Engagements." *National Identities* 18 (1): 35–51.

Lüthi, Lorenz M. (2010). *The Sino-Soviet Split: Cold War in the Communist World*. Princeton, NJ: Princeton University Press.

Lynn-Jones, Sean M. (1995). "Offense–Defense Theory and Its Critics." *Security Studies* 4(4): 660–691.

MacDonald, Paul K. (2009). "Is Imperial Rule Obsolete? Assessing the Barriers to Overseas Adventurism." *Security Studies* 18(1): 79–114.

Manners, Ian (2002). "Normative Power Europe: A Contradiction in Terms." *Journal of Common Market Studies* 40(2): 235–258.

Mastanduno, Michael (2019). "Partner Politics: Russia, China, and the Challenge of Extending US Hegemony after the Cold War." *Security Studies* 28(3): 479–504.

Mattern, Janice. B. and Ayşe Zarakol (2016). "Hierarchies in World Politics." *International Organization* 70(3): 623–654.

McConaughey, Meghan, Paul Musgrave, and Daniel H. Nexon (2018). "Beyond Anarchy: Logics of Political Organization, Hierarchy, and International Structure." *International Theory* 10(2): 181–218.

McGill, William J. (1971). "The Roots of Policy: Kaunitz in Vienna and Versailles, 1749–1753." *The Journal of Modern History* 43(2): 228–244.

McGlinchey, Eric (2011). *Chaos, Violence, Dynasty: Politics and Islam in Central Asia*. Pittsburgh, PA: University of Pittsburgh Press.

Medeiros, Evan S. (2005). "Strategic Hedging and the Future of Asia-Pacific Stability." *The Washington Quarterly* 29(1): 145–167.

Medeiros, Evan S. and M. Taylor Fravel (2003). "China's New Diplomacy." *Foreign Affairs* 82(6): 22–35.

Meirsheimer, John (1994). "The False Promise of International Institutions." *International Security* 19(3): 5–49.

Menon, Rajan and Eugene B. Rumer (2015). *Conflict in Ukraine: The Unwinding of the Post–Cold War Order*. Cambridge, MA: The MIT Press.

Merton, Robert C. (1973). "An Intertemporal Capital Asset Pricing Model." *Econometrica* 41(5): 867–887.

Morozov, Viatcheslav and Bahar Rumelili (2012). "The External Constitution of European Identity: Russia and Turkey As Europe-Makers." *Cooperation and Conflict* 47(1): 28–48.

Morse, Julia. C. and Robert. O. Keohane (2014). "Contested Multilateralism." *The Review of International Organizations* 9(4): 385–412.

Mortensen, Bent and Ole Gram (2013). "The Quest for Resources – The Case of Greenland." *Journal of Military and Strategic Studies* 15(2): 93–128.

Motyl, Alexander J. (2001). *Imperial Ends: The Decay, Collapse, and Revival of Empires*. New York: Columbia University Press.

Murdoch, James C. (1995). "Military Alliances: Theory and Empirics," pp. 89–108 in Keith Hartley and Todd Sandler (eds.) *Handbook of Defense Economics, Vol. 1*. Amsterdam: Elsevier.

Musgrave, Paul and Daniel Nexon (2018). "Defending Hierarchy from the Moon to the Indian Ocean: Symbolic Capital and Political Dominance in Early Modern China and the Cold War." *International Organization* 72 (3): 561–590.

Müller, Matthias (2015). "Schweiz Unterzeichnet Gründungsvertrag Der AIIB. China Zelebriert Diplomatischen Erfolg," June 29. www.nzz.ch/wirtschaft/china-zelebriert-diplomatischen-erfolg-1.18570980.

Myers, Margaret and Carol Wise (eds.) (2016). *The Political Economy of China–Latin America Relations in the New Millennium: Brave New World*. New York: Routledge.

Naim, Moisés (2007). "Rogue Aid." *Foreign Policy*, March/April.

Neumann, Iver B. (2015). "Institutionalizing Peace and Reconciliation Diplomacy: Third-Party Reconciliation As Systems Maintenance," pp. 140–167 in Ole Jacob Sending, Vincent Pouliot, and Iver B. Neumann (eds.) *Diplomacy and the Making of World Politics*. Cambridge: Cambridge University Press.

Nexon, Daniel (2009). "The Balance of Power in the Balance." *World Politics* 61(2): 330–359.

Nexon, Daniel H. and Iver B. Neumann. (2018). "Hegemonic-Order Theory: A Field-Theoretic Account." *European Journal of International Relations* 24(3): 662–686. https://doi.org/10.1177/1354066117716524.

Nexon, Daniel H. and Thomas Wright (2007). "What's at Stake in the American Empire Debate". *American Political Science Review* 101(2): 253–271.
New York Times (2011). "Chinese Deal for Iceland Property Founders over Distrust," September 21. www.nytimes.com/2011/09/22/world/asia/22iht-letter22.html.
New York Times (2013). "Teeing Off at Edge of the Arctic? A Chinese Plan Baffles Iceland," March 22. www.nytimes.com/2013/03/23/world/europe/iceland-baffled-by-chinese-plan-for-golf-resort.html?pagewanted=all&_r=0.
Nolte, Ditlef (2013). "The Dragon in the Backyard: US Visions of China's Relations toward Latin America." *Papel Político* 18(2): 587–598.
Norrlof, Carla (2010). *America's Global Advantage: US Hegemony and International Cooperation*. Cambridge: Cambridge University Press.
Norrlof, Carla (2014). "Dollar Hegemony: A Power Analysis." *Review of International Political Economy* 21(5): 1042–1070. https://doi.org/10.1080/09692290.2014.895773.
Norrlof, Carla (2018). "Hegemony and Inequality: Trump and the Liberal Playbook." *International Affairs* 94(1): 63–88. https://doi.org/10.1093/ia/iix262.
Oatley, Thomas (2015). *A Political Economy of American Hegemony*. New York: Cambridge University Press.
Oatley, Thomas, W. , Kindred Winecoff, Andrew Pennock, and Sarah Bauerle Danzman. (2013). "The Political Economy of Global Finance: A Network Model." *Perspectives on Politics* 11(01): 133–153. https://doi.org/10.1017/S1537592712003593.
Olcott, Martha Brill (1996). *Central Asia's New States: Independence, Foreign Policy, and Regional Security*. Washington, DC: United States Institute of Peace Press.
Olson, Mancur (1973). *The Logic of Collective Action: Public Goods and the Theory of Groups*. Cambridge, MA: Harvard University Press.
Onea, Tudor A. (2014). "Between Dominance and Decline: Status Anxiety and Great Power Rivalry". *Review of International Studies* 40: 125–152.
Oneal, John R. (1990). "The Theory of Collective Action and Burden Sharing in NATO." *International Organization* 44(03): 379–402.
O'Neill, Jim. (2001). "Building Better Global Economic BRICs." Goldman Sachs, Global Economics Paper No. 66.
Organski, Abramo Fimo Kenneth (1958). *World Politics*. 2nd ed. New York: Knopf.
Organski, Abramo Fimo Kenneth and Jacek Kugler (1980). *The War Ledger*. Chicago, IL: University of Chicago Press.
Ostrom, Elinor, Roy Gardner, and James Walker (1994). *Rules, Games, and Common-Pool Resources*. Ann Arbor, MI: University of Michigan Press.

Over the Circle (2018). "Greenland's Airport Saga: Enter the US?," September 18. https://overthecircle.com/2018/09/18/greenlands-airport-saga-enter-the-us/.

Owen, John M. (2012). *The Clash of Ideas in World Politics: Transnational Networks, States, and Regime Change, 1510–2010*. Princeton, NJ: Princeton University Press.

Oxley, Audrey (2012). "Dragon Training at Home. Exploring the Possibilities for Collaboration between the U.S. and Chinese Navies in the Western Hemisphere." Policy paper, Brookings Institution, Washington, DC.

Pape, Robert A. (2005). "Soft Balancing against the United States." *International Security* 30(1): 7–45.

Pardo, Rodrigo and Juan G. Tokatlian (1989). *Política exterior colombiana.: De la subordinación a la autonomía?* Bogotá: Tercer Mundo.

Park, Jae Jeok (2011). "The US-Led Alliances in the Asia-Pacific: Hedge against Potential Threats or an Undesirable Multilateral Security Order?" *The Pacific Review* 24(2): 137–158.

Paul, T. V. (2004). "Introduction: The Enduring Axioms of Balance of Power Theory and Their Contemporary Relevance," pp. 1–25 in T. V. Paul, James J. Wirtz, and Michel Fortmann (eds.) *Balance of Power: Theory and practice in the 21st century*. Stanford, CA: Stanford University Press.

Paul, Thazha Varkey (2005). "Soft Balancing in the Age of U.S. Primacy." *International Security* 30(1): 46–71.

Paul, T. V., Deborah. W. Larson, and William. C. Wohlforth (eds.) (2014). *Status in World Politics*. Cambridge: Cambridge University Press.

Pempel, T. J. (2010). "Soft Balancing, Hedging, and Institutional Darwinism: The Economic-Security Nexus and East Asian Regionalism." *Journal of East Asian Studies* 10(2): 209–238.

Peng, Zhongzhou and Sow Keat Tok (2016). "The AIIB and China's Normative Power in International Financial Governance Structure." *China Political Science Review* 1: 736–753.

Peou, Sorpong (2002). "Realism and Constructivism in Southeast Asian Security Studies Today: A Review Essay." *The Pacific Review* 15(1): 119–138.

Perlez, Jane (2015). "China Creates a World Bank of Its Own, and the U.S. Balks." *The New York Times*, December 4.

Permanyer, Inaki (2013). "A Critical Assessment of the UNDP's Gender Inequality Index." *Feminist Economics* 19(2): 1–32.

Petersen, Nikolaj (2011). "SAC at Thule. Greenland in the U.S. Polar Strategy." *Journal of Cold War Studies* 13(2): 90–115.

Petursson, Gustav (2014). "Icelandic Security in a Changing Regional and Geopolitical Seascape: Limited Capabilities and Growing

Responsibilities," pp. 28–40 in Lassi Heninen (ed.) *Security and Sovereignty in the North Atlantic*. Basingstoke, UK: Palgrave Macmillan.

Pham, J. P. (2013). "Pirates and Dragon Boats: Assessing the Chinese Navy's Recent East African Deployments." *The Journal of the Middle East and Africa* 4(1): 87–108.

Phillips, Andrew (2013). "From Global Transformation to Big Bang – A Response to Buzan and Lawson." *International Studies Quarterly* 57 (3): 640–642. https://doi.org/10.1111/isqu.12089.

Philpott, Daniel (2001). "Usurping the Sovereignty of Sovereignty?" *World Politics* 53 (January): 297–324.

Piccone, Ted (2016). *The Geopolitics of China's Rise in Latin America*. Washington, DC: Brookings Institution.

Poe, Steven C., Carey, Sabine C., and Tanya C. Vasquez (2001). "How Are These Pictures Different? A Quantitative Comparison of US State Department and Amnesty International Human Rights Reports, 1976-1995." *Human Rights Quarterly* 23(3): 650–677.

Pomfret, Richard (1995). *The Economies of Central Asia*. Princeton, NJ: Princeton University Press.

Pouliot, Vincent (2016). *International Pecking Orders: The Politics and Practice of Multilateral Diplomacy*. Cambridge: Cambridge University Press.

Powers, Benjamin (2017). "An Abandoned US Nuclear Base in Greenland Could Start Leaking Toxic Waste Because of Global Warming." *Mother Jones*, 12 June. www.motherjones.com/environment/2017/06/camp-century-global-warming/#.

Randall, Stephen J. (1992). *Colombia and the United States: Hegemony and interdependence (Vol. 6)*. Athens, GA: University of Georgia Press.

Randolph, Sean R. (1986). *The United States and Thailand: Alliance Dynamics, 1950–1985*. Berkeley, CA: University of California Press.

Reisen, Helmut (2015). "Will the AIIB and the NDB Help Reform Multilateral Development Banking?" *Global Policy* 6(3): 297–304.

Reus-Smit, Christia. (1997). "Constructing Anarchy: The Constitutional Structure of International Society and the Nature of Fundamental Institutions." *International Organization* 51(4): 555–589.

Reuters (2019). "Denmark Approves New U.S. Consulate in Greenland," 18 December. https://ca.reuters.com/article/topNews/idCAKBN1YM21L.

Reykjavik Economics (2016). "The Economic Impact of the Russian Counter-Sanctions on Trade between Iceland and the Russian Federation." www.forsaetisraduneyti.is/media/Skyrslur/TheEconomicImpactoftheRussianSanctionsonTradebetweenIcelandandRussia.pdf.

Rubin, Barnett R. (1993). "The Fragmentation of Tajikistan." *Survival* 35 (4): 71–91.

Rumelili, Bahar (2007). *Constructing Regional Community and Order in Europe and Southeast Asia*. Basingstoke, UK: Palgrave.

Ryan, John (2015). "Chinese Renminbi Arrival in the Tripolar Global Monetary Regime." *China & World Economy* 23(6): 44–55.

Rynning, Sten, and Jens Ringsmose (2008). "Why Are Revisionist States Revisionist? Reviving Classical Realism as an Approach to Understanding International Change." *International Politics* 45: 16–39.

Saldinger, Adva (2017). "AIIB President Jin Liqun: 'We're Lean, Clean and Green, but Not mean'." *Devex*, April 26. www.devex.com/news/aiib-president-jin-liqun-we-re-lean-clean-and-green-but-not-mean-90140.

Sanderson, Henry and Michael Forsythe (2012). *China's Superbank: Debt, Oil and Influence – How China Development Bank is Rewriting the Rules of Finance*. Singapore: John Wiley & Sons.

Sandler, Todd and Keith Hartley (2001). "Economics of Alliances: The Lessons for Collective Action." *Journal of Economic Literature* 39(3): 869–896.

Sandler, Todd and John Tschirhart (1997). "Club Theory: Thirty Years Later." *Public Choice* 93(3–4): 335–355.

Savage, Mike, Alan Warde, and Fiona Devine (2005). "Capitals, Assets, and Resources: Some Critical Issues." *The British Journal of Sociology* 56(1): 31–46.

Schake, Kori (2017). *Safe Passage*. Cambridge, MA: Harvard University Press.

Schake, Kori (2018). "The Trump Doctrine Is Winning and the World Is Losing." *New York Times*, June 15. www.nytimes.com/2018/06/15/opinion/sunday/trump-china-america-first.html.

Schake, Kori (2019). "Back to Basics: How to Make Right What Trump Gets Wrong." *Foreign Affairs*, August 28. www.foreignaffairs.com/articles/2019-04-16/back-basics.

Schatz, Edward and Renan Levine (2010). "Framing, Public Diplomacy, and Anti-Americanism in Central Asia." *International Studies Quarterly* 54(3): 855–869.

Schimmelfennig, Frank (1998). "Nato Enlargement: A Constructivist Explanation." *Security Studies* 8(2): 198–234.

Schueth, Sam (2011). "Assembling International Competitiveness: The Republic of Georgia, USAID, and the Doing Business Project." *Economic Geography* 87(1): 51–77.

Schweller, Randall L. (1996). "Neorealism's Status-Quo Bias: What Security Dilemma?" *Security Studies* 5(3): 90–121.

Schweller, Randall L. (2006). *Unanswered Threats: Political Constraints on the Balance of Power*. Princeton, NJ: Princeton University Press.

Schweller, Randall L. and Xiaoyu Pu (2011). "After Unipolarity: China's Visions of International Order in an Era of U.S. Decline." *International Security* 36(1): 41–72. https://doi.org/10.1162/ISEC_a_00044.

Schweller, Randall L. and William C. Wohlforth (2000). "Power Test: Evaluating Realism in Response to the End of the Cold War." *Security Studies* 9(3): 60–107.

Sending, Ole Jacob (2015). "Diplomats and Humanitarians in Crisis Governance," pp. 256–283 in Ole Jacob Sending, Vincent Pouliot, and Iver B. Neumann (eds.) *Diplomacy and the Making of World Politics*. Cambridge: Cambridge University Press.

Sending, Ole Jacob (2017). "Recognition and Liquid Authority." *International Theory* 9(2): 311–328.

Sharman, Jason (2017). "Sovereignty at the Extremes: Micro-States in World Politics," *Political Studies* 65(3): 559–575.

Shekhovtsov, Anton (2015). "Far-right Election Observation Monitors in the Service of the Kremlin's Foreign Policy," pp. 223–243 in Marlene Laruelle (ed.) *Eurasianism and the European Far Right: Reshaping the Europe–Russia Relationship*. Lanham, MD: Lexington Books.

Simmons, Beth A. (2009). *Mobilizing for Human Rights: International Law in Domestic Politics*. New York: Cambridge University Press.

Skaale, S. (2015). "R 8 Udenrigsministerens sikkerhedspolitiske redegørelse 2015." *Resume, Meeting No. 46, Folketinget*. www.ft.dk/samling/20151/redegoerelse/r8/beh1/220/forhandling.htm?startItem=.

Sofka, James R. (2001). "The Eighteenth Century International System: Parity or Primacy?" *Review of International Studies* 27(5): 147–163. https://doi.org/10.1017/S0260210501008063.

Soldatov, Andrei and Irina Borogan (2010). *The New Nobility: The Restoration of Russia's Security State and the Enduring Legacy of the KGB*. New York, NY: Public Affairs.

Stensvold, Anne (ed.) (2017). *Religion, State and the United Nations*. London: Routledge.

Stoeckl, Kristina (2018). "Transnational Norm Mobilization: The World Congress of Families in Georgia and Moldova." *Foreign Policy Centre*, July 18. https://fpc.org.uk/transnational-norm-mobilization-the-world-congress-of-families-in-georgia-and-moldova/.

Stokes, Doug (2018). "Trump, American Hegemony and the Future of the Liberal International Order." *International Affairs* 94(1): 133–150. https://doi.org/10.1093/ia/iix238.

Strauss, Julia C. and Ariel. C. Armony (eds.) (2012). *From the Great Wall to the New World: China and Latin America in the 21st Century* . Cambridge: Cambridge University Press.

Strüver, Georg (2017). "China's Partnership Diplomacy: International Alignment Based on Interests or Ideology." *The Chinese Journal of International Politics* 10(1): 31–65.

Stuenkel, Oliver (2020). *The BRICS and the Future of Global Order.* Lanham, MD: Lexington Books.

Sun, Yun (2015a). "China and the Evolving Asian Infrastructure Investment Bank," pp. 27–42 in Daniel Bob (ed.) *Asian Infrastructure Investment Bank: China As Responsible Stakeholder?* Washington, DC: Sasakawa Peace Foundation USA.

Sun, Yun (2015b). "How the International Community Changed China's Asian Infrastructure Investment Bank." *The Diplomat*, July 31. http://thediplomat.com/2015/07/how-the-international-community-changed-chinas-asian-infrastructure-investment-bank/.

Suzuki, Shogo (2008). "Seeking 'Legitimate' Great Power Status in Post-Cold War International Society: China's and Japan's Participation in UNPKO." *International Relations* 22(1): 45–63.

Symons, Jonathan and Dennis Altman (2015). "International Norm Polarization: Sexuality as a Subject of Human Rights Protection." *International Theory* 7(1): 61–95.

Taagholt, Jørgen and Kent Brooks (2016). "Mineral Riches: A Route to Greenland's Independence." *Polar Record* 52(2): 360–371.

Tajfel, Henry and John C. Turner (1979). "An Integrative Theory of Intergroup Conflict," pp. 33–47 in William G. Austin and Stephen Worchel (eds.). *The Social Psychology of Intergroup Relations.* Monterey, CA: Brooks Cole.

Tan-Mullins, May, Giles Mohan, and Marcus Power (2010). "Redefining 'Aid' in the China–Africa Context." *Development and Change* 41(5): 857–881.

Taylor, Paul and William James (2015). "How Europe and U.S. Stumbled into Spat over China-Led Bank." *Reuters*, March 22. www.reuters.com/article/us-china-bank-europe-insight-idUSKBN0MI0ER20150322.

Tessman, Brock and Wojtek Wolfe (2011). "Great Powers and Strategic Hedging: The Case of Chinese Energy Security Strategy." *International Studies Review* 13(2): 214–240. https://doi.org/10.1111/j.1468-2486.2011.01022.x.

Têtu, Pierre-Louis and Frédéric Lasserre (2017). "Chinese Investment in Greenland's Mining Industry: Toward a New Framework for Foreign Direct Investment." *The Extractive Industries and Society* 4(3): 661–671.

The Economist (2017). "The World's most Powerful Man," October 14.

Thomas, Andrea and Charles Hutzler (2015). "Germany, France, Italy to Join China-Backed Development Bank." *Wall Street Journal*, March 17. www.wsj.com/articles/germany-france-italy-to-join-china-backed-development-bank-1426597078.

Thomas, Ward (2001). *The Ethics of Destruction: Norms and Force in International Relations*. Ithaca, NY: Cornell University Press.

Thorhallsson, Baldur (2013). "Iceland's Contested European Policy: The Footprint of the Past – A Small and Insular Society." Jean Monnet Occasional Papers No.1, Institute of European Studies.

Thorhallsson, Baldur and Petur Gunnarsson (2017). "Iceland's Alignment with the EU–US Sanctions on Russia: Autonomy versus Dependence." *Global Affairs* 3(3): 307–318.

Tickner, Arlene B. (2002). "Colombia es lo que los actores estatales hacen de ella': Una (re)lectura de la política exterior Colombiana hacia los Estados Unidos," pp. 353–398 in Martha Ardila, Diego Cardona, and Arlene B. Tickner (eds.) *Prioridades y Desafíos de la Politica Exterior Colombiana*. Bogotá: Friedrich Ebert Stiftung/ Hanss Seidel Stiftung.

Tickner, Arlene B. (2003a). "Colombia and the United States: From Counternarcotics to Counterterrorism." *Current History* 102(661): 77.

Tickner, Arlene B. (2003b). "US Subordinate, Autonomous Actor, or Something in Between?" pp. 165–184 in J. F. Aviel, R. Berríos, and L. Bizzozero et al. (eds.) *Latin American and Caribbean foreign policy*. Lanham, MD: Rowman & Littlefield.

Toal, Gerard (2017). *Near Abroad: Putin, the West, and the Contest over Ukraine and the Caucasus*. New York: Oxford University Press.

Towns, Ann (2009). "The Status of Women as a Standard of 'Civilization'." *European Journal of International Relations* 15(4): 681–706. https://doi.org/10.1177/1354066109345053.

Towns, Ann (2010). *Women and States. Norms and Hierarchies in International Society*. Cambridge: Cambridge University Press.

Towns, Ann (2012). "Norms and Social Hierarchies: Understanding Policy Diffusion from Below." *International Organization* 66(2): 179–209.

Towns, Ann and Bahar Rumelili (2017). "Taking the Pressure: Unpacking the Relation between Norms, Social Hierarchies, and Social Pressures on States." *European Journal of International Relations* 23(4): 756–779. https://doi.org/10.1177/1354066116682070.

Tsygankov, Andrei P. and David Parker (2015). "The Securitization of Democracy: Freedom House Ratings of Russia" *European Security* 24(1): 77–100.

Tynan, Deirdre (2009). "Ashgabat Hosts US Refueling and Resupply Operations." *Eurasianet*, July 8.

UK.gov. (2015) "UK Announces Plans to Join Asian Infrastructure Investment Bank." www.gov.uk/government/news/uk-announces-plans-to-join-asian-infrastructure-investment-bank.

United Nations (2020). "Troop and Police Contributors Financing Peacekeeping." https://peacekeeping.un.org/en/troop-and-police-contributors.
United Nations (n.d.). "Peacekeeping – How We Are Funded." https://peacekeeping.un.org/en/how-we-are-funded.
United Nations Development Programme (2016). "Table 5. Gender Inequality Index," *2016 Human Development Report*. United Nations Development Programme, Geneva. http://hdr.undp.org/en/composite/GII.
Veblen, Thorstein (1908). "On the Nature of Capital." *The Quarterly Journal of Economics* 22(4):517–542.
Vestergaard, Cindy (2015). "Greenland, Denmark and the Pathway to Uranium Supplier Status." *The Extractive Industries and Society* 2015 (2): 153–161.
Vestergaard, Jakob and Robert H. Wade (2013). "Protecting Power: How Western States Retain the Dominant Voice in the World Bank's Governance." *World Development* 46: 153–164.
Vitalis, Robert (2015). *White World Order, Black Power Politics: The Birth of American International Relations*. Ithaca, NY: Cornell University Press.
Volgy, Thomas J. and Stacey Mayhall (1995). "Status Inconsistency and International War: Exploring the Effects of Systemic Change." *International Studies Quarterly* 39(1): 67–84. https://doi.org/10.2307/2600724.
Vreeland, James Raymond. (2003). *The IMF and Economic Development*. Cambridge: Cambridge University Press.
Vreeland, James Raymond and Axel Dreher (2014). *The Political Economy of the United Nations Security Council: Money and Influence*. New York: Cambridge University Press.
Vucetic, Srdjan (2011). *The Anglosphere: A Genealogy of a Racialized Identity in International Relations*. Stanford, CA: Stanford University Press.
Walker, Christopher (2018). "What Is 'Sharp Power'?" *Journal of Democracy* 29(3): 9–23. https://doi.org/10.1353/jod.2018.0041.
Walker, Christopher and Alexander Cooley (2013). "Vote of the Living Dead," Foreign Policy, October 31.
Walker, Christopher and Jessica Ludwig (2017). "The Meaning of Sharp Power." *Foreign Affairs*, November 16. www.foreignaffairs.com/articles/china/2017-11-16/meaning-sharp-power.
Walt, Stephen M. (1985). "Alliance Formation and the Balance of Power." *International Security* 9(4): 2–43.
Walt, Stephen M. (2009). "Alliances in a Unipolar World." *World Politics* 61(1): 86–120.
Waltz, Kenneth N. (1979). *Theory of International Politics*. New York: Addison-Wesley.

Waltz, Kenneth N. (2000). "Structural Realism after the Cold War." *International Security* 25(1): 5–41.

Ward, Steven (2013). "Race, Status, and Japanese Revisionism in the Early 1930s." *Security Studies* 22(4): 607–639.

Ward, Steven (2017). *Status and the Challenge of Rising Powers*. Cambridge: Cambridge University Press.

Ward, Steven (2019). "Logics of Stratified Identity Management in World Politics." *International Theory* 11(2): 211–238.

Ward-Perkins, Bryan (2005). *The Fall of Rome and the End of Civilization*. Oxford: Oxford University Press.

Watt, Nicholas, Paul Lewis, and Tania Branigan (2015) "US Anger at Britain Joining Chinese-Led Investment Bank AIIB." *The Guardian*, March 13. www.theguardian.com/us-news/2015/mar/13/white-house-pointedly-asks-uk-to-use-its-voice-as-part-of-chinese-led-bank.

Way, Lucan A. and Steven Levitsky (2007). "Linkage, Leverage, and the Post-Communist Divide." *East European Politics and Societies* 21(1): 48–66.

Webb, Michael C. and Stephen D. Krasner (1989). "Hegemonic Stability Theory: An Empirical Assessment." *Review of International Studies* 15(2): 183–198.

Weitsman, Patricia A. (2004). *Dangerous Alliances: Proponents of Peace, Weapons of War*. Stanford, CA: Stanford University Press.

Welsh, Alexander (2008). *What Is Honor? A Question of Moral Imperatives*. New Haven, CT: Yale University Press.

Wendt, Alexander and Daniel Friedheim (1995). "Hierarchy under Anarchy: Informal Empire and the East German State." *International Organization* 49(4): 689–721.

Wesley, Michael (2015). "Trade Agreements and Strategic Rivalry in Asia." *Australian Journal of International* Affairs 69(5): 479–495.

Whitaker, Beth Elise (2010). "Soft Balancing among Weak States? Evidence from Africa." *International Affairs* 86(5): 1109–1127.

Whitmore, Brian (2013). "Vladimir Putin, Conservative Icon." *The Atlantic*, Dec 20. www.theatlantic.com/international/archive/2013/12/vladimir-putin-conservative-icon/282572/.

Wiener, Antje (2008). *The Invisible Constitution of Politics. Contested Norms and International Encounters*. Cambridge: Cambridge University Press.

Wildau, Gabriel and Tom Mitchell (2016). "China's New Asia Development Bank Will Lend in US Dollars." Financial Times, June 15.

Wilkinson, David (1999). "Unipolarity without Hegemony." *International Studies Review* 1(2): 141–172.

Wilson, Page (2017). "An Arctic 'Cold Rush'? Understanding Greenland's (In)Dependence Question." *Polar Record* 53(5): 512–519.

Winger, Gregory and Gustav Petursson (2016). "Return to Keflavik Station: Iceland's Cold War Legacy Reappraised." *Foreign Affairs*, February 24.

Wohlforth, William C. (1999). "The Stability of a Unipolar World." *International Security* 24(1): 5–41.

Wohlforth, William C., Stuart J. Kaufman, and Richard Little (2007). "Introduction: Balance and Hierarchy in International Systems," pp. 1–21 in Stuart Kauffman, Richard Little, and William Wohlforth (eds.) *The Balance of Power in World History*. New York: Palgrave.

Wohlforth, William, Benjamin De Carvalho, Halvard Leira, and Iver B. Neumann (2018). "Moral Authority and Status in International Relations: Good States and the Social Dimension of Status Seeking." *Review of International Studies* 44(3): 526–546.

Wolf, Reinhard (2011). "Respect and Disrespect in International Politics: The Significance of Status Recognition." *International Theory* 3(1): 105–142.

Woods, Ngaire (2008). "Whose Aid? Whose Influence? China, Emerging Donors and the Silent Revolution in Development Assistance." *International Affairs* 84(6): 1205–1221.

World Bank (1992). *Statistical Handbook: States of the Former USSR*. Washington, DC: World Bank.

World Bank Group (2015). "Despite Progress, Laws Restricting Economic Opportunity for Women Are Widespread Globally, Says WBG Report," September 9. www.worldbank.org/en/news/press-release/2015/09/09/des pite-progress-laws-restricting-economic-opportunity-for-women-are-widespread-globally-says-wbg-report.

Wuthnow, Joel, Li Xin, and Qi Lingling (2012). "Diverse Multilateralism: Four Strategies in China's Multilateral Diplomacy." *Journal of Chinese Political Science* 17: 269–290.

Zarakol, Ayse (2010). *After Defeat. How the East Learned to Live with the West*. Cambridge: Cambridge University Press.

Zeuthen, Jesper (2017). "Part of the Master Plan? Chinese Investment in Rare Earth Mining in Greenland," *Arctic Yearbook 2017*.

Zhang, Feng (2015). *Chinese Hegemony: Grand Strategy and International Institutions in East Asian History*. Stanford, CA: Stanford University Press.

Zhang, Xiaojun (2004). "Land Reform in Yang Village: Symbolic Capital and the Determination of Class Status." *Modern China* 30(1): 3–45.

Index

9/11 attacks, 107, 109
Abkhazia
  election observers in, 123
  Russia and, 52
Academic capital, 20–1
Adamson, Fiona B., 105
ADB (*See* Asian Development Bank)
Addition, 13–14
Adler-Nissen, Rebecca, 21, 26–7, 78–9, 180, 182–3
Afghanistan
  Central Asia, United States military presence in, 107–9
  China and, 111–12
  consensus regarding war, 110
  Operation Enduring Freedom (OEF), 15, 107
  Quadrilateral Cooperation and Coordination Mechanism (QCCM), 111–12
Africa, LGBTQ persons in, 63–4, 84–6
AIIB (*See* Asian Infrastructure Investment Bank)
Aircraft carriers, 22
Akayev, Askar, 108
American Conservative Union Foundation, 85
Amnesty International, 73
Andean Community, 138
Andean Development Corporation, 131–2
Andean Pact, 138
Andersen, Morten Skumsrud, 26, 178, 181–2, 184
Ansoms, An, 81
Architecture of international order
  distribution of power versus, 36
  normative goods and, 182

positionalist strategy and, 31, 182
reformist strategy and, 31, 39, 42, 182
revolutionary strategy and, 31, 37–8, 182
status quo strategy and, 31, 41, 182
Arctic Council, 158, 167, 169
Argentina
  China and, 130
  debt owed to China, 59
Armenia, election observers and, 122
Armony, Ariel C., 142
Asian Development Bank (ADB)
  Asian Infrastructure Investment Bank and, 90, 92, 93
  Central Asia generally and, 113
  Japan and, 96, 100
Asian Infrastructure Investment Bank (AIIB) (*See also specific country*)
  generally, x, 24–5, 53, 90
  overview, 101–3
  Articles of Agreement (AOA), 91, 98, 100, 101
  Asian Development Bank and, 90, 92, 93
  Australia and, 88, 91, 95, 96, 100
  Bangladesh and, 90–1
  Belt and Road Initiative and, 115
  Brazil and, 98
  BRICS countries and, 98
  in context of existing international financial order, 90–1
  counter-hegemonic strategy of, 89, 91–4
  Egypt and, 98
  France and, 97–8
  Germany and, 97–8
  goods substitution and, 11, 89, 101–3, 186–7

Index

hedging and, 98
herding and, 99
historical background, 90–1
IMF and, 90
India and, 90–1, 92, 98
integration into existing financial structures, 99–101
international financial institutions and, 89, 92–4
Israel and, 98
Italy and, 97
Japan and, 92, 96, 97
Kuwait and, 90–1
Luxembourg and, 91
Mongolia and, 90–1
Nepal and, 90–1
New Zealand and, 91, 98
Oman and, 90–1
Pakistan and, 90–1
Qatar and, 90–1
renminbi and, 91–2
Russia and, 98
South Africa and, 98
South Korea and, 88, 91, 92, 95, 96
Sri Lanka and, 90–1
United Kingdom and, 88, 91, 97–8
United States and, 41–2, 88, 91, 92, 95–6, 97, 99, 101–2, 180
World Bank and, 47, 90, 92–3, 100
Asia–Pacific Economic Cooperation (APEC), 90, 95, 132–3
Assets versus goods, 7, 128, 185–6
Association of Southeast Asian Nations (ASEAN), 90–1
Australia
  Asian Infrastructure Investment Bank and, 88, 91, 95, 96, 100
  Russia and, 46
Austria, alliances and, 14

Bader, Julia, 24–5, 42, 53, 180, 181
Bahrain, Israel and, 148
Bakiyev, Kurmanbek, 15, 108, 109, 110–11
Bangladesh, Asian Infrastructure Investment Bank and, 90–1
Beckley, Michael, 29
Belarus
  election observers and, 122
  Russia and, 52

Belt and Road Initiative (BRI)
  generally, 30–1, 53, 89, 102
  Asian Infrastructure Investment Bank and, 115
  Central Asia generally and, 115–16
  "civilizational diversity" and, 120
  goods substitution and generally, 11
  Greece and, 2–3
  Kyrgyzstan and, 116
  Tajikistan and, 116
Biden, Joseph, 87
Bolivarian Alliance (ALBA), 127, 133, 135, 150 (*See also* Ecuador; Venezuela)
Bolivia
  debt owed to China, 130
  shifting of ties in, 130
Bottom-up drivers of goods substitution, 17–19, 152–5
Bourdieu, Pierre, 20–1, 182 (*See also* Capital; Fields)
Bradley, Christopher G., 73
Brazil
  Asian Infrastructure Investment Bank and, 98
  in BRICS countries (*See* BRICS countries)
  Colombia and, 139–40, 144
  energy-backed loans from China, 54
Bretton Woods system, 47, 100, 101, 102–3, 138
BRI (*See* Belt and Road Initiative)
BRICS countries (*See also specific country*)
  Asian Infrastructure Investment Bank and, 98
  IMF and, 46
  international financial institutions and, 45, 46
  New Development Bank, 47, 53, 100–1, 115
  positionalist strategy and, 46
  reformist strategy and, 47
  revolutionary strategy and, 46
  rise of, 45
  status quo strategy and, 45–6
  Syria and, 46
  World Bank and, 46
  World Trade Organization and, 45
Bukovansky, Mlada, 72

Bush, George W.
  Colombia and, 141
  reformist strategy of, 40, 181
  Uzbekistan and, 108

Cameron, David, 97
Campbell, Kurt M., 4
Capital
  academic capital, 20–1
  cultural capital, 20–1
  defined, 20
  diplomatic capital, 20–1, 35
  economic capital, 35
  fields, relation to, 20–1, 182
  meta-capital, 32–3
  social capital, 20–1
  symbolic capital, 21–2
Carr, E. H., 62–3
Central Asia (*See specific country*)
Chavez, Hugo, 142
Chile
  China and, 130
  normative goods and, 83
Chin, Gregory T., 93
China
  Afghanistan and, 111–12
  alliances and, 14
  in Arctic Council, 167, 169
  Argentina and, 130
  Asian Infrastructure Investment Bank (*See* Asian Infrastructure Investment Bank)
  Belt and Road Initiative (BRI) (*See* Belt and Road Initiative)
  in BRICS countries (*See* BRICS countries)
  Chile and, 130
  China Development Bank (CDB), 54, 55–6, 58
  China National Petroleum Corporation (CNPC), 57–8, 114–15
  "civilizational diversity" and, 120–1
  Colombia and, 130, 139–42, 143–4, 145, 146–7
  counter-hegemonic strategies in, 88, 178
  COVID-19 pandemic and, ix, 4, 5
  Denmark and, 175
  development assistance and, 179
  Ecuador and, 126, 127, 133, 135
  energy-backed loans from (*See* Energy-backed loans from China)
  Exim Bank, 115
  Faroe Islands and, 173, 175
  foreign debt owed to (*See* Debt owed to China)
  global performance indices and, 70–1, 73–4
  goods substitution and generally, ix, 5
  Greece and, 2–3
  Greenland and, 152, 166–7, 168–71, 175, 180
  as hegemonic power, 30–1
  Iceland and, 161–5, 175
  international order and, 42
  Israel and, 148
  Kazakhstan and, 114–15, 124
  Kyrgyzstan and, 111, 114–15, 124
  Latin America generally, trade with, 125, 133
  Middle East and, 149
  Ming Dynasty as hegemonic power, 1
  Ministry of Foreign Affairs, 169
  multilateralism in, 188
  normative goods and, 62, 64, 83, 86–7
  North Atlantic generally and, 157, 158–9
  Pakistan and, 111–12
  Peru and, 130
  Philippines and, 17
  positionalist strategy in, 48, 180, 182
  power transitions and, 2, 30–1
  Quadrilateral Cooperation and Coordination Mechanism (QCCM), 111–12
  "re-engineering" in, 89
  reformist strategy in, 48, 180, 181, 182
  revolutionary strategy in, 48
  Serbia and, 4
  "shadow diplomacy" in, 89
  Shanghai Cooperation Organization (*See* Shanghai Cooperation Organization)
  Silk Road Maritime Belt, 115
  Tajikistan and, 111–12, 114–15, 124
  Turkmenistan and, 114–15, 124
  Uighurs in, 50, 109

Index 221

United Nations and, 88–9, 102
United States and, 2, 30–1
Uzbekistan and, 109–10, 114–15, 124
Venezuela and, 126, 127, 133, 135
"Civilizational diversity," 120–1
Club goods, 8, 32, 179
Cold War
　club goods and, 16
　Colombia and, 137
　development assistance and, 15
　Faroe Islands and, 171
　Iceland and, 161
　North Atlantic generally and, 151
　nuclear weapons and, 16–17
Collective Security Treaty Organization (CSTO), 107, 109, 110, 124
Colombia
　Brazil and, 139–40, 144
　China and, 130, 139–42, 143–4, 145, 146–7
　Cold War and, 137
　Cuba and, 143
　demand-side factors in, 27–8
　diversification of ties in, 126–7, 136, 144–7
　"dry canal" proposal, 140–1
　Foreign Ministry, 136
　foreign policy in, 136–8
　free trade agreement, 141, 142–4
　Global War on Terror and, 140
　goods substitution in, 26, 126, 135–6, 149–50
　hedging in, 136, 138–40, 144, 146–7
　hierarchical relations and, 126, 136, 139–40
　leverage in, 130, 136, 140–4, 146–7
　Ministry of Defence, 136
　National Police, 136
　Panama and, 137
　"Plan Colombia," 137, 139
　positionalist strategy in, 147
　power transitions in, 26, 126, 135–6, 149–50
　respice polum in, 137, 143, 144–5, 147
　respice similia in, 137–8, 140–1, 143, 144, 147
　Revolutionary Armed Forces of Colombia (FARC), 144
　Russia and, 145

　as security asset for United States, 126, 140
　supply-side factors in, 184
　United States and, 126, 136–47, 150
　Venezuela and, 140, 142–3
Colonization, 21, 22
Color Revolutions, 119, 122
Common pool goods, 8
Commonwealth of Independent States (CIS), 105, 119–20, 122–3
Competition strategy for acquisition of normative goods, 65, 77–8, 82–4
Competitiveness, 71, 75, 80–1, 83
Confucianism, 1
Cooley, Alexander, ix–x, 12, 22–3, 25–6, 64, 81, 178, 180, 181–2, 183, 188
Coproduction of goods, 28, 183–7
Correa, Rafael, 55
Corruption, 72, 82, 83
Corruption Perception Index, 72, 83
Counter-hegemonic strategies
　generally, 22–3, 59–61
　of Asian Infrastructure Investment Bank, 89, 91–4
　bottom-up goods substitution as, 153–5
　in China, 88, 178
　energy-backed loans from China as, 132
　goods ecologies and, 178–9
　normative goods and, 64, 68–9, 86–7
　in North Atlantic generally, 175–6
　positionalist strategy (*See* Positionalist strategy)
　reaction of United States to, 187–8
　reformist strategy (*See* Reformist strategy)
　revisionist states and, 29–30
　revolutionary strategy (*See* Revolutionary strategy)
　status quo strategy (*See* Status quo strategy)
　against United States, 59–61
COVID-19 pandemic
　generally, ix
　China and, ix, 4, 5
　European Union and, ix
　goods substitution and, ix
　Italy and, ix

COVID-19 pandemic (cont.)
  Russia and, ix
  Serbia and, ix, 4
  Spain and, ix
  United States and, 4
Creativity strategy for acquisition of normative goods, 65, 78, 84–6
Credit rating agencies, 83, 91
Cuba
  Colombia and, 143
  global performance indices and, 73, 74
Cultural capital, 20–1

Davidson, Jason W., 11
Debt owed to China
  Argentina, 59
  Bolivia, 130
  Ecuador, 59, 127–8, 130, 132
  Kyrgyzstan, 116
  Myanmar, 59
  Russia, 59
  Sri Lanka, 59
  Tajikistan, 116
  Venezuela, 59, 130, 132
Debusscher, Petra, 81
de Carvalho, Benjamin, 26–7, 77, 180, 182–3
Decoupling, 39
Defensive positionalism, 38
Deglobalization, ix
Democracy Index, 68, 70–1
Deng Menmin, 57
Denmark
  China and, 175
  Faroe Islands and, 151, 155, 157, 171, 172, 174
  Greenland and, 151, 155, 157, 165–7, 170–1
  North Atlantic generally and, 152, 174, 176
  Norway and, 155
  United States and, 157, 185
Devine, Fiona, 21
Diplomatic capital, 35
Diplomatic Revolution of 1756, 14
Distribution of power
  architecture of international order versus, 36
  goods ecologies and, 182
  positionalist strategy and, 31, 38, 182
  reformist strategy and, 31, 40, 182, 183
  revolutionary strategy and, 31, 38, 182
  status quo strategy and, 31, 41, 182
Distributive revisionists, 11–12
Diversification of ties
  generally, 128
  in Colombia, 126–7, 136, 144–7
  as demand-side mechanism of goods substitution, 129
  hedging and, 129, 130 (*See also* Hedging)
  hierarchical relations and, 129–30, 134–5, 147
  leverage and, 129, 130 (*See also* Leverage)
  shifting of ties versus, 125–6, 147
  transaction costs and, 128
Doshi, Rush, 4
Drezner, Daniel W., 29
Duque, Iván, 145, 146
Duterte, Rodrigo, 17, 60

Ease of Doing Business Index (EDBI), 71, 80–1, 83, 86–7
East Asian financial crisis, 47
Economic assistance, 18–19
Economic capital, 20–1, 35
Economic Intelligence Unit, 68, 70–1
Ecuador
  China and, 126, 127, 133, 135
  debt owed to China, 59, 127–8, 130, 132
  energy-backed loans from China, 31–2, 49, 55–6, 131
  shifting of ties in, 130
Egypt
  Asian Infrastructure Investment Bank and, 98
  IMF and, 18
  international financial institutions and, 19
  Kuwait and, 18–19
  Qatar and, 18–19
  Saudi Arabia and, 18–19
  shifting of ties in, 186
  United Arab Emirates and, 18–19
  United States and, 18–19

Index

World Bank and, 18
Energy-backed loans from China
  generally, 54–5
  Brazil, 54
  as counter-hegemonic strategy, 132
  Ecuador, 31–2, 49, 55–6, 131
  Kazakhstan, 54
  Russia, 54
  Turkmenistan, 31–2, 49, 56–9
  Venezuela, 54, 131
Erdogan, Recep Tayyip, 53–4, 60
Eurasian Economic Union, 52
"Eurasianism," 121
European Bank for Reconstruction and Development (EBRD), 100, 105–6, 113
European Economic Area (EEA), 156
European Free Trade Association (EFTA), 156
European Union (See also specific country)
  Central Asia generally and, 105
  COVID-19 pandemic and, ix
  Faroe Islands and, 156
  Greenland and, 156, 165
  Iceland and, 156
  Iran and, 179
  Turkey and, 53–4
  Ukraine and, 2–3, 18
Excludability of goods, 7–8
Exiting, 13, 14 (See also Shifting of ties)

Faller, Craig, 145
Family Prosperity Index, 85, 87
Faroe Islands
  bottom-up goods substitution in, 152–3
  China and, 173, 175
  Denmark and, 151, 155, 157, 171, 172, 174
  European Union and, 156
  goods substitution in, 26–7, 173–4
  home rule in, 155
  power transitions and, 26–7, 152–3
  Russia and, 152, 171–4, 175
  small population of, 157–8
  strategic importance of, 151–2
  United Kingdom and, 171
  United States and, 171, 173–4, 175
Fields
  capital, relation to, 20–1, 182
  defined, 21
  symbolic capital and, 21–2
France
  alliances and, 14
  Asian Infrastructure Investment Bank and, 97–8
Freedom House, 70–1, 73, 74, 81, 82
Freedom in the World Index, 73

Gender equality, 80, 81, 85
Gender Inequality Index (GII), 71–2
Georgia
  Abkhazia (See Abkhazia)
  elections in, 119
  normative goods and, 80–1
  Russia and, 43, 52
  South Ossetia (See South Ossetia)
  World Bank and, 80–1
Germany
  Asian Infrastructure Investment Bank and, 97–8
  North Atlantic generally and, 151
  Turkmenistan and, 58
  United Kingdom and, 30
Global Competitiveness Index (GCI), 75, 81
Global Gender Gap Index, 80
Global hegemony, 42–3
Global performance indices (GPIs) (See also specific index)
  generally, 62, 65, 69–70
  China and, 70–1, 73–4
  composite indicators, 72–3
  Cuba and, 73, 74
  independence of, 73
  meaning of norms, specifying and concretizing, 71–4
  moral status, allocation of, 74–7
  organizational preferences, 73
  policymaking, role in, 69–70
  public and comparable standards, providing, 70–1
  Qatar and, 73
  Russia and, 70–1, 73–4
  Singapore and, 71
  United States and, 74
  Western bias of, 73–4
  World Bank and, 73

Global War on Terror (GWOT), 107, 109, 140
Goods
  generally, 6
  assets versus, 7, 128, 185–6
  club goods, 8, 32, 179
  common pool goods, 8
  defined, 7
  excludability of, 7–8
  non-rival goods, 7–8
  normative goods (*See* Normative goods)
  performance as, 20
  private goods, 8
  public goods, 7–8, 32
  rival goods, 7–8
  social construction of, 20–2, 182–3
  specificity of, 8–9
  status as, 6–7, 21–2
  symbolic goods, 6–7, 21–2, 32–3
Goods ecologies
  counter-hegemonic strategies and, 178–9
  development assistance and, 179
  distribution of power and, 182
  goods substitution in, 129
  international order as, 10–12, 178
  revisionist states and, 10–12
Goods substitution (*See also specific topic or country*)
  Asian Infrastructure Investment Bank and, 11, 89, 101–3, 166–7
  bottom-up drivers of, 17–19, 152–5
  competition strategy for acquisition of normative goods and, 83
  demand-side factors in, 27–8
  dynamics of, 5–6, 150
  economic assistance and, 18–19
  extrinsic factors, 17–18
  in goods ecologies, 129
  "hard balancing" and, 34–5
  hegemonic powers and, 32–3
  hierarchical relations and, 150
  international order and, 12–13
  intrinsic factors, 17
  logics of (*See* Logics of goods substitution)
  politics of, 5–6, 31
  positionalist aim (*See* Positionalist strategy)
  power transitions and, x, 33–4
  reasons for, 31
  reformist aim (*See* Reformist strategy)
  revolutionary aim (*See* Revolutionary strategy)
  social contract view of, 178, 183–4, 186
  "soft balancing" and, 34–5
  status quo aim (*See* Status quo strategy)
  synthetic approach to, 6
  top-down drivers of, 15–17
GPIs (*See* Global performance indices)
Greece
  Belt and Road Initiative (BRI) and, 2–3
  China and, 2–3
  NATO and, 10
  normative goods and, 81–2
Greenland
  bottom-up goods substitution in, 152–3
  China and, 152, 166–7, 168–71, 175, 180
  Denmark and, 151, 155, 157, 165–7, 170–1
  difficulty of investing in, 168–9
  European Union and, 156, 165
  goods substitution in, 26–7, 167–8
  home rule in, 155, 165–6
  Japan and, 168
  mining in, 166, 168, 169
  NATO and, 167
  Philippines and, 168
  potential independence of, 165–7
  power transitions and, 26–7, 152–3
  Russia and, 168, 175
  Self Government Act, 165
  small population of, 157–8
  South Korea and, 168
  strategic importance of, 151–2
  Thailand and, 168
  United States and, 151–2, 156–7, 165, 166, 167, 168–9, 170–1, 174
Greico, Joseph, 38
Grímsson, Ólafur Ragnar, 160–1
Group of 77, 138
Gulf States (*See specific country*)

Index 225

Haarde, Geir, 160
Haley, Nikki, 146
"Hard balancing," 34–5
Hedging
  generally, 13, 14–15
  alliances and, 17–18
  Asian Infrastructure Investment Bank
    and, 98
  in Colombia, 136, 138–40, 144,
    146–7
  diversification of ties and, 129, 130
    (*See also* Diversification of ties)
  power transitions and, 34
Hegemonic powers
  club goods and, 32
  counter-hegemonic strategies (*See*
    Counter-hegemonic strategies)
  global hegemony, 42–3
  goods substitution and, 32–3
  power transitions and, 2
  public goods and, 32
  regional hegemony, 42–3
  rise and decline of, 1–2, 29
  symbolic goods and, 32–3
Hezbollah, 43
Hierarchical relations
  Colombia and, 126
  diversification of ties and, 129–30,
    134–5, 147
  goods substitution and, 150
Hill, James T., 139–40
Hirai, Tadashi, 71
Human Development Index (HDI), 71,
  72–3, 75–6
Humanitarian assistance, 185–6
Hungary in NATO, 124

Iceland
  Aurora Observatory, 162
  bottom-up goods substitution in,
    152–3
  China and, 161–5, 175
  Cold War and, 161
  demand-side factors in, 27–8
  economic crisis in, 159–60, 174
  European Union and, 156
  free trade agreement with China,
    162–3
  goods substitution in, 26–7, 152–3
  IMF and, 160

  Keflavik airbase, 151, 156–7,
    159–60, 161, 174
  leverage in, 164–5
  NATO and, 156–7, 159
  power transitions and, 26–7, 152–3
  Russia and, 152, 159–61, 163–5, 175
  small population of, 157–8
  Soviet Union and, 161
  strategic importance of, 151–2
  United States and, 151–3, 156–7,
    159–60, 161, 174
Identity, 184–5
IFIs (*See* International financial
    institutions)
Ikenberry, G. John, 63
IMF (*See* International Monetary
    Fund)
India
  Asian Infrastructure Investment Bank
    and, 90–1, 92, 98
  in BRICS countries (*See* BRICS
    countries)
  Israel and, 148
  Shanghai Cooperation Organization
    and, 50, 52–3
Inter-American Development Bank, 56,
  126, 131–2
International Criminal Court (ICC), 63,
  187
International financial institutions (IFIs)
  (*See also* International Monetary
    Fund (IMF); World Bank)
  Asian Infrastructure Investment Bank
    and, 89, 92–4
  BRICS countries and, 45, 46
  Central Asia generally and, 105–6,
    112
  Egypt and, 19
International Monetary Fund (IMF)
  generally, 33
  Asian Infrastructure Investment Bank
    and, 90, 92–3
  BRICS countries and, 46
  Central Asia generally and, 105–6,
    113
  Egypt and, 18
  Iceland and, 160
  Latin America generally and, 131–2
  Malaysia and, 47
  United States and, 96, 99, 187

International order
  generally, 6
  Asian Infrastructure Investment Bank in context of, 90–1
  China and, 42
  defined, 9–10
  distributive revisionists, 11–12
  as goods ecology, 10–12, 178
  goods substitution and, 12–13
  military capabilities and, 12
  normative revisionists, 11–12
  radical revisionists, 11–12, 29, 37–8
  revisionist states, 10–12 (*See also* Revisionist states)
International rankings (*See* Normative goods)
International Students Association, x
Internet Corporation for Assigned Names and Numbers (ICANN), 46
INTERPOL, 120
Iran
  European Union and, 179
  Israel and, 43
  Joint Comprehensive Plan of Action, 179, 188
  Russia and, 43
  Saudi Arabia and, 43
  United States and, 179
Iraq
  Abu Ghraib prison, 118
  insurgency in, 118
Israel
  Asian Infrastructure Investment Bank and, 98
  Bahrain and, 148
  China and, 148
  India and, 148
  Iran and, 43
  Oman and, 148
  Russia and, 148
  Saudi Arabia and, 148
  United States and, 148, 150
Italy
  Asian Infrastructure Investment Bank and, 97
  COVID-19 pandemic and, ix

Japan
  Asian Development Bank and, 96, 100
  Asian Infrastructure Investment Bank and, 92, 96, 97
  Central Asia generally and, 113
  Greenland and, 168
  United States and, 32
Johnson, Stephen, 125

Karimov, Islam, 108, 109–10
Kazakhstan
  anti-Americanism in, 118
  Asian Infrastructure Investment Bank and, 90–1
  China and, 54, 114–15, 124
  "civilizational diversity" and, 120–1
  economics of, 104–5
  election fraud in, 3–4
  election observers in, 122–3
  energy-backed loans from China, 54
  extrication from Soviet system, 104
  goods substitution and, 25–6, 106–7
  illiberal regimes in, 118, 119–22
  IMF and, 105–6, 113
  independence, "unwanted" nature of, 104
  LGBTQ persons in, 121
  liberalism in, 104
  nongovernmental organizations (NGOs), opposition to, 119–20
  noninterference and, 120–1
  Organization for Security and Co-operation in Europe and, 3–4, 14–15
  regional order and, 105
  regional trade in, 113–14
  Russia and, 105, 124
  Shanghai Cooperation Organization and, 50, 107
  Soviet Union and, 112–13
  "traditional values" and, 121
  transition economics in, 113
  United States and, 104, 105–6, 113, 124
  World Bank and, 105–6
Kelley, Judith G., 69, 71, 73–4, 123
Kennedy, John F., 22
Keohane, Robert O., 142
Kindleberger, Charles, 32
Kissinger, Henry, 37
Krasner, Stephen D., 32
Krebs, Ronald R., 10

Index 227

Kuwait
  Asian Infrastructure Investment Bank and, 90–1
  Egypt and, 18–19
Kyoto Protocol, 63, 187
Kyrgyzstan
  anti-Americanism in, 118
  Belt and Road Initiative and, 116
  China and, 111, 114–15, 124
  "civilizational diversity" and, 120–1
  debt owed to China, 116
  economics of, 104–5
  election observers in, 122–3
  elections in, 119
  extrication from Soviet system, 104
  goods substitution and, 25–6, 106–7
  illiberal regimes in, 118, 119–22
  IMF and, 105–6, 113
  independence, "unwanted" nature of, 104
  Kant military base, 109, 111
  LGBTQ persons in, 121
  liberalism in, 104
  Manas Air Base, 52, 109, 110–11
  Manas Transit Center, 15, 107–8
  nongovernmental organizations (NGOs), opposition to, 119–20
  noninterference and, 120–1
  political reform in, 116–18
  regional order and, 105
  regional trade in, 113–14
  Russia and, 52, 105, 109, 111, 124
  Shanghai Cooperation Organization and, 50, 107
  Soviet Union and, 112–13
  "traditional values" and, 121
  transition economics in, 113
  United States and, 15, 104, 105–6, 107–8, 109, 110–11, 113, 124
  World Bank and, 105–6

Lake, David A., 32, 178, 186
Larson, Deborah Welch, 77
Latin America (*See specific country*)
Legitimization, 186
Leira, Halvard, 26–7, 180, 182–3
Leverage
  overview, 13, 15
  in Colombia, 130, 136, 140–4, 146–7
  diversification of ties and, 129, 130 (*See also* Diversification of ties)
  in Iceland, 164–5
Levine Renan, 118
LGBTQ persons
  in Africa, 63–4, 84–6
  in Central Asia, 121
  in Kazakhstan, 121
  in Kyrgyzstan, 121
  in Uganda, 84–6
Liberalism
  in Central Asia, 104, 105–6
  normative goods and, 63, 64, 68, 86
Libya
  no-fly zone in, 45
  Responsibility to Protect (R2P) and, 45
Li Xiaopeng, 146
Logics of goods substitution
  generally, 6
  addition, 13–14
  diversification of ties (*See* Diversification of ties)
  exiting, 13, 14
  hedging (*See* Hedging)
  leverage (*See* Leverage)
  shifting of ties (*See* Shifting of ties)
Luxembourg, Asian Infrastructure Investment Bank and, 91

Mabus, Ray, 175
Makled, Walid, 142–3, 144
Malaysia, IMF and, 47
Manas Air Base, 52, 109, 110–11
Manners, Ian, 77
McCaffrey, Barry, 139
McCaul, Michael, 143
Medvedev, Dmitry, 110
Michelsen, Alfonso Lopez, 137–8
Minsk Treaty, 119–20
Mobility strategy for acquisition of normative goods, 65, 77, 79–82
Mohammed Bin Salman, 148–9
Mongolia, Asian Infrastructure Investment Bank and, 90–1
Morningstar, Richard, 58
Morse, Lulia C., 142
Morsi, Mohamed, 18–19
Mubarak, Hosni, 18–19

Multipolarity, 12, 16, 29–30, 44–5, 124, 187
Mutually Assured Destruction, 10
Myanmar, debt owed to China, 59

NATO (*See* North Atlantic Treaty Organization)
Nazarbayev, Nursultan, 3–4
Nepal, Asian Infrastructure Investment Bank and, 90–1
Netherlands, United States and, 185
Neumann, Iver B., 28, 77
New Development Bank (NDB), 47, 53, 100–1, 115
New International Economic Order, 138
New Zealand, Asian Infrastructure Investment Bank and, 91, 98
Nexon, Daniel, ix–x, 12, 22–3, 64, 178, 181–2, 183, 188
Non-Aligned Movement, 138
Nongovernmental organizations (NGOs), opposition to in Central Asia, 119–20
Non-rival goods, 7–8
Normative goods (*See also specific country*)
  generally, 23–4, 86–7, 179
  architecture of international order and, 182
  behavioral standards, 66, 68
  competition strategy for acquisition of, 65, 77–8, 82–4
  conversion of rankings to goods, 64, 65
  counter-hegemonic strategies and, 64, 68–9, 86–7
  counter-stigmatization, 78–9
  creation of norms, 67–8
  creativity strategy for acquisition of, 65, 78, 84–6
  critical perspective and, 62
  esteem as, 66–7
  global performance indices (*See* Global performance indices)
  historical background, 62–4
  honor as, 66–7
  identity as, 185
  liberalism and, 63, 64, 68, 86
  mobility strategy for acquisition of, 65, 77, 79–82
  nature of, 65–9
  pluralism and, 68
  realist perspective and, 62
  status as, 67
  stigma-management strategies and, 78–9
  stigma recognition, 78
  stigma rejection, 79
  strategies for acquisition generally, 77–9
Normative revisionists, 11–12
North American Free Trade Agreement (NAFTA), 133
North Atlantic (*See specific island*)
North Atlantic Treaty Organization (NATO)
  Central Asia generally and, 105
  club goods and, 8, 32, 179
  Greece and, 10
  Greenland and, 167
  Hungary in, 124
  Iceland and, 156–7, 159
  North Atlantic and, 151–2
  Poland in, 124
  Russia and, 2–3, 10
  Shanghai Cooperation Organization and, 51, 53
  Turkey and, 10
  United States and, 30, 32, 39
Norway
  Denmark and, 155
  humanitarian assistance and, 185–6
  identity and, 184
  North Atlantic generally and, 152, 155
  Norwegian Institute of International Affairs (NUPI), x
  Norwegian Research Council, x
  Palestinian Authorities and, 185–6
  Sweden and, 155
  United States and, 184, 185–6
Nubo, Huang, 163

Obama, Barack, 41–2, 96
Offensive positionalism, 38
Oman
  Asian Infrastructure Investment Bank and, 90–1
  Israel and, 148
O'Neill, Jim, 45

Orban, Viktor, 60
Organisation for Economic Co-operation and Development (OECD), 13, 101, 179
Organization for Security and Co-operation in Europe (OSCE)
  generally, 60
  Central Asia generally and, 105
  "civilizational diversity" and, 120–1
  election observers and, 122, 123
  Kazakhstan and, 3–4, 14–15
  Office of Democratic Institutions and Human Rights (ODIHR), 3–4, 122, 123
Organization of Islamic States, 85
Organski, Abramo Fimo Kenneth, 102
Osborne, George, 88, 97
OSCE (*See* Organization for Security and Co-operation in Europe)
Otunbayeva, Roza, 111

Pakistan
  Asian Infrastructure Investment Bank and, 90–1
  China and, 111–12
  Quadrilateral Cooperation and Coordination Mechanism (QCCM), 111–12
  Shanghai Cooperation Organization and, 50, 52–3
Palestinian Authorities, Norway and, 185–6
Panama, Colombia and, 137
Paris Agreement on Climate Change, 187
Pastrana, Andres, 139
Performance as goods, 20
Permanent Structured Cooperation (PESCO), 179
Permanyer, Inaki, 72
Peru, China and, 130
Philippines
  China and, 17
  Greenland and, 168
  Russia and, 17
  shifting of ties in, 186
Pizano, Eduardo, 139–40
Pluralism, normative goods and, 68
Poe, Steven C., 73
Poland in NATO, 124

Positionalist strategy, 38–9
  generally, 31, 36–7, 177, 181–2
  architecture of international order and, 31, 182
  BRICS countries and, 46
  in China, 48, 180, 182
  in Colombia, 147
  defensive positionalism, 38
  distribution of power and, 31, 38, 182
  intentions and effects, 41, 42
  in Latin America generally, 133
  in North Atlantic generally, 174–5
  offensive positionalism, 38
  shifting of ties as, 133
  United States, against, 44–5
Power transitions
  in Central Asia generally, 25–6, 106–7
  China and, 2, 30–1
  in Colombia, 26, 126, 135–6, 149–50
  goods substitution and, x, 33–4
  hedging and, 34
  hegemonic powers and, 2
  in North Atlantic generally, 26–7, 152–3
  politics of goods substitution in, 31
  theory of, 102
  in Ukraine, 2–3
  uneven economic growth and, 30
  United States and, 2, 30–1, 59–61
Prestige (*See* Status)
Private goods, 8
Prussia, alliances and, 14
Pu, Xiaoyu, 39
Public goods, 7–8, 32
Putin, Vladimir V.
  Faroe Islands and, 173
  gender equality and, 85
  terrorism and, 107
  Ukraine and, 2–3

Qatar
  Asian Infrastructure Investment Bank and, 90–1
  Egypt and, 18–19
  global performance indices and, 73
Quadrilateral Cooperation and Coordination Mechanism (QCCM), 111–12

Radical revisionists, 11–12, 29, 37–8
Rankings (*See* Normative goods)
Realism, 16, 34–5, 38, 62–3
Reformist strategy, 39–40
   generally, 31, 36–7, 177, 181–2
   architecture of international order and, 31, 39, 42, 182
   BRICS countries and, 47
   in China, 48, 180, 181, 182
   distribution of power and, 31, 40, 182, 183
   intentions and effects, 41, 42
   in Latin America generally, 133–4
   rules versus distribution of power, 183
   Shanghai Cooperation Organization and, 53
   shifting of ties as, 133–4
   against United States, 44–5
   in United States, 40, 181
Regional Comprehensive Economic Partnership (RCEP), 132–3
Regional hegemony, 42–3
Relationalism, 180
Renminbi (RMB) (currency), 91–2, 97
Responsibility to Protect (R2P), 45, 63
Restrepo, Carlos Lleras, 138
Revisionist states
   generally, 177, 180–2
   counter-hegemonic strategies and, 29–30
   distributive revisionists, 11–12
   goods ecologies and, 10–12
   in international order, 10–12
   normative revisionists, 11–12
   radical revisionists, 11–12, 29, 37–8
   Russia as, 181, 182
Revolutionary strategy, 37–8
   generally, 31, 36–7, 177, 181–2
   architecture of international order and, 31, 37–8, 182
   BRICS countries and, 46
   in China, 48
   distribution of power and, 31, 38, 182
   in Russia, 43
   against United States, 44–5
Rival goods, 7–8
"Rogue states," 140, 149
Rohrabacher, Dana, 139

Rome (Ancient) as hegemonic power, 1
Rumelili, Bahar, 23–4, 182–3
Rumsfeld, Donald, 51
Russia (*See also* Soviet Union)
   Abkhazia and, 52
   in Arctic Council, 167
   Asian Infrastructure Investment Bank and, 98
   Australia and, 46
   Belarus and, 52
   in BRICS countries (*See* BRICS countries)
   Colombia and, 145
   COVID-19 pandemic and, ix
   Crimea, annexation of, 2–3, 46
   debt owed to China, 59
   election observers and, 122–3
   energy-backed loans from China, 54
   Faroe Islands and, 152, 171–4, 175
   Gazprom, 56, 57–8
   Georgia and, 43, 52
   global performance indices and, 70–1, 73–4
   goods substitution and generally, ix, 5
   Greenland and, 168, 175
   Iceland and, 152, 159–61, 163–5, 175
   Iran and, 43
   Israel and, 148
   Kazakhstan and, 105, 124
   Kyrgyzstan and, 52, 105, 109, 111, 124
   Middle East and, 149
   Ministry of Finance, 160
   NATO and, 2–3, 10
   normative goods and, 62, 64, 77–8, 82, 83, 85, 86–7
   North Atlantic generally and, 157, 158–9
   Philippines and, 17
   as regional hegemonic power, 43
   Responsibility to Protect (R2P) and, 63
   as revisionist state, 181, 182
   revolutionary strategy in, 43
   Rosneft, 56
   sanctions against, 2–3, 152, 172
   Saudi Arabia and, 148–9

Shanghai Cooperation Organization and, 31, 48–9, 50, 51–3, 107 (*See also* Shanghai Cooperation Organization)
South Ossetia and, 52
Syria and, 43
Tajikistan and, 105, 109, 111, 124
"traditional values" and, 121
Turkmenistan and, 56, 57–8, 105, 124
Ukraine and, 2–3, 18, 43, 46, 63
United States and, 2–3
Uzbekistan and, 105, 109–10, 124
World Trade Organization and, 114
Rwanda
Constitution, 80
normative goods and, 80, 81

Saakashvili, Mikheil, 119
Santos, Juan Manuel, 140–1, 142–4
Saudi Arabia
Egypt and, 18–19
Iran and, 43
Israel and, 148
Russia and, 148–9
United States and, 150
Savage, Mike, 21
Schatz, Edward, 118
Schengen Area, 156
Schock, Aaron, 143
Schueth, Sam, 81
Schweller, Randall L., 39
SCO (*See* Shanghai Cooperation Organization)
Sending, Ole Jacob, 28
Serbia
China and, 4
COVID-19 pandemic and, ix, 4
Shanghai Cooperation Organization (SCO), 49–54
generally, 31, 48–9, 124
"civilizational diversity" and, 120–1
Counterterrorism Treaty, 50
economic cooperation, 51
election monitoring, 51
emergency fund, 52
India and, 50, 52–3
Kazakhstan and, 50, 107
Kyrgyzstan and, 50, 107
NATO and, 51, 53
Pakistan and, 50, 52–3
"Peace Missions," 50
reformist strategy of, 53
Regional Anti-Terror Structure (RATS), 50, 120
Russia and, 31, 48–9, 50, 51–3, 107
Tajikistan and, 50, 107
"three evils," 50
Turkey and, 53–4
United States and, 181
Uzbekistan and, 50, 107
Shevchenko, Alexei, 77
Shifting of ties
generally, 128
in Bolivia, 130
as demand-side mechanism of goods substitution, 129
diversification of ties versus, 125–6, 147
in Ecuador, 130
in Egypt, 186
in Philippines, 186
as positionalist strategy, 133
as reformist strategy, 133–4
transaction costs and, 128
in Turkey, 186
in Venezuela, 130
Simmons, Beth, 69, 71, 73–4, 106
Singapore
Economic Development Board, 80, 82
global performance indices and, 71
normative goods and, 80, 82, 84
al-Sisi, Abdel Fattah, 18–19
Skaale, Sjúrdur, 172
Slovenia, normative goods and, 80, 84
Social capital, 20–1
Social competition strategy for acquisition of normative goods, 65, 77–8, 82–4
Social construction of goods, 20–2, 182–3
Social contract view of goods substitution, 178, 183–4, 186
Social creativity strategy for acquisition of normative goods, 65, 78, 84–6
Social mobility strategy for acquisition of normative goods, 65, 77, 79–82

Society of Worldwide Interbank Financial Telecommunications (SWIFT), 179
"Soft balancing," 34–5
South Africa
  Asian Infrastructure Investment Bank and, 98
  in BRICS countries (*See* BRICS countries)
South Korea
  Asian Infrastructure Investment Bank and, 88, 91, 92, 95, 96
  Greenland and, 168
  normative goods and, 84
South Ossetia
  election observers in, 123
  Russia and, 52
Soviet Union (*See also* Russia)
  alliances and, 14
  Iceland and, 161
  Kazakhstan and, 112–13
  Kyrgyzstan and, 112–13
  as regional hegemonic power, 42–3
  Tajikistan and, 112–13
  Turkmenistan and, 112–13
  United States and, 15, 16–17, 22, 30
  Uzbekistan and, 112–13
Spain
  COVID-19 pandemic and, ix
  decline of monarchy, 30
Specificity of goods, 8–9
Sri Lanka
  Asian Infrastructure Investment Bank and, 90–1
  debt owed to China, 59
Status
  as good, 6–7, 21–2
  as normative good, 67 (*See also* Normative goods)
Status quo strategy, 41
  generally, 31, 36–7, 177, 181–2
  architecture of international order and, 31, 41, 182
  BRICS countries and, 45–6
  distribution of power and, 31, 41, 182
  intentions and effects, 41–2
Stigma-management strategies, normative goods and, 78–9
Strauss, Julia C., 142

Suarez, Marco Fidel, 137
Sun, Yun, 94
Sweden
  normative goods and, 80
  Norway and, 155
Symbolic capital, 21–2
Symbolic goods, 6–7, 21–2, 32–3
Syria
  BRICS countries and, 46
  Russia and, 43

Tajfel, Henry, 77
Tajikistan
  anti-Americanism in, 118
  Belt and Road Initiative and, 116
  China and, 111–12, 114–15, 124
  "civilizational diversity" and, 120–1
  debt owed to China, 116
  economics of, 104–5
  election observers in, 122–3
  extrication from Soviet system, 104
  goods substitution and, 25–6, 106–7
  illiberal regimes in, 118, 119–22
  IMF and, 105–6, 113
  independence, "unwanted" nature of, 104
  liberalism in, 104
  nongovernmental organizations (NGOs), opposition to, 119–20
  noninterference and, 120–1
  Nurek space observation center, 109
  Quadrilateral Cooperation and Coordination Mechanism (QCCM), 111–12
  regional order and, 105
  regional trade in, 113–14
  Russia and, 105, 109, 111, 124
  Shanghai Cooperation Organization and, 50, 107
  Soviet Union and, 112–13
  "traditional values" and, 121
  transition economics in, 113
  United States and, 104, 105–6, 113, 124
  World Bank and, 105–6
Tessman, Brock, 34, 187
Thailand
  Greenland and, 168
  United States and, 17
Thorhallsson, Baldur, 164

Index   233

Tillerson, Rex, 145
Tokayev, Kassym-Jomart, 3–4, 123
Top-down drivers of goods substitution, 15–17
Towns, Ann, 21, 23–4, 182–3
"Traditional values," 121
Transaction costs, 128
Transnistria, election observers in, 123
Trans-Pacific Partnership (TPP), 125, 132–3
Transparency International, 72, 73, 83
Trujillo, Carlos Holmes, 146
Trump, Donald
  alliances and, 16
  Brexit and, 187
  China and, 133
  Colombia and, 143, 145–6
  European Union and, 187
  foreign aid and, 34
  Greenland and, 151, 174
  international order and, 42, 87
  NATO and, 187
  Paris Agreement and, 187
  reformist strategy of, 181
  revisionist strategy of, 40
  Russian interference in election of, 2–3
  shifting of ties and, 131
  transactional approach, 187
  Trans-Pacific Partnership and, 125, 132–3
  World Health Organization and, ix, 4–5
Turkey
  European Union and, 53–4
  NATO and, 10
  normative goods and, 63, 82–3
  Shanghai Cooperation Organization and, 53–4
  shifting of ties in, 186
Turkmenistan
  anti-Americanism in, 118
  Bagtyarlyk (South Yolotan) oil field, 57
  China and, 114–15, 124
  "civilizational diversity" and, 120–1
  economics of, 104–5
  election observers in, 122–3
  energy-backed loans from China, 31–2, 49, 56–9
  extrication from Soviet system, 104
  Galkynysh (South Yolotan) oil field, 58
  Germany and, 58
  goods substitution and, 25–6, 106–7
  illiberal regimes in, 118, 119–22
  IMF and, 105–6, 113
  independence, "unwanted" nature of, 104
  liberalism in, 104
  nongovernmental organizations (NGOs), opposition to, 119–20
  noninterference and, 120–1
  regional order and, 105
  regional trade in, 113–14
  Russia and, 56, 57–8, 105, 124
  Soviet Union and, 112–13
  "traditional values" and, 121
  transition economics in, 113
  United States and, 104, 105–6, 108, 113, 124
  World Bank and, 105–6
Turner, John C., 77
Tymoshenko, Yulia, 18

Uganda, LGBTQ persons in, 84–6
Ukraine
  election observers in, 122–3
  elections in, 119
  European Union and, 2–3, 18
  Maidan movement, 2–3
  power transitions in, 2–3
  Russia and, 2–3, 18, 43, 46, 63
Unipolarity, 33, 36
United Arab Emirates, Egypt and, 18–19
United Kingdom
  alliances and, 14
  Asian Infrastructure Investment Bank and, 88, 91, 97–8
  Brexit, 187
  Faroe Islands and, 171
  Germany and, 30
  as hegemonic power, 1, 30, 42–3
  United States and, 1–2
United Nations
  China and, 88–9, 102
  Development Programme (UNDP), 71, 72–3
  gender equality and, 85

United Nations (cont.)
  global performance indices and, 73
  Human Rights Council, 121
  Security Council, 20, 45
United States
  9/11 attacks, 107, 109
  Agency for International
    Development (USAID), 80–1, 110
  alliances and, 16
  in Arctic Council, 167
  Asian Infrastructure Investment Bank
    and, 41–2, 88, 91, 92, 95–6, 97,
    99, 101–2, 180
  Central Asia, military presence in,
    107–9
  China and, 2, 30–1
  Colombia and, 126, 136–47, 150
  Commerce Department, 46
  counter-hegemonic strategies against,
    59–61
  COVID-19 pandemic and, 4
  Denmark and, 157, 185
  development assistance and, 179
  dollar as global currency, 92
  Egypt and, 18–19
  Export–Import Bank, 56
  Faroe Islands and, 171, 173–4, 175
  foreign aid and, 34
  global performance indices and, 74
  Global War on Terror, 107, 109, 140
  Greenland and, 151–2, 156–7, 165,
    166, 167, 168–9, 170–1, 174
  Guantánamo Bay, 63
  as hegemonic power, 30, 42–3
  hegemonic self-harm in, 188
  Iceland and, 151–3, 156–7, 159–60,
    161, 174
  IMF and, 96, 99, 187
  International Criminal Court and, 63
  Iran and, 179
  Israel and, 148, 150
  Japan and, 32
  Kazakhstan and, 104, 105–6, 113,
    124
  Kyoto Protocol and, 63
  Kyrgyzstan and, 15, 104, 105–6,
    107–8, 109, 110–11, 113, 124
  moon landing, 22
  NATO and, 30, 32, 39
  Netherlands and, 185
  normative goods and, 63, 64, 68–9,
    83, 86–7
  North Atlantic generally and, 175,
    176
  Norway and, 184, 185–6
  Operation Enduring Freedom, 15,
    107
  positionalist strategy against, 44–5
  power transitions and, 2, 30–1,
    59–61
  reaction to counter-hegemonic
    strategies in, 187–8
  reformist strategy against, 44–5
  reformist strategy in, 40, 181
  revolutionary strategy against, 44–5
  Russia and, 2–3
  Saudi Arabia and, 150
  Shanghai Cooperation Organization
    and, 181
  Soviet Union and, 15, 16–17, 22, 30
  State Department, 73, 108–9
  Tajikistan and, 104, 105–6, 113, 124
  Thailand and, 17
  Turkmenistan and, 104, 105–6, 108,
    113, 124
  unipolarity and, 33, 36
  United Kingdom and, 1–2
  Uzbekistan and, 51, 104, 105–6, 107,
    108–10, 113, 124
  World Health Organization and, ix,
    4–5
Uribe, Álvaro, 141, 144
Uzbekistan
  Andijon massacre, 108–10
  anti-Americanism in, 118
  Asian Infrastructure Investment Bank
    and, 90–1
  China and, 109–10, 114–15, 124
  "civilizational diversity" and, 120–1
  economics of, 104–5
  election observers in, 122–3
  extrication from Soviet system, 104
  goods substitution and, 25–6, 106–7
  illiberal regimes in, 118, 119–22
  IMF and, 105–6, 113
  independence, "unwanted" nature
    of, 104
  Karshi-Khanabad (K2) airfield, 51,
    107, 109–10
  liberalism in, 104

nongovernmental organizations
    (NGOs), opposition to, 119–20
noninterference and, 120–1
Regional Anti-Terror Structure
    (RATS) in, 50
regional order and, 105
regional trade in, 113–14
Russia and, 105, 109–10, 124
Shanghai Cooperation Organization
    and, 50, 107
Soviet Union and, 112–13
"traditional values" and, 121
transition economics in, 113
United States and, 51, 104, 105–6,
    107, 108–10, 113, 124
World Bank and, 105–6

Vatican, gender equality and, 85
Venezuela
    China and, 126, 127, 133, 135
    Colombia and, 140, 142–3
    debt owed to China, 59, 130, 132
    energy-backed loans from China, 54,
        131
    shifting of ties in, 130
Vikings, 155
Vučić, Aleksandar, 4

Ward, Steven, 29, 31, 41
Warde, Alan, 21
Washington Consensus, 46
Webb, Michael C., 32
Wohlforth, William C., 36
Wolfe, Wojtek, 34, 187
World Bank

generally, 54, 56, 126
Asian Infrastructure Investment Bank
    and, 47, 90, 92–3, 100
BRICS countries and, 46
Central Asia generally and, 105–6,
    113
Ease of Doing Business Index (*See*
    Ease of Doing Business Index
    (EDBI))
Egypt and, 18
Georgia and, 80–1
global performance indices and, 73
Latin America generally and, 131–2
World Congress of Families, 121
World Economic Forum, 80
World Health Organization (WHO), ix,
    4–5
World Trade Organization (WTO), 45,
    114
World War I, 30, 151
World War II, 30, 151

Xi Jinping
    Asian Infrastructure Investment Bank
        and, 90
    Belt and Road Initiative and, 89,
        115
    goods substitution and, 4
    Latin America generally and, 125
    Regional Comprehensive Economic
        Partnership and, 132–3

Yanukovych, Viktor, 2–3, 122–3

Zhang, Xiaojun, 21

Milton Keynes UK
Ingram Content Group UK Ltd.
UKHW020838110324
439289UK00018B/114